1836-1886

Sri Ramakrishna

B133.R2A3

THE GOSPEL OF RAMAKRISHNA

Revised by
SWAMI ABHEDANANDA
From
M.'s Original English Text

Foreword by
Christopher Isherwood

KANSAS SCHOOL OF RELIGION
UNIVERSITY OF KANSAS
1300 OREAD AVENUE
LAWRENCE, KANSAS 66044

Published by
The Vedanta Society

34 West 71st Street
New York

COPYRIGHT, 1947, by
THE VEDANTA SOCIETY, NEW YORK.

Printed in the United States of America. All rights in this book are reserved. No part of the book may be reproduced in any manner whatsoever without written permission except in the case of brief quotations embodied in critical articles and reviews.

FOREWORD

There is a story in the Old Testament which may well be used as a cautionary foreword to the occidental reader who is about to begin this book. It is the story of the prophet Elisha and of Naaman the leper.

"So Naaman came with his horses and with his chariot, and stood at the door of the house of Elisha. And Elisha sent a messenger unto him, saying, 'Go and wash in Jordan seven times, and thy flesh shall come again to thee, and thou shalt be clean.'

"But Naaman was wroth, and went away, and said, 'Behold, I thought, "He will surely come out to me, and stand, and call on the name of the Lord his God, and strike his hand, and recover the leper." Are not Abana and Pharpar, rivers of Damascus, better than all the waters of Israel? May I not wash in them and be clean?' So he turned and went away in a rage.

"And his servants came near, and spoke unto him, and said, 'My father, if the prophet had bid thee do some great thing, wouldest thou not have done it? How much rather then, when he saith to thee, "Wash and be clean"?'"

Naaman, in fact, was a snob. Most of us are snobs when it comes to recognizing spiritual truth. This snobbery is, actually, nothing but a defense which the mind raises against the challenge of new ideas. We do not entirely wish to be cured of our "leprosy"—our fixed habits of thinking, our materialistic sloth—but we refuse to admit to this unwillingness. So, instead, we criticize the prophet and his methods. We object to the way he talks and behaves. We find fault with his clothes or the cut of his beard. Why, we ask with Naaman, should we listen to an obscure, nineteenth-century Hindu in preference to one of our modern know-all psychologists or learned university professors? Are not the Thames and the Mississippi better than all the waters of India?

If we consider Ramakrishna from this hostile viewpoint, it will be very easy to find him comic, odd, alien and hopelessly lacking in the kind of theatrical impressiveness which the motion-picture and the popular novel have taught us to expect of our spiritual leaders. Indeed, Ramakrishna himself will encourage us to laugh at him—for he is a born comedian and dearly loves to tease and embarrass prigs. But it is we who are ridiculous, not he—we who demand to be healed, if we must be healed at all, with the circumstances and solemnity which befit our wealth, our dignity, our rank. Naaman's servants were wiser. Being simple people, they were gratefully content to receive the truth where they could find it, and to follow its instructions without carping.

That is the spirit in which we should read this book. I believe that anybody who does so with an open mind—avoiding the twin pitfalls of intellectual prejudice and sentimental reverence—will have to admit that here is one of the very greatest teachers and saints the world has ever known.

CHRISTOPHER ISHERWOOD

PREFACE

THIS is the authorized English edition of the "Gospel of Râmakrishna." For the first time in the history of the world's Great Saviours, the exact words of the Master were recorded *verbatim* by one of His devoted disciples. These words were originally spoken in the Bengali language of India. They were taken down in the form of diary notes by a householder disciple, "M." At the request of Srî Râmakrishna's Sannyâsin disciples, however, these notes were published at Calcutta during 1902-1903 A.D., in Bengali, in two volumes, entitled "*Râmakrishna Kathâmrita.*"

At that time "M" wrote to me letters authorizing me to edit and publish the English translation of his notes, and sent me the manuscript in English which he himself translated, together with a true copy of a personal

PREFACE

letter * which Swâmi Vivekânanda wrote to him.

At the request of "M" I have edited and remodelled the larger portion of his English manuscript; while the remaining portions I

---

* Swâmi Vivekânanda's letter to "M."

(True Copy.)

DEHRA DOON,
24th Nov., 1897.

My dear Master Mahasaya:

Many thanks for your second leaflet. It is indeed wonderful. The move is quite original, and never the life of a great teacher was brought before the public untarnished by the writer's mind as you are doing. The language also is beyond all praise. So fresh, so pointed, and withal so plain and easy.

I cannot express in adequate terms how I have enjoyed them. I am really in a transport when I read them. Strange, isn't it? Our teacher and Lord was so original and each one of us will have to be original or nothing. I now understand why none of us attempted his life before. It has been reserved for you, this great work. He is with you evidently. With all love and namaskar.

(Sd.) VIVEKÂNANDA.

P.S.—Socratic dialogues are Plato all over. You are entirely hidden. Moreover, the dramatic part is infinitely beautiful. Everybody likes it—here or in the West.

(Sd.) V.

This letter of Swami Vivekânanda shows that the words of the Master were accurately recorded by "M."

viii

PREFACE

have translated directly from the Bengali edition of his notes. The marginal headings, foot-notes, and index, as well as the division of the Gospel into fourteen chapters, were added by me. I have endeavored to make every word of this edition as literal, simple, and colloquial as possible.

Some repetitions are purposely kept to show how the Master used the same illustrations on different occasions during the course of His eloquent conversations.

The completed work is now offered to the Western World with the sincere hope that the sublime teachings of Srî Râmakrishna may open the spiritual sight of seekers after Truth, and bring peace and freedom to all souls struggling for realization.

SWÂMI ABHEDÂNANDA.

NEW YORK,
December 15, 1907.

Niranjanam Nityam anantarupam,
Bhaktânukampâ dhritavigraham vai;
Ishâvatâram Paramesham Idyam,
Tam Râmakrishnam Shirashâ Namâmah.

Salutations to Bhagavân Srî Râmakrishna, the perfect Embodiment of the Eternal Truth which manifests Itself in various forms to help mankind, and the Incarnation of the Supreme Lord who is worshipped by all.

HARI OM TAT SAT.

CONTENTS

	PAGE
Introduction	1
I. Srî Râmakrishna at the Temple of Dakshineswara	21
II. Srî Râmakrishna with His Disciples at the Temple	36
III. The Bhagavân with Certain of His Householder Disciples	62
IV. Visit to the Pandit Vidyâsâgara	99
V. Day on the River with Keshab Chunder Sen	142
VI. Sunday at the Temple	179
VII. Some Incidents in the Life of Srî Râmakrishna (as told by Himself)	207
VIII. Feast at the Garden-house of Surendra	225
IX. Visit to a Hindu Pandit and Preacher	261
X. Gathering of Disciples at the Temple	289
XI. Srî Râmakrishna at the Sinti Brâhmo-Samâj	319
XII. At the House of Balarâm, a Disciple	347
XIII. A Day at Shâmpukur	379
XIV. Cossipur Garden-house	411

INTRODUCTION

The Lord declares:—
"Whenever true religion declines and irreligion prevails, I manifest myself and in every age I incarnate to establish spiritual law and to destroy evil."—*Bhagavad Gitâ*.

India has produced many great spiritual leaders who are recognized and worshipped as
Saviours. Saviours of mankind. The life and character of each of these were as wonderful, superhuman, and divine as were those of the illustrious Son of Man. Each has been like the embodiment of all Divine attributes; each has been the giver of new life to the old spiritual truths, and the generator of that tidal wave of spirituality which has again and again inundated the religious world, surmounting the

barriers of superstition and prejudice and carrying the stream of individual souls toward the ocean of Divinity.

The present upheaval of the spiritual tide, the waves of which, traversing nearly half the world, have touched the shores of America, was produced by the Christlike character and Divine personality of Bhagavân Srî Râmakrishna—revered and worshipped in India to-day as an ideal manifestation of the Divine glory. His life was so extraordinary and unparalleled that within ten years after His departure from earth it aroused the admiration, wonder and reverence not only of all classes of people in His own country, but of many distinguished English and German scholars of the nineteenth century.

A short account of the life of Bhagavân Srî Râmakrishna appeared for the first time in the January number of the "Imperial and Quarterly Review" of 1896 under the title of "A Modern Hindu Saint." It was an able article penned by Prof. C. H. Tawney, who was for many years the professor of Sanskrit in Calcutta University and the distinguished Librarian of India House in London. This article excited the interest of many

Life of Sri Râmakrishna by European Scholars.

European scholars, among whom Professor Max Muller showed his appreciation by publishing in the August number of the "Nineteenth Century" of 1896 a short sketch of this Hindu Saint's life entitled "A Real Mahâtman." In this celebrated article, which was for some time the subject of most severe criticism both in England and India among many of the Christian missionaries and the Theosophists, the noted Professor showed the difference between the imaginary Mahâtmas of the Theosophists and the Real Mahâtman or the Great Soul of India who had reached God-consciousness and had manifested Divinity in all the actions of His daily life. He gave a brief account of the extraordinary life of Bhagavân Srî Râmakrishna, paying Him the highest tribute of honor and respect that a Christian scholar could give to a Divine manifestation in the so-called heathen land. Later, in 1898, he compiled and published "Râmakrishna, His Life and Sayings," collecting more facts of His life and the sayings of this exemplary character perfumed with Divine personality.

Professor Max Muller was deeply impressed by the originality of this great Saint and real Mahâtman, who was not brought up within the precincts of any university and who drew the water of His wisdom neither from any book nor Scripture nor from any ancient prophet but directly from the eternal Fountainhead of all Knowledge and Wisdom.

Râmakrishna a real Mahâtman.

He was also struck by the broad, liberal and absolutely unsectarian spirit which pervades the utterings of Bhagavân Srî Râmakrishna. Indeed the life and sayings of the Bhagavân have given a death-blow to the sectarian bigotry and fanaticism of the so-called religious world. Whosoever has read His Sayings is impressed with the universality of His spiritual ideals which embraced the ideals of all mankind.

From His childhood Srî Râmakrishna fought against all sectarian doctrines and dogmas, but yet at the same time He showed that all sects and creeds were but the paths which lead sincere and earnest souls to the one universal goal of all religions. Having realized the highest ideal of every religion by following the methods and practices of the various sects and creeds of the world, Bhagavân Srî Râmakrishna gave to humanity whatever spiritual experience and realization He had acquired. Every idea which He gave was fresh from above and unadulterated by the product of human intellect, culture or scholastic education. Each step of His life from babyhood to the last moment was extraordinary. Every stage was like the unfoldment of a chapter of a new scripture especially written out by the Unseen Hand to fit the minds of the East and the West and to fulfil the spiritual needs of the twentieth century.

Bhagavân Srî Râmakrishna is not only the greatest saint of modern India but He is the "Real Mahâtman." A real Mahâtman as described in the Bhagavad Gitâ (Chapter VII, verse 19) is one who, having realized the Absolute, perceives the Divine Being in all animate and inanimate objects of the universe. His heart and soul never turn away from God. He lives in God-consciousness, and Divine qualities constantly flow through his soul. He cares neither for fame nor power nor worldly prosperity. A true Mahâtman has no attachment to His body or to sense-pleasures; He is a living God; He is absolutely free and His inner nature is illumined by the self-effulgent light of Divine wisdom and His heart is overflowing with Divine Love. His soul becomes the playground of the Almighty, His body and mind become the instrument of the Divine will. And Bhagavân Srî Râmakrishna was such a real Mahâtman.

Even in this age when the vast majority of educated people do not believe in the existence of God and of the human soul, when scientific knowledge has turned the minds of students away from the path of spirituality, when sense-pleasures and the luxuries of life have become the ideals of earthly existence and human beings have degenerated into money-making machines, we have witnessed with our eyes a Great Soul who is recognized as a Real Mahâtman by hundreds and thousands of thoughtful men and women of India, Europe and America. This Great Soul manifested His Divine qualities and lived in God-consciousness at every moment of His earthly career, and to-day thousands of people prostrate before His picture and worship Him as the latest manifestation of Divinity. Whosoever has heard of His most wonderful life has felt in his soul that Râmakrishna was the perfect Ideal of mankind.

He made His appearance in an obscure part of Bengal where He passed His early boyhood, but His youth and maturity were spent near Calcutta, the capital of British India, as cosmopolitan a city as London, New York, or any other large city of the civilized world and the seat of education, refinement and scientific knowledge. He allowed the sceptical minds of the students and professors of colleges and universities as well as of educated men and women of the world to come in direct touch with the self-effulgent light of Divine wisdom which was shining in its full glory through His childlike, soft, and tender form. Scholars and intelligent people of all classes poured from every quarter to that spot which was sanctified by the presence of the Bhagavân. He was the living example of the spiritual greatness and Divinity which had been manifested by the great Incarnations like Christ, Buddha, Krishna, Râma, Chaitanya* and other Saviours of the world.

<small>Râmakrishna's influence upon the mind of Scholars.</small>

We know a number of sceptics and agnostics who had never believed in Christ or Buddha or Krishna as Divine Incarnations, who had never accepted the authority of the Scriptures, but on

---

* Chaitanya, the Founder of a sect of the Vaishnavas, is regarded in India as the Incarnation of Krishna. He is also known as the "Prophet of Nuddea," for Nuddea (or Navadvipa) in Bengal was his birthplace. His other name is Lord Gaurânga (see p. 9). He was born in 1485 A.D., and was a contemporary of Luther.

GOSPEL OF RAMAKRISHNA

the contrary had maintained that the lives of Christ and of other Saviours were but exaggerated accounts based upon the imagination of their disciples, anxious to deify their human masters—such sceptics and unbelievers when they met Râmakrishna and watched His superhuman life, were convinced that the lives of Christ, Buddha, Krishna, and other Avatâras must have been true and real. The same sceptics, when they beheld His Divine powers, were so deeply impressed with His personality that they prostrated before Him, kissed the dust of His holy feet and realized that He was the Personification of the Sermon on the Mount, the Incarnation of Divinity on earth, and the remanifestation of Christ, Buddha, Krishna, and Chaitanya in one form. All the special qualities and Divine powers that had adorned the wonderful character of each of these great personages were witnessed by them in this uncommon Divine manifestation of the nineteenth century.

<u>Have we not watched with admiration when the followers of all the great religions of the world recognized in Srî Râmakrishna their Divine Ideals?</u> Have we not seen how Quakers and orthodox Christians knelt and prayed before

GOSPEL OF RAMAKRISHNA

Him and worshipped Him as the Christ when the Bhagavân went into superconscious com-
munion with the Heavenly Father after hearing the holy name of Jesus of Nazareth? The Mahometan saints who came to see Him, prostrated at His holy feet and recognized in Him the highest Ideal of Islam. The Buddhists regarded Him as Sambuddha, the Enlightened. The followers of Chaitanya, like Vaishnava Charan,* and others, worshipped Him as the second Prophet of Nuddea when Bhagavân Srî Râmakrishna occupied the altar which was reverentially dedicated to Srî Chaitanya by hundreds of devoted Vaishnavas, who always prostrated before that altar and prayed to their Lord Guarânga. The worshippers of Krishna called Him the Incarnation of Krishna. The devotees of the Divine Mother realized that the Mother of the universe was playing through Him; the followers of Shiva declared that Bhagavân Srî Râmakrishna was their living Deity; while the Sikhs, the faithful votaries of Guru Nânaka,†

Ramakrishna as the Divine Ideal of all Sects.

---

* Vaishnava Charan was a great Hindu saint and a true follower of Chaitanya, whom he worshipped as the Ideal Incarnation of Divine Love.

† Guru Nânaka was the founder of the sect known as the

regarded Him as their Holy Master. His followers, seeing all these powers, marvelled at His greatness and believed that His many-sided personality was the living example and the consummation of all the previous Avatâras and Divine manifestations. And the truth of this was again and again verified and confirmed by His acts as well as by His own words: "He who was Krishna, Râma, Christ, Buddha, Chaitanya has *now* become Râmakrishna." Bhagavân was always conscious of this truth and spoke of it before the world as well as before His dearest disciples.

As His Divine personality was many-sided yet one, so was His great mission. It was to **His mission.** show the underlying unity in the variety of religions and to establish that universal religion of which sectarian religions are each but partial expressions. Like all other Saviours the life of the Bhagavân exemplified His mission. He spent the best part of His life in practising in full the different

---

Sikhs, or disciples. He was born near Lahore in the Punjab (India) in the year 1469 A.D. and died in 1538 A.D. He was the first of the ten Gurus or spiritual masters among the Sikh people. He is regarded by His followers as a manifestation of Divinity.

GOSPEL OF RAMAKRISHNA

methods of Yoga. He went through every minute detail of the devotional exercises and different forms of worship ordained by the Scriptures of different nations and practised by the followers of the various sects and creeds of the world. His object in devoting so much time to these practices was to find out whether they had any real value in the path which leads to perfection.

Râmakrishna's mind was always open to Truth. He would not accept anything on second-hand authority. He would not believe in anything because it was written in a book or because it was declared by some great personage. He must know the Truth first hand. Before accepting any statement, He must realize it in His own life and then He would speak of His personal experience to others in order that they might gain benefit from it. For nearly twelve years before He appeared in public or made any disciples Srî Râmakrishna, like a scientific investigator, inquired into the beliefs of the various sects of every religion, followed their methods and performed their rituals and ceremonies with perfect faith and earnest devotion that He might realize the goal which could be reached by each of them. To His great surprise, however, He discovered that He arrived at God-consciousness through each sectarian method. Whenever, furthermore, He desired to follow any particular path, there came to Him a perfected soul of each sect who had realized the Ideal, to direct Him in that path. Everyone of these great saints recognized in Srî Râmakrishna the manifestation of Divine powers, when in a short time He attained to that which they had not been able to acquire during years of austerity, worship and extreme devotion.

Having finished His investigations, He was ready to proclaim His message and give to the world the fruits of His own experience and realization. But unlike other spiritual teachers, He did not go out in search after His disciples and followers. As a fragrant flower does not hunt for bees but waits patiently for the bees to come, so the full-blown flower of spirituality in the form of Srî Râmakrishna waited for His disciples to come to Him in the Temple garden at Dakshineswara on the bank of the Ganges.

When Râmakrishna had attained to the highest ideal of each Yoga and had realized the spiritual oneness with the Absolute Brahman and the Mother of the universe, rumor spread from mouth to mouth that Râmakrishna had reached perfection in this life. People from all quarters began to crowd around Him. Pandits and scholars of every nationality as well as hundreds of devout men and women of all sects came to see Him and listen to His original and wonderful teachings. This was the beginning of His public life as spiritual leader and guide, which continued for nearly sixteen years. During this period He did nothing but help mankind by freely distributing the priceless jewels of spiritual truths which he had earned through such struggle, hardship and austerities.

Râmakrishna had a marvellous intellect and keen insight into the true nature of things and events, and using the commonest occurrences of every-day life as illustrations, He succeeded in making the dull minds of worldly people grasp the spiritual depth, beauty and grandeur of His sublime ideals. He poured new life into every word that He uttered so as to touch the soul of His hearers. People listened with wonder and admiration to His original discourses on the most difficult problems concerning life and death, the nature and origin of the soul, the origin of the universe and our relation to God.

His spiritual insight.

In this age of scientific rationalism Bhagavân Srî Râmakrishna has shown to the world how the Lord of the universe can be realized **Realization of God.** and attained in this life, and no one except Him has ventured to go through all the tests of sceptics and agnostics to prove that He had attained to God-consciousness. Those who have seen Him, lived with Him for years and watched Him by day and by night, have proclaimed before the world that He was the embodiment of the highest spiritual ideals of all nations, and that whoever worships Him with faith and reverence worships the latest manifestation of Divinity.

The Bhagavân proved by His example that wherever there is extreme longing to see God, there is the nearness of the realization of the absolute Truth. His life has given to the world a grand demonstration that even in this age Divinity can be reached and Divine perfection can be acquired by one who is pure, chaste, simple and whose devotion is whole-hearted and whole-souled. We have neither seen nor heard of a character purer, simpler, more chaste, more truthful and more godly than that of this ideal Mahâtman. He was like the personification of purity and chastity and the embodiment of truthfulness.

His life was the life of absolute renunciation. Earthly pleasures and comforts meant nothing to Him. The only pleasure, comfort or happiness which He cared for was the blissful state of Samâdhi or God-consciousness, when His soul, liberated from the bondage of body and mind, soared high in the infinite space of the Absolute. This Samâdhi was a natural state with Râmakrishna. He never had to make a special effort to attain it. We often heard Him say that when He was four years old He went into Samâdhi at the sight of the beautiful coloring of a tropical cloud. This realization He always remembered and often described in His conversation. And as He grew older His Samâdhi or ecstasy became stronger and deeper.

In His Samâdhi His body would become absolutely motionless, His pulse and heart-beat imperceptible, His eyes would be half open and if anyone pressed His eyeball with the finger, His body would not move or show the least sign of sensation. He would remain in this state sometimes for a few minutes, sometimes for half an hour or an hour, and on one occasion He continued in it for three days and nights. Then He would come down on the plane of sense-consciousness and relate His

His Samâdhi.

experiences. He had the power to separate Himself from the cage of the physical organism and to go into this state of Divine communion at His will and stay there as long as He wished. Frequently He told us that He reached such a height in Samâdhi that if He had been like an ordinary mortal He could never have returned to His body; that no mortal had ever come back from that kind of Samâdhi; and that the Divine Mother gave Him this power to return to this plane simply to help mankind and to establish His mission.

To Him God was father, mother, brother, sister, and everything. He recognized no earthly relations. He never coveted wealth, nor had He any earthly possession. He realized that gold had no more value than earth and became ab-

His renunciation. solutely unattached to riches, understanding the transitoriness of the objects which can be acquired by wealth. He often said that immortality could not be purchased by money, and emphasized by His example the true meaning of the Vedic passage: "Neither by meritorious deed, nor by progeny, nor by wealth, but by renunciation alone the Immortal Truth can be acquired." Renunciation of the attachment to worldly things is the

GOSPEL OF RAMAKRISHNA

gate to God-consciousness. Christ, Buddha, Chaitanya, Sankarâchârya and all other Saviours and spiritual leaders of the world exemplified this by living the life of absolute renunciation. It is very rare to find in this age a perfect ideal of the renunciation of lust and of worldly attachment. Bhagavân Srî Râmakrishna practised the ideal of the renunciation of riches to such an extent that He was able to make His body respond involuntarily to the touch of coin by shrinking from it even in sound sleep. We have often seen Him suffer pain when he was obliged to touch a coin of any metal. Who could be a more perfect ideal of renunciation in this age of materialism!

He uplifted womanhood. Srî Râmakrishna taught that every woman, old or young, was the representative of the Divine Mother. He worshipped God as the Mother of the universe and frequently declared that His Divine Mother had shown Him that all women represent Divine Motherhood on earth. For the first time in the religious history of the world was this ideal preached by any Divine Incarnation. And upon this depends the salvation of men and especially of women of all countries from immorality, corruption and such other vices as prevail in a civilized community.

17

By His living example the Bhagavân established the truth of spiritual marriage on the soul plane even in this age of sensuality. He had a wife whom He always treated with reverence and whom He regarded as the manifestation of His Divine Mother. He never had any sex relation with her or with any woman on the physical plane. <u>His wife, the Blessed Virgin Sâradâ Devi, is still living like an embodiment of Holy Motherhood with innumerable spiritual children around Her</u>. She in turn has always regarded the Bhagavân as Her Blessed Mother Divine in a human form. Up to the last moment of His earthly career the Bhagavân was absolutely pure, chaste, and a perfect child of His Divine Mother of the universe. <u>Furthermore, Râmakrishna uplifted the ideal of womanhood on the spiritual plane by accepting His first Guru or spiritual instructor in a woman form.</u> No other Saviour or spiritual leader has ever given such an honor to womanhood in the annals of religious history.

<u>The mission of Bhagavân Srî Râmâkrishna was to show by His living example how a truly</u>

His mission. <u>spiritual man, being dead to the world of senses, can live on the spiritual plane of God-consciousness; it was to prove</u>

GOSPEL OF RAMAKRISHNA

that each individual soul is immortal and potentially Divine. His mission was to establish harmony between religious sects and creeds. For the first time it was absolutely demonstrated by Râmakrishna that all religions are like so many paths leading to the same Goal, that the realization of the same Almighty Being is the highest Ideal of Christianity, Mahometanism, Judaism, Zoroastrianism, Hinduism, as well as of all other smaller religions of the world. Srî Râmakrishna's mission was to proclaim the eternal Truth that God is one but has many aspects, and that the same one is worshipped by different nations under various names and forms; that He is personal, impersonal and beyond both; that He is with name and form and yet nameless and formless. His mission was to establish the worship of the Divine Mother and thus to elevate the ideal of womanhood into Divine Motherhood. His mission was to show by His own example that true spirituality can be transmitted and that salvation can be obtained through the grace of a Divine Incarnation. His mission was to declare before the world that psychic powers and the power of healing are obstacles in the path of the attainment of God-consciousness.

GOSPEL OF RAMAKRISHNA

Bhagavân Srî Râmakrishna possessed all the Yoga powers but He seldom exercised those **His Divine powers.** powers, especially the power of healing diseases. Moreover, He always prevented His disciples from either seeking or exercising those powers. But one power which we have seen Him frequently exercise was the Divine power to transform the character of a sinner and to lift a worldly soul to the plane of superconsciousness by a single touch. He would take the sins of others upon His own shoulders and would purify them by transmitting His own spirituality and opening the spiritual eyes of His true followers.

The days of prophecy have passed before our eyes. The manifestations of the Divine powers of One who is worshipped to-day by thousands as the latest Incarnation of Divinity, we have witnessed with our eyes. Blessed are they who have seen Him and touched His holy feet. May the glory of Srî Râmakrishna be felt by all nations of the earth; may His Divine power be manifested in the earnest and sincere souls of His devotees of all countries in all ages to come, is the prayer of His child and servant,

ABHEDÂNANDA.

CHAPTER I

SRÎ RÂMAKRISHNA AT THE TEMPLE OF DAKSHINESWARA

BHAGAVÂN* SRÎ RÂMAKRISHNA lived for many years in Râni Râshmoni's celebrated _{Where} Temple garden on the eastern bank _{Râmakrishna} of the Ganges in the village of _{lived.} Dakshineswara about four miles north of Calcutta. This Temple with the garden attached was dedicated by its foundress (Râni Râshmoni) to the Divine Mother (Kâli). In the northwest corner of the spacious Temple-compound is a small room which faces on the west the waters of the sacred river Ganges. This room with its holy surroundings was con-

---

* "Bhagavân" is a Sanskrit word meaning "The Blessed Lord." When the word is used without the accent on "a" of the last syllable it signifies the vocative case used in addressing a Saviour.

secrated as the dwelling-place for many years of Bhagavân Srî Râmakrishna, whose Divine Presence made the spot holier and more sacred. It was from this retired corner that the rays of His Divine glory, emanating from His God-intoxicated soul, dazzled the eyes of the seekers after Truth and attracted them to Him as a blazing fire attracts moths from all quarters. Hundreds of educated men and women were drawn towards this superhuman personality to listen with the deepest reverence to the words of wisdom uttered by One who had realized God and who lived in constant communion with the Divine Mother of the universe.

One Sunday in the month of March, 1882, Mahendra, hearing from a friend about this Divine Man, was so deeply impressed that he came to the Temple garden to pay Him a respectful visit. It was the day of a special religious festival and people had gathered in great numbers in Srî Râmakrishna's room and on the veranda. The Bhagavân was seated on a raised platform, and on the floor around Him were Kedâr, Suresh, Râm, Manmohan, Bijoy, and many other devotees. They gazed up into His radiant face and drank the nectar of the living words of Divine wisdom

Mahendra's visit to the Temple.

GOSPEL OF RAMAKRISHNA

that fell from His hallowed lips. With a smiling face Srî Râmakrishna was speaking to them of the power of the Lord's Holy Name and true Bhakti as the means of attaining God-vision. Addressing Bijoy,* He asked: What do you say is the means of attaining to God?

Bijoy: Bhagavan, by the repetition of His Holy Name. In this age the Holy Name of the Lord has saving powers.

Bhagavân: Yes, the Holy Name has saving powers, but there must be earnest longing with it. Without earnest longing of the heart no one can see God by mere repetition of His Name. One may repeat His Name, but if one's mind be attached to lust and wealth, that will not help much. When a man is bitten by a scorpion or a tarantula, mere repetition of a *mantram* will not do; a special remedy is necessary.

Power of the Lord's Holy Name.

Bijoy: If that be the case, Bhagavan, then how did Ajâmila,† who was the greatest of

---

* Bijoy was the first name of Bijoy Krishna Goswami, the celebrated preacher, lecturer, writer and spiritual teacher (Âchârya) of the Brâhmo Samâj in Calcutta.

† Ajâmila was the name of a sinner who received salvation by repeating the name of the Lord (which was also the name

23

GOSPEL OF RAMAKRISHNA

sinners and committed all sorts of crimes, obtain salvation by repeating the Name of the Lord at the time of his death?

Râmakrishna: Perhaps in his previous incarnations Ajâmila was righteous and performed a great many good deeds. Besides, it is said that he practised asceticism later in this life. It may also be said that at the last moment of his life the repetition of the Holy Name purified his heart and therefore he attained salvation. When an elephant is washed, immediately he throws dust and dirt over himself; but if he is kept in a clean stall after his bath, then he cannot cover himself with dirt. By the power of the Holy Name a man may be purified, but he may once more commit sinful acts because his mind is weak. He cannot promise that he will never sin again. The water of the Ganges may wash away past sins, but there is a saying that sins perch on the top of trees. When a man comes out of the Ganges and stands under a tree, the sins drop over his shoulders and seize upon him; these old sins ride him, as it were. Therefore, repeat the Holy Name of the Lord,

---

of his son) at the last moment of his life. The story of his life is given in the Purânas and is well known to the Hindus.

GOSPEL OF RAMAKRISHNA

but at the same time pray to Him that you may have true love and devotion for Him, and that your love for wealth, fame and the pleasures of the body may decrease because they are transitory, they last only until to-morrow.

When there is true devotion and love, one can reach God by any of the sectarian religions. **All religions lead to God.** The Vaishnavas, the worshippers of Krishna, will attain God in the same way as the Sâktas, the worshippers of the Divine Mother or the followers of Vedânta. Those who belong to the Brâhmo-Samâj,* the Mahometans and Christians, will also realize God through their respective religions. If you follow any of these paths with intense devotion, you will reach Him. If there be any mistake in the path chosen, He will correct the mistake in the long run. The man who wishes to see Jagannâth † may go towards the South instead of

---

* Brâhmo Samâj is the name of the Hindu Unitarian church founded by Râjâ Râmmohun Roy in 1830 A.D. It has now various branches in India. The original organization is now known as the Âdi Samâj Keshab Chunder Sen was the founder of the sect called "New Dispensation," while Shivanâth Sâstri was the founder of the Sâdhâran Brâhmo Samâj.

† Jagannâth literally means the "Lord of the Universe." There is a great Temple at Puri in India where the Car festival

towards the North, but some one will sooner or later direct him in the right way and he will surely visit Jagannâth in the end. The one thing necessary for realization is whole-hearted and whole-souled devotion to God.

<u>Vaishnavas, Mahometans, Christians and Hindus are all longing for the same God; but</u> **Many names of one God.** <u>they do not know that He who is Krishna is also Shiva, Divine Mother, Christ and Allah. God is one, but He has many names.</u> The Substance is one, but is worshipped under different names according to the time, place and nationality of His worshippers. All the different Scriptures of the world speak of the same God. He who is described in the Vedas as Absolute Existence-Intelligence-Bliss or Brahman, is also described in the Tantras * as Shiva, in the Purânas † as Krishna, in the Koran as Allah, and in the Bible as Christ. Yet

---

takes place every year. Hence the common expression "The Car of Juggernath."

* Tantras are sacred writings of the Shaiva and Sâkta sects among the Hindus.

† Purânas are the sacred Scriptures of the Hindus next in authority to the Vedas. There are 18 Great Purânas and many smaller Purânas.

GOSPEL OF RAMAKRISHNA

the various sects quarrel with one another. The worshippers of Krishna, for instance, say that nothing can be achieved without worshipping Krishna; those who are devoted to the Divine Mother think that the worship of the Divine Mother is the only way to salvation; similarly, the Christians say that no one can reach heaven except through Christ; He is the only way and Christianity is the only religion, all other religions are false. This is narrow-mindedness.

Bigotry is not right. "My religion is true while that of others is false,"—this kind of belief is not right. It is not our business to correct the errors of other religions. He who has created the world will correct them in time. Our duty is in some way or other to realize Him. God can be reached through many paths; each of these sectarian religions points out a path which ultimately leads to Divinity. Yes, all religions are paths, but the paths are not God. I have seen all sects and all paths I do not care for them any more People belonging to these sects quarrel so much! After trying all religions, I have realized that God is the Whole and I am His part; that He is the Lord and I am His servant; again I realize, He is I; I am He

People dispute among themselves, saying: "God is personal, with form. He cannot be impersonal and formless,"—like the Vaishnavas who find fault with those who worship the Impersonal Brahman. When realization comes, then all these questions are settled. He who has seen God can tell exactly what He is like. As Kavira* said: "God with form is my Mother, God without form is my Father. Whom shall I blame, whom shall I praise? The balance is even." He is with form, yet He is formless. He is personal, yet He is impersonal, and who can say what other aspects He may have!

God Personal and Impersonal.

Four blind men went to see an elephant. One touched a leg of the elephant and said: "The elephant is like a pillar." The second touched the trunk and said: "The elephant is like a thick club." The third touched the belly and said: "The

Parable of the elephant and the blind men.

---

* Kavira was a Hindu saint who lived between 1488 and 1512 A.D. Rising from the low caste of a weaver he became the founder of a Vaishnava sect called after his name "Kavira Panth." His teachings were so broad and universal that they were accepted by the Mahometans as well as the Hindus of all castes. Even now there are thousands among the lower classes of the Hindus who regard him as their spiritual master.

elephant is like a huge jar." The fourth touched the ears and said: "The elephant is like a big winnowing-basket." Then they began to dispute among themselves as to the figure of the elephant. A passer-by, seeing them thus quarrelling, asked them what it was about. They told him everything and begged him to settle the dispute. The man replied: "None of you has seen the elephant. The elephant is not like a pillar, its legs are like pillars. It is not like a big water-jar, its belly is like a water-jar. It is not like a winnowing-basket, its ears are like winnowing-baskets. It is not like a stout club, its trunk is like a club. The elephant is like the combination of all these." In the same manner do those sectarians quarrel who have seen only one aspect of the Deity. He alone who has seen God in all His aspects can settle all disputes.

Again: Two persons were hotly disputing as to the color of a chameleon. One said: "The chameleon on that palm-tree is of a red color." The other, contradicting him, replied: "You are mistaken, the chameleon is not red but blue." Not being able to settle the matter by argument, both went to the person who always lived under

Parable of the chameleon.

that tree and had watched the chameleon in all its phases of color. One of them asked him: "Sir, is not the chameleon on that tree red?" The person replied: "Yes, sir." The other disputant said: "What do you say? It is not red, it is blue." The person again humbly replied: "Yes, sir." The person knew that the chameleon is an animal which constantly changes color; thus it was that he said "yes" to both these conflicting statements. <u>The Sat-chit-ânanda (the Absolute Existence-Intelligence-Bliss) likewise has many forms. The devotee who has seen God in one aspect only, knows Him in that aspect</u> alone. But he who has seen Him in manifold aspects is alone in a position to say with authority: "All these forms are of one God and God is multiform." He is formless and with form, and many are His forms which no one knows.

God is not only personal and with form but <u>He can take the form of Krishna, Christ or any other Incarnation</u>. It is true that He manifests Himself in infinite forms to fulfil the desires of His devotees. It is also true that He is formless Indivisible Existence-Intelligence-Bliss Absolute. The Vedas have described Him to be both

Different aspects of Divinity.

GOSPEL OF RAMAKRISHNA

personal, with form and attributes, and impersonal, beyond all form and attributes. Do you know how this is? He is like the infinite ocean of Absolute Existence-Intelligence-Bliss. As in the ocean intense cold will freeze a portion of the water into ice which may float in various forms on the water, similarly intense devotion (Bhakti) may condense a portion of Divinity and make it appear in different forms. The Personal God with form exists for the sake of His Bhaktas (dualistic devotees). When the sun of wisdom rises, the block of ice melts and becomes water once more; above, below, and on every side the Infinite Being pervades. Therefore there is a prayer in the Scriptures: "O Lord, Thou art personal with form. Thou art also impersonal and formless. Thou hast manifested Thyself in a human form and hast lived in our midst, but in the Vedas Thou art described as beyond speech and mind, Unspeakable, Imperceptible and Unthinkable." But it can be said that for a certain class of Bhaktas He is eternally personal and always with form. There are places where the ice never melts, it becomes crystallized.

Relation between God Personal and Impersonal.

31

Kedâr:* Bhagavan, it is also said in the Scriptures: "O Lord, Thou art beyond speech and mind, but I have described Thy Personal form only, do Thou forgive me for this offense."

Bhagavân: Yes, God is with form and also formless. No one can say positively that He is so much and no more. To a devotee (Bhakta, or lover of God) the Lord appears as a Personal Being with form, but to one who has attained to the state of selfless Samâdhi through the path of discrimination and knowledge He is the formless, Impersonal and Absolute Brahman.

Night had fallen and the priests were moving the lights before the shrines to the accompani-

Evening at the Temple. ment of bells, cymbals, and drums. From the southern end of the garden was wafted the sweet music played by the Temple musicians upon flutes and other instruments—the music being carried far over the Ganges until it was lost. The breeze blowing from the south was gentle and fragrant with the sweet odor of many flowers. The moon was rising and the garden was soon bathed in

---

* Kedâr was a great dualistic Bhakta, or a lover of God. He belonged to the Vaishnava sect of Chaitanya. He regarded Râmakrishna as the Incarnation of Divine Love.

GOSPEL OF RAMAKRISHNA

its soft silvery light. It seemed as if nature as well as man was rejoicing and holding herself in readiness for the sacred ceremony of the Ârati (evening service).

One by one the disciples began to take their leave. Mahendra * and his friend, who had been visiting the different temples, now wended their way back through the grand quadrangle to Srî Râmakrishna's chamber. Coming up to the door of the room, they noticed that it was closed. Near the door stood a maid-servant named Brindâ. Mahendra spoke to her, saying: Well, my good woman, is the Holy Man in?

Brindâ: Yes, He is in His room.

Mahendra: I suppose He has many books to read and study?

Brindâ: Oh dear no; not a single one. Everything, even the highest truths, is spoken by His tongue. His words are all inspired.

---

* Mahendra is the first name of Babu Mahendra Nath Gupta. He was a professor of English literature in Calcutta University. He is a devoted householder disciple of Râmakrishna. He is the author of "Râmakrishna Kathâmrita" (or The Nectar of the Sayings of Râmakrishna) in Bengali. It was he who kept a diary of the events which are now translated and embodied in the present volume.

Mahendra: Indeed! Is He now going through the evening service? May we go in? Will you kindly tell Him of our anxiety to see Him?

Brindâ: Why, you may go in, my children. Go in and take your seats before Him.

Thereupon they entered the room. No other people were there. Bhagavân Srî Râmâkrishna was alone, seated as in the afternoon on the platform beside His bed. Incense was burning and the doors were closed. Mahendra saluted the Bhagavân with folded hands. A mat was pointed out on the floor. At His word Mahendra and his friend took their seats upon it. The Bhagavân asked him: What is your name? Where do you live? What are you? What has brought you to Barâhanagore?*

Mahendra answered each of these questions, but he noticed that in the course of the conversation Srî Râmakrishna's mind was fixed upon some other object, on which He was meditating. He was only half-conscious of the physical plane and His attitude resembled that of a man quietly seated rod in hand, intent on catching fish. When the float trembles and the fish bites, the man eagerly looks at the float,

---

* Barâhanagore is a suburb of Calcutta.

grasping the rod with all his strength. He does not talk to anyone, but his whole mind is fixed upon the float. Such was the Bhagavân's concentration at this moment. Mahendra learned afterwards that this was the state of Samâdhi or God-consciousness which invariably came over Him every day during the evening service. Very often in this state He would become absolutely unconscious of the external world. Mahendra, observing His abstraction, said to Srî Râmakrishna: I am afraid, Bhagavan, that Thou wouldst prefer to go through the evening service (Sandhyâ) alone. In that case we will not disturb Thee any more, but will call some other time.

Srî Râmakrishna replied: Oh no, you need not be in a hurry.

But He was silent again for a time. He then opened His lips and said: Sandhyâ? Evening service? It is not that.

A short while after, Mahendra saluted the Bhagavân, who in turn bade him good-bye, saying, "Come again."

CHAPTER II

SRÎ RÂMAKRISHNA WITH HIS DISCIPLES AT THE TEMPLE

THE Bhagavân was in His room seated in His usual place on the small platform beside His bed. It was Sunday and the room was filled with a large number of devotees. Among them was a young college student only nineteen years of age named Narendra, who afterwards became the world-renowned Swâmi Vivekânanda. Everyone noticed even at that time that he was a sincere and earnest seeker after Truth and that his mind was above all worldly concerns. His eyes were shining with spiritual light, his face was aglow with innocence and simplicity, and his words were full of spiritual power. The Bhagavân was discoursing on worldly people who ridicule the worshippers of God. Especially addressing Narendra, He asked: What do you say, Narendra? Worldly

GOSPEL OF RAMAKRISHNA

men will speak all manner of things against godly people, but they should act like the elephant. When an elephant passes through a public road, dogs run after him and bark at him; but the elephant turns a deaf ear to their barking and goes on his own way. Suppose, my boy, people should speak ill of you behind your back, what would you think of them?

Narendra: I would look upon them as a lot of barking dogs.

The Bhagavân laughed and said: No, my friend, do not go so far as that. You should love everyone; no one is a stranger; God dwells in all beings; without Him nothing can exist. When Prahlâda* realized Him, the Lord asked him to crave a boon. Prahlâda replied: "When I have seen Thee, what other boon do I need?" The Lord asked him again. He then prayed: "If Thou wishest to grant me a boon, do Thou forgive those who have persecuted me." Prahlâda meant that by persecuting him they had persecuted the Lord dwelling within him. Know that God resides in all things animate and inanimate. Hence everything is an object of worship, be

---

* See note page 128.

it men, beasts or birds, plants or minerals In our relation with men all that we can do is to take heed to ourselves that we mix with good people and avoid bad company. It is true, however, that God resides in bad people also, yes, even in a tiger; but surely it does not follow that we should embrace a tiger. It may be asked: Why should we run away from a tiger when God is dwelling in that form? To this the answer is that God abiding in our hearts directs us to run away from the tiger. Why should we not obey His will?

In a certain forest there lived a sage who had a number of disciples. He taught his disciples the truth: "God dwells in all things. Knowing this, you should bend your knee before every object." One day a disciple went out into the forest for wood. On his way he saw a man riding a mad elephant and shouting: "Get out of the way, get out of the way! This is a mad elephant." The disciple, instead of running away, remembered his master's teaching and began to reason: "God is in the elephant as well as in me. God cannot be hurt by God, so why should I run away?" Thus thinking, he stood where he was and saluted the elephant

Parable of the disciple and the mad elephant.

GOSPEL OF RAMAKRISHNA

as he came nearer. The driver (Mâhoot) kept on shouting: "Get out of the way!" but the disciple would not move, until he was snatched up by the mad elephant and dashed to one side. The poor boy, bruised and bleeding, lay on the ground unconscious. The sage, hearing of the accident, came with his other disciples to carry him home. When after some time the unfortunate pupil recovered consciousness, he described what had happened. The sage replied: My boy, it is true that God is manifest in everything. But if He is in the elephant, is He not equally manifest in the driver (Mâhoot)? Tell me why you did not pay heed to the warning of the driver?

The Bhagavân continued: In the sacred Scriptures it is written, "God dwells in water"; but some water can be used for divine service, **God in everything.** or for drinking purposes, some for bathing or washing, while dirty water cannot be touched even. In the same manner, although God resides in all human beings, still there are good men and bad men, there are lovers of God and those who do not love God. <u>We should recognize Divinity in all, but we should not mix with bad people or with those who do not love God.</u> Our relation with them must not be very close. It is wise to avoid the company of such people.

Narendra:* What attitude should we hold when wicked people come to disturb our peace or do actually offend us?

Bhagavân: A person living in society should have a little Tamas (the spirit of resisting evil) **Resistance of** for purposes of self-protection. But **evil.** this is necessary only for outward show, its object being to prevent the wicked from doing harm to you. At the same time you should not do actual injury to another on the ground that he has done injury to you.

There was a large venomous snake in a field. No one dared to go that way. One day a holy **Parable of the** man (Mahâtmâ) passed by that road **snake and the** and the serpent ran after the sage to **holy man.** bite him. But when the snake approached the holy man, he lost all his ferocity and was overpowered by the gentleness of the Yogi. Seeing him, the sage said: "Well, my friend, think you to bite me?" The snake was abashed and made no reply. At this the sage continued: "Hearken, friend; do not injure anyone in future." The snake bowed and nodded

---

* Narendra was a Sannyâsin disciple of Râmakrishna. He was afterwards known as the Swâmi Vivekânanda.

assent. The sage went his way, and the snake entered his hole and thenceforward began to live a life of innocence, without attempting to harm anyone. In a few days all the neighborhood concluded that the snake had lost his venom and was no longer dangerous; so everyone began to tease him. They pelted him with stones or dragged him mercilessly by the tail, and there was no end to his troubles. Fortunately the sage again passed that way, and seeing the bruised and battered condition of the snake, was very much moved and inquired the cause. "Holy Sir," the snake replied, "this is because I do not injure anyone after your advice. But alas! they are so merciless!" The sage smilingly said: "My friend, I simply advised you not to bite anyone; but I did not tell you not to frighten others. Although you should not bite any living creature, still you should keep people at a distance by hissing at them." And Srî Râmakrishna added: <u>There is no harm in "hissing" at wicked men and at your enemies, showing that you can protect yourself and know how to resist evil.</u> Only you must be careful not to pour your venom into the blood of your enemy. Resist not evil by causing evil in return.

GOSPEL OF RAMAKRISHNA

One of the devotees present said: But when a person is annoyed with me, Bhagavan, I feel unhappy. I feel that I have not been able to love everyone equally.

Love for all.

Râmakrishna: When you feel that way, you should have a talk with that person and try to make peace with him. If you fail after such attempts, then you need not give it further thought. <u>Take refuge with the Lord. Think upon Him. Do not let your mind be disturbed by any other thing.</u>

Devotee: Christ and Chaitanya have both taught us to love all mankind.

Râmakrishna: You should love everyone because God dwells in all beings. But to wicked people you should bow down at a distance. (To Bijoy, smiling) Is it true that people blame you because you mix with those who believe in a Personal God with form? A true devotee of God should possess absolute calmness and never be disturbed by the opinions of others. Like a blacksmith's anvil, he will endure all blows and persecutions and yet remain firm in his faith and always the same. Wicked people may say many things about you and blame you; but if you long for God, you should endure with patience.

A true devotee always calm.

Company of the wicked.

One can think on God even dwelling in the midst of wicked people. The sages of ancient times, who lived in forests, could meditate on God although surrounded by tigers, bears, and other wild beasts. The nature of the wicked is like that of a tiger or bear. They attack the innocent and injure them. You should be especially cautious in coming in contact with the following: First, the wealthy. A person who possesses wealth and many attendants can easily do harm to another if he so desires. You should be very guarded in speaking with him; sometimes it may even be necessary to agree with him in his opinion. Second, a dog. When a dog barks at you, you must not run, but talk to him and quiet him. Third, a bull. When a bull chases you, you should always pacify him by talking to him. Fourth, a drunkard. If you make him angry, he will call you names and swear at you. You should address him as a dear relative, then he will be happy and obliging.

When wicked people come to see me, I am very careful. The character of some of them is like that of a snake. They may bite you unawares. It may take a long time and much discrimination to recover from the effects of

GOSPEL OF RAMAKRISHNA

that bite. Or you may get so angry at them that you will wish to take revenge. It is necessary, however, to keep occasionally the company of holy men. Through such association right discrimination will come.

There are four classes of *Jivas*, or individual souls: First, *Baddha*, the bound; second, *Mumukshu*, the seeker after freedom; third, *Mukta*, the emancipated; and fourth, *Nitya-mukta*, the eternally free. This world is like a net, the soul is the fish, and the Lord of the phenomenal world is the fisherman. When a fisherman draws in his net, some of the fish try to escape by rending the net, that is, they struggle for freedom. So are the souls of the second class, the *Mumukshus*, the seekers after freedom. But among the fish that struggle, only a few escape. Similarly, a few souls only attain to freedom and they belong to the third class, the *Muktas*. There are some fish, however, that are naturally cautious and never fall into the net. Such are the souls of the fourth class, the *Nitya-muktas*, who are never caught in the net of the phenomenal world, but who remain eternally free, like Nârada* and others like him. Most of the fish,

<small>Four classes of individual souls.</small>

---
* See note page 168.

GOSPEL OF RAMAKRISHNA

however, fall into the net and have not the sense to know that they are going to die there. When caught, they try to run away and hide in the mud at the bottom by swimming with the net. They make no effort to get out of the net, but go deeper and deeper into the mud. These may be compared to the souls who are bound fast in the world. They are caught in the net, but they delude themselves by thinking that they are happy. <u>They remain attached to worldliness. They plunge into the mire of worldly evils and are content, while those who are seeking after freedom or who are emancipated do not like worldliness and do not care for sense-pleasures</u>.

Those who are thus caught in the net of the world are the *Baddha*, or bound souls. No one can awaken them. They do not come to their senses even after receiving blow upon blow of misery, sorrow and indescribable suffering. The camel loves thorny bushes, and although his mouth bleeds when he eats them, still he does not cease to love them dearly and no one can keep him away from them. The bound souls may meet with great grief and misfortune, but after a few days they are just as they were before. The wife

Bound souls.

may die or become unchaste, the man will marry again; his son may die, he will be extremely sorrowful, but he will soon forget him. The mother of the boy may be overwhelmed with grief for a short time, but in a few days she will once more be concerned for her personal appearance and will deck herself with jewels and finery. Such worldly people may be left paupers after marrying their sons and daughters, yet they will still beget children every year. They may lose their fortune by a lawsuit, but they will again go to the courts. They may not be able to support their children, to educate, feed, clothe, or house them properly, still they will continue to have more. They are like the snake with a musk-rat in its mouth. As the snake cannot swallow the rat because of its strong odor, neither can it throw it out because of its own bent teeth, so these bound souls, *Baddhas*, although they may occasionally feel that the world is unreal, can neither give it up nor can they fix their minds on the Reality of the universe. I once saw a relative of Keshab Chunder Sen, who was quite old, still playing cards as if the time for meditating on God had not come for him.

There is another sign of a *Baddha*, or worldly

soul. If you remove him from the world and put him in a better place, he will pine away and die. He will work like a slave to support his family, and he will not hesitate to tell lies, to deceive or to flatter in order to earn his livelihood. He looks upon those who worship God or who meditate on the Lord of the universe as insane. He never finds time or opportunity to think of spiritual subjects. Even at the hour of death he will think and talk of worldly things. Whatever thought is strongest in the minds of worldly people comes out at the time of death. If they become delirious, they rave of nothing but material objects. They may go to places of worship, but so long as their minds are attached to the world, worldly thoughts will rise at the last moment. As a parrot may be taught to utter the Lord's Holy Name, but when attacked by a cat, screams and gives its natural cry; so they may repeat the Holy Name of the Lord, but when attacked by death, the natural tendency of their minds will predominate. It is said in the Bhagavad Gîtâ that the future is determined by the thought that is uppermost at the moment of death, and in the Purâna there is a story that King Bharata was born as a deer

What thou thinkest thou shalt become.

GOSPEL OF RAMAKRISHNA

because when he died, his mind was fixed on the thought of a deer. He who passes away thinking of God and meditating on Him, does not come back to this world.

A devotee: Bhagavan, will a man who thinks of God, but who does not meditate on Him at the time of death, be born again?

Srî Râmakrishna: An ordinary soul who has no faith in God may think of Him for a time, but easily forgets Him again and becomes attached to the world. If, however, he concentrates his mind upon God at the last moment of his life, his heart and soul become purified and remain so even after death. People suffer so much because they have no faith in God. In order to be able to think of God at the time of death we must prepare our mind by constant practice. The practice of meditation on God will create a tendency of mind to think of Him spontaneously even at the last moment.

Concentration and meditation.

A devotee: Bhagavan, what condition of mind is necessary for a worldly person to attain to freedom?

Râmakrishna: If by the Grace of the Lord strong dispassion for worldly things arises in his mind, then such a person becomes free from

GOSPEL OF RAMAKRISHNA

all earthly attachment. What is this *strong* dispassion? Let me tell you. Ordinary dispassion
Dispassion. makes the mind think of the Lord occasionally, but there is no longing in the heart. Strong dispassion, on the contrary, makes the mind dwell constantly on the Lord with the same intense longing as a mother feels for her only child. He who has strong dispassion does not want anything but the Lord. He looks at the world as a deep well and is always fearful lest he may fall into it. Earthly relations seem to him very distant. He does not seek their company. His whole heart and soul yearn for God. He does not think of his family, nor does he think of the morrow. He also possesses great spiritual force.

Let me explain this to you by a parable: In a certain place there had been a long drought.
Parable of the farmer and the canal. The farmers were irrigating their fields by canals, bringing water from a long distance. One farmer had great determination and force of character. One morning he made up his mind that he would continue to dig his canal until he had connected it with the river and brought the water to his field. He was so busy digging that he lost account of time. The hour for luncheon came

49

GOSPEL OF RAMAKRISHNA

and passed. His wife called him to come home, wash and eat. "The luncheon is getting cold. Leave your work until to-morrow," she urged. At first he paid no heed to her words, but when she repeated her request, he bade her go home and not disturb him any more. "You have no sense," he said, "with this terrible drought we cannot grow anything. There will be no food for the children, the whole family will die of starvation. I have resolved that this very day I shall bring the water of the river to my field; then I shall think of washing and eating." Hearing this, his wife ran home. The farmer worked hard the whole day and toward evening he joined the canal to the river and sat on one side with great delight as he saw the stream of water running into his field. His mind was then peaceful and happy. He went home and called his wife, saying: "Now give me a little oil and fill my pipe," and he washed, ate a hearty dinner and enjoyed a sound sleep. This kind of determination and firmness of purpose must be at the back of strong dispassion. Another farmer who was trying to bring water to his field was likewise called by his wife at the hour of the noonday meal. "It is getting late, come home, and wash and eat," she said, and at once he dropped his spade and replied: "My dear, when you ask me to go, I must go." So his field remained dry. As a farmer cannot irrigate his field, so a devotee cannot attain to God without firm determination.

When God is attained through such strong dispassion, all worldly attachment fades away. A householder may then live with his family, but he becomes unattached and there is no more danger for him. If there be two magnets, one very large and the other very small, which do you suppose will attract a piece of iron? The larger one of course. God is the greatest magnet. Compared to Him the attraction of the world is small and powerless.

A devotee: Bhagavan, why are we so bound to the world that we cannot see God?

Râmakrishna: The sense of "I" in us is the greatest obstacle in the path of God-vision. It

Sense of "I." covers the Truth. When "I" is dead, all troubles cease. If by the mercy of the Lord one realizes "I am a non-doer," instantly that man becomes emancipated in this life. This sense of "I" is like a thick cloud. As a small cloud can hide the glorious sun, so this cloud of "I" hides the glory of the Eternal

51

GOSPEL OF RAMAKRISHNA

Sun. If the cloud is dispersed by the mercy of a Guru, or spiritual master, the glory of the Infinite becomes visible. When Râma, the Divine Incarnation in a human form, was walking in the forest, Lakshmana (the individual soul), who was at a short distance, could not see Him because Sitâ or Mâyâ, or the sense of "I," was standing between. Look at me. I cover my face with this handkerchief and you cannot see me; still my face is there. So God is the nearest of all, but because of the sense of "I" you do not see Him. The soul in its true nature is absolute Existence, Intelligence and Bliss, but on account of Mâyâ or the sense of "I," it has forgotten its real Self and has become entangled in the meshes of the various limitations of mind and body.

Each attribute limits the soul and modifies its nature. He who dresses smartly will naturally sing love-songs, play cards and carry a cane, and such things will appeal to him. If you have a pencil in your hand, you will unconsciously scribble on anything; such is the power of the pencil. Money has great power. When a man becomes wealthy his nature is entirely changed. He is a different being. A poor Brâhmin, for in-

Money is power.

52

stance, used to come here. He was very humble. He lived on the other side of the Ganges. One day as I was landing from a boat, I saw him sitting at the riverside. Seeing me, he shouted in a disrespectful tone, "Hello! is it you, my good fellow?" Immediately I understood by his manner that he had got hold of some money, otherwise he would not dare to address me thus. A toad had a Rupee in its hole. An elephant was coming that way and passed over the hole. The toad was very angry; it came out and was about to kick the elephant, saying: "How darest thou pass over me?" Such is the power of wealth! It makes one so egotistic.

This sense of "I," however, vanishes at the approach of Divine wisdom, which leads to superconsciousness (Samâdhi) and eventually to God-consciousness. But it is very difficult to acquire this Divine wisdom. It is said in the Vedas that when the mind reaches the seventh stage of spiritual evolution, the soul enters into Samâdhi and instantly its sense of "I" disappears. The mind naturally dwells in the first three stages, the realm of worldly tendencies and animal propensities, and becomes attached to lust and

Seven stages of spiritual evolution.

53

wealth. When the mind dwells in the purified heart, spiritual light is perceived by the soul. At that time the soul exclaims: "What is this! What is this!" When it rises near the throat and remains there, the devotee loves to hear and speak of God. When the mind rises still higher, near the space between the eyebrows, it beholds the vision of the Infinite Being, whose nature is absolute Existence-Intelligence-Bliss. The soul then desires to touch and embrace that Being, but fails. As a light within a lantern can be seen but cannot be touched from outside, so the soul beholds the vision but cannot lay hold on it, cannot enter into it, cannot become one with it. In the seventh stage, however, the mind is bereft of the sense of "I," enters into God-consciousness and realizes its oneness with the Infinite.

Devotee: Bhagavan, what happens after reaching the seventh stage when Divine wisdom comes? What does the man see?

Râmakrishna: It cannot be described by words. In the seventh stage when the mind goes into its causal form, Samâdhi comes and what happens then no one can tell.

This sense of "I" which makes one worldly

GOSPEL OF RAMAKRISHNA

and attached to lust and wealth is the cause of bondage. <u>The difference between the Supreme and the individual soul is created by this sense of "I"</u> which stands between. If you hold a stick on the surface of a stream, the water will appear to be divided into two parts, but in reality the water is one. It appears as two because of the stick. The sense of "I" may be compared to this stick. Remove this limiting adjunct and the current will be one and unbroken. What is this sense of "I" which clings to man? That which says: "I am this, I am that. I possess so much wealth. I am great and powerful; who is greater than I?" If a thief has stolen ten Rupees and been detected, the owner takes his money first, then beats him, then hands him over to the police and finally puts him in jail. The worldly "I" says: "Doesn't he know that he stole ten Rupees which belonged to me? How dared he?"

Difference between soul and God.

The worldly "I."

Devotee: Bhagavan, if we cannot get rid of worldliness except by losing the sense of "I" in Samâdhi, is it not better to follow the path of wisdom which leads to Samâdhi, since in the path of devotion the sense of "I" still remains?

Râmakrishna: <u>Very few can get rid of the sense of "I" through Samâdhi</u>. It generally **Difficult to be rid of "I."** clings to us. We may discriminate a thousand times, but the sense of "I" is bound to return again and again. You may cut the branches of a fig-tree to-day, but to-morrow you will see that new twigs are sprouting. <u>If this sense of "I" will not leave, then let it stay as the servant of God</u>. "O God! Thou art my Lord, I am Thy servant!" Think in this way: "I am His servant, I am His **Servant "I" of a Bhakta.** Bhakta, devotee." There is no harm in this kind of "I." Sweet things cause dyspepsia and acidity, but crystallized sugar-candy is harmless. The path of wisdom is very difficult. It cannot be followed so long as the sense of "I" is connected with the body. In this age the consciousness of the body and the sense of "I" cannot be overcome easily. But in the path of devotion, through prayer and the repetition of His Holy Name with extreme longing, God can be reached without fail.

Devotee: Bhagavan, dost Thou teach us to renounce the worldly "I" and not the sense of the servant "I"?

Râmakrishna: Yes, the servant "I" or "I am the servant of God," "I am His devotee," this egoism is not bad but on the contrary it helps us to realize God.

Devotee: Bhagavan, does he who has the sense of the servant "I" possess passion and anger?

Râmakrishna: If this attitude of a servant be genuine and perfect, then passion and anger will drop off leaving only a scar in the mind. This "I" of a Bhakta or devotee does no harm to any living creature. It is like a sword which, after touching the Philosopher's Stone, is turned to gold. The sword retains the same form but it cannot cut or injure anyone. The dry leaves of the cocoanut-tree drop off in the wind, leaving a mark on the trunk; that mark proves that there was a leaf there at one time. Similarly, the scar of the sense of "I" remains in the mind of one who has realized God, but his whole nature is transformed into that of an innocent child. The child's sense of "I" is not attached to worldly objects. He may like a thing at one moment, but the next moment he may dislike it. You can take from him an object of great value by giving him a doll worth a penny. To a child everyone is equal, there is none greater or smaller. Therefore a child has no sense of caste or creed. If his

A child's "I."

mother says: "He is your brother," however low his caste may be, the child will sit with him and eat with him without feeling dislike or difference of any kind.

<u>Some Bhaktas after attaining to Samâdhi or God-consciousness, when they return, retain the sense of "I" as "I am His servant, I am His devotee."</u> They do not lose the sense of "I" entirely but keep a small portion of it to repeat the Holy Name of the Lord, to sing His praises, to love and serve Him. Again, those who constantly practise this sense of "servant I" eventually reach the Supreme Lord. This is the path of Bhakti or devotion. But true devotion is very rare. True devotion leads to intense love for God; and when that intense love comes, the Divine Being is not very far. In that intense love the sense of worldliness is wiped out entirely and the whole heart and soul rest upon nothing but the Lord of the universe. Some are born with this intense love for God; it is natural with them. Its expression is to be found even in their childhood. At that tender age even, they cry for God. There are many examples of such born Bhaktas like Prahlâda and others. Ordinary devotion which is confined by scriptural

GOSPEL OF RAMAKRISHNA

laws of sacrifice and worship is preparatory. As in hot weather one fans oneself for a breath of air so long as the breeze is not blowing, but when the breeze springs up, the fan is no longer needed; so when the breeze of intense love begins to blow in the soul, all devotional exercises like repetition of the Name of the Lord, sacrifice, prayers and asceticism become unnecessary. Devotion without intense love is the sign of unripe Bhakti. When it ripens, it leads into Divine Love, which is perfect and which brings the highest realization.

A disciple: Bhagavan, how can God be realized?

Râmakrishna: <u>God can be realized by the purified heart alone</u>. <u>Ordinarily the mind is stained with worldliness</u>. The mind

Pure heart.

may be compared to a needle. If a needle be covered with thick mud, it is not

God is like a magnet.

attracted by the magnet; but when the mud is washed off, the magnet attracts it. Similarly, when the mind is covered with the mud of worldliness, it does not feel the attraction of the Lord; but whosoever re-

Power of repentance.

pents, saying: "O Lord, I shall never again commit such an act," and sheds tears of true repentance, washes off all impurities and the magnet of the Lord then attracts the needle of the mind. Instantly superconsciousness comes and is followed by God-vision.

A man may make thousands of attempts, but nothing can be accomplished without the mercy of the Lord. Without His mercy no one can see Him. Nor is it an easy thing to obtain His mercy. The egotistic sense of "I" which says: "I am the doer," must be abandoned entirely before the Divine mercy can be felt. So long as there is a steward in charge of the storehouse, if any come to the master and beg him, saying: "Master, wilt thou not come to the storehouse and give me this thing?" he will reply: "The steward is there, what need have I to go?" In like manner, so long as the ego thinks of himself as the "doer" and the master of the storehouse of the heart, the Real Master does not enter there. The mercy of the Lord is the surest way to God-vision. He is the sun of wisdom. A single ray of this Eternal Sun illumines this world, and by that light we are conscious of ourselves and of one another and we acquire various kinds of knowledge. If He turns that light towards His

The mercy of the Lord.

God, the Sun of wisdom.

own face, then He becomes visible to His Bhakta or devotee. In the night the watchman goes from place to place holding in his hand the bull's-eye lantern. By its light he sees everyone's face and people see each other, but no one can see him. If any one wishes to see the watchman, he must beg him to turn the light towards himself. Similarly, he who wishes to see the Lord must pray to Him thus: "O Lord, in Thy mercy do Thou turn the light of Thy wisdom towards Thine own face that I may behold Thee." If there be no light in a house, that is the sign of extreme poverty. Therefore one must light the lamp of wisdom within the heart. "O mind, why dost thou not see the face of the Divine Mother by lighting the lamp of wisdom in the chamber of the soul!"

Illustration of a bull's-eye lantern.

CHAPTER III

THE BHAGAVÂN WITH CERTAIN OF HIS HOUSEHOLDER DISCIPLES

ONE day in winter a certain householder disciple, who was a college professor, came to see the Bhagavân. Srî Râmakrishna was seated on the southern veranda of His room, and He was smiling. After a short conversation He asked: "Do you prefer to meditate on God with form or without form?" The disciple hesitated and answered: "I prefer to meditate upon God as the formless Being rather than as a Being with form." The Bhagavân replied: "That is good. There is no harm in looking at Him from this or the other point of view. Yes, to think of Him as the formless Being is quite right. But do not go away with the idea that that alone is true and that all else is false. Meditating

God is formless and with form.

GOSPEL OF RAMAKRISHNA

upon Him as a Being with form is equally right. You, however, must hold on to your particular conception of God until you have realized and seen God."

The disciple asked: "Bhagavan, one may believe that God is with form, but surely He is **Image** not in the earthen images that are **worship.** worshipped?" Srî Râmakrishna replied: "My dear sir, why do you say earthen images? The image of the Divine Being is made of the spirit." The disciple could not understand the meaning of this, but answered: "Yet should it not be one's duty to make clear to those who worship images that God is not the same as the images and that at the time of worship they should think of God Himself and not of the image made of clay?" The Bhagavân said: "The Lord of the universe teaches mankind. He who has made the sun and moon, men and brutes; He who has created things for them to live upon, parents to tend and rear them; He who has done so many things will surely do something to bring them to the light. The Lord dwells in the temple of the human body. He knows our innermost thoughts. If there is anything wrong in image worship, does He not know that all worship is meant for Him? He will be pleased to accept it knowing that it is for Him. Why should you worry yourself about things which are beyond your reach? Try to realize God and love Him. This is your first duty.

"You speak of images made of clay. Well, there often comes a necessity for worshipping such images and symbols. In Vedânta it is said, the absolute Existence-Intelligence-Bliss pervades the universe and manifests itself through all forms. What harm is done by worshipping the Absolute through images and symbols? We see little girls with their dolls. How long do they play with them? So long as they are not married. After marriage they put away those dolls. Similarly, one needs images and symbols so long as God is not realized in His true form. It is God Himself who has provided these various forms of worship. The Master of the universe has done all this to suit different men in different stages of spiritual growth and knowledge. The mother so arranges the food for her children that each one gets what is best for him. Suppose a mother has five children with one fish to cook for all. She will make different dishes of it that she may give to each just what suits him,—the rich *polâo* for one, soup for another, fried fish for a third, fish with sour tamarind for a fourth, and so on, exactly according to the power of digestion of each. Do you now understand?"

The disciple replied: "Yes, Bhagavan, now I do. But, Revered Sir, how can one fix one's mind on God?"

Srî Râmakrishna: To that end one must always sing forth the Holy Name of God and talk without ceasing of His glory and attributes. Then one must seek the company of holy men. One must from time to time visit the Lord's devotees or those who have given up attachment to the things of the world for the sake of the Lord. It is, however, difficult to fix one's mind upon God in the midst of worldly cares and anxieties; hence the necessity of going into solitude now and again with a view to meditating on Him. In the first stage of one's spiritual life one cannot do without solitude. When plants are young, they stand in need of fences around them for their protection; otherwise goats and cattle will destroy them. The depth of the heart, the retired corner, and the forest are the three places for meditation.

How to fix one's mind on God.

Solitude necessary.

GOSPEL OF RAMAKRISHNA

One should also practise discrimination. One should discriminate between the Real and the unreal, between matter and spirit. It is thus that one will shake off one's love for the things of the world and attachment to sensual pleasures, wealth, fame, power.

Turning to Bijoy, who had come in the Bhagavân continued.: Shivanâth, the leader of the Brâhmo Samâj, has great cares, he has to edit a newspaper and do various other works In attending to worldly affairs, one naturally loses peace of mind and is overwhelmed with worries and anxieties. It is said in the Bhâgavat that Avadhuta * made twenty-four Gurus. The kite was one of them. In a certain place some fishermen were catching fish, a kite swooped down and snatched a fish. Seeing the kite with the fish in its claw, hundreds of crows flew after him and began to caw, making a great noise. In whatever direction the kite flew, the crows followed. When he flew to the

Marginal note: Avadhuta and a kite.

---

* "Avadhuta" is a Sanskrit title which is given to one who has become the absolute master of nature and who has realized God. Such a great soul was Dattâtreya. In the Purânas he is called the Avadhuta. He was also the author of the "Avadhuta Gitâ," a famous work on the Advaita Vedânta.

south, they pursued him; when he flew to the north, they were after him, and he found no peace in any direction. At last the kite dropped the fish. Then the crows flew after the fish and the kite rested calmly on the branch of a high tree. He thought within himself: "That fish was the cause of all this trouble. Now that I no longer have it, I am happy and in perfect peace." The Avadhuta learned from this kite that as long as a man is attached to worldly objects, so long he has toil, cares, anxiety, unrest and unhappiness. When attachment is gone, all works end, and then comes peace. But work without attachment is good; it does not bring unrest.

It is very difficult, however, to work and remain unattached. A few only can accomplish it. Those who have attained to God-consciousness, like the sage Nârada, work for the good of humanity. Avadhuta made another Guru —a bee. What trouble a bee takes to collect honey! But it is not for its own use; some one else comes and takes the honey from the comb. The Avadhuta learned from the bee that it is not wise to collect anything. Truly spiritual men should depend absolutely upon God and should not

Avadhuta and a bee.

desire to possess anything. But this is not possible for householders. They will have to support their families and therefore they should gather and possess. A fowl does not gather into barns, but when it has a number of young ones, then it brings food for them in its bill.

<u>Perform all your duties with your mind always fixed on God</u>. As for your parents, wife and children, serve them as your own, but always remember they do not belong to you, that they are the children of God. You are also a child of God and your own people are those who love God. The tortoise moves about in the water in quest of food; where do you think her mind is? On the water's edge where her eggs are laid. In the same manner you may go about in the world, but take good care that your mind always rests upon the hallowed feet of the Lord.

Practice of non-attachment.

Suppose you have not acquired true love for the Lord? If in this state you enter the world, then you will surely get entangled. Misfortune, grief, misery, sorrow, suffering and the various diseases of the body will disturb the balance of your mind; and the more you will throw yourself into the affairs of the world and trouble yourself about worldly matters, the more your attachment to the world will be increased. Rub your hand with oil if you desire to break open the jackfruit, else the milky exudation of the fruit will stick to your hands. First rub your soul with the oil of love and devotion to the Lord, then you may come in contact with the affairs of the world. But to this end solitude is the one thing needful. If you want butter, you must curdle the milk and set it in a place where no one can disturb it; otherwise the curd will not stand. Then churn it and the butter will rise. Similarly the neophyte should sit in solitude and not be disturbed by worldly-minded people; then through the churning of the settled mind by the practice of meditation the butter of Divine Love will be acquired. If you give your mind to God in solitude, you will obtain the spirit of true renunciation and absolute devotion. If you give the same mind to the world, it will grow worldly and think of woman and gold.

Need of solitude.

The world may be likened to water, and the mind to milk. Pure milk once mixed with water cannot be separated from it; but if it is first turned into butter and then placed in water,

GOSPEL OF RAMAKRISHNA

it can remain separate. Let the milk of your mind be turned into the butter of Divine Love by means of religious practices in solitude. The mind then will never get mixed with the water of worldliness, but will rise above and remain unattached to the world. Having attained true knowledge and devotion the mind will stand apart from the world.

Along with this, practise discrimination. "Lust and gold" are unreal; God is the one Reality. What uses has money? It can give one food, clothes, house, the luxuries and comforts of life, but it cannot bring spiritual perfection or God-vision. Therefore the acquisition of wealth should not be the highest end and aim of life. In this manner you should discriminate. Similarly by discrimination you will overcome your attachment to personal beauty. Think what the body of a beautiful woman is made of. Like all bodies it is of flesh and blood, skin and bones, fat and marrow, etc. The wonder is that man loses sight of God and gives his mind purely to such transitory objects of sense.

Lust and gold unreal.

The disciple asked: "Bhagavan, is it possible to see God?"

Srî Râmakrishna: Certainly. The following

are some of the means of seeing God: Going from
Means of God-vision. time to time into solitude; singing forth His name and His attributes; discrimination.

The disciple: Bhagavan, what state of mind leads to God-vision?

Srî Râmakrishna: Cry to God with a yearning heart and then you will see Him. People will shed a jugful of tears for the sake of their wife or children; they will be carried away by a stream of their own tears for the sake of money; but who sheds a tear for God? Cry for Him, not for show, but with a longing and yearning heart. The rosy light of the dawn comes before the rising sun; likewise a longing and yearning heart is the sign of God-vision that comes after.

Extreme longing is the surest way to God-vision. Through extreme longing the mind remains fixed on the Supreme Being. One should have faith like that of an innocent child and such longing as a child has when it wants to see its mother. There was a boy named Jatila. He used to go to school alone through the woods. Often he felt lonely and afraid. He told his mother about it and she said to him: "Why art thou fearful, my child? Thou must call Krishna whenever thou art frightened." "Who is Krishna, mother?" the boy asked. The mother answered: "Krishna is thy brother." After that when Jatila was passing through the woods alone and felt frightened, he called aloud, "Brother Krishna!" When no one came, he cried again: "O Brother Krishna, where art thou? Come to me and protect me; I am frightened." Hearing the call of this faithful child, Krishna could no longer remain away. He appeared in the form of a young boy and said: "Here am I, thy brother! Why art thou frightened? Come with me, I will take thee to school." Then having escorted him to school, Lord Krishna said to him: "I will come to thee whenever thou callest me; do not be afraid." Such is the power of true faith and true longing.

Power of true faith and true longing.

You can see God if your love for Him be as strong as the strength of these three attachments put together: namely, the attachment of a miser to his wealth, that of a mother to her new-born child, and that of a chaste wife to her husband.

How to love God.

To see God one must love Him with the whole heart and soul. One must make one's prayers

GOSPEL OF RAMAKRISHNA

reach the Divine Mother. Absolute self-resignation to the will of the Divine Mother is the surest way to God-vision. As the kitten resigns itself to the will of its mother, so a devotee shall resign himself to the will of the Divine Mother. The kitten knows nothing more than to cry "Mew, mew," and the mother-cat may keep her young one on the bare floor of the kitchen or on the downy bed of the householder. The kitten is always contented. Similarly the true devotee should always cry unto the Divine Mother and be contented with whatever She wishes to do with him.

God-consciousness does not come so long as there are three things in the heart,—shame, hatred and fear. These three and caste pride are the fetters of the soul. When these fetters are broken, freedom is attained. Bound by fetters is Jiva (the ego), free from fetters is Shiva (God).

Fetters of the soul.

Every man has certain debts to pay,—a debt to the Divine Spirit, a debt to the sages, debt to mother, to father, to the wife. No man can renounce everything without paying off these debts. But if his soul be intoxicated with Divine Love and become mad after God, then he is free from all duties and debts. Then who is his father, who is his mother and who is his wife? He behaves like a madman who is free **Madness of** from all bondage and who has no duty **Divine Love.** to perform. Do you know what that madness of Divine Love is? In that state one forgets the world and becomes unconscious of one's own body which is so dear to one. Chaitanya Deva possessed this madness of ecstasy. He had neither hunger, nor thirst, nor sleep, nor consciousness of his physical form. The meaning of the word Chaitanya is "indivisible and absolute intelligence." Vaishnava Charan used to say that Chaitanya Deva, the Incarnation of Divine Love, was like a bubble on the ocean of that Absolute Intelligence.

Divine Love is the rarest thing in the world. He who can love God as a devoted wife loves **Divine Love** her husband, attains to Divine Love. **and ecstasy.** Pure love is difficult to acquire. In pure love the whole heart and soul must be absorbed in God. Then will come ecstasy. In ecstasy a man remains dumb with wonder. Outward breathing stops entirely, but inward breathing continues; as when aiming a gun, a man remains speechless and without breathing. In Divine Love one entirely forgets the external world with all its charms and attractions; even one's own body, which is so dear to one, is easily forgotten. In ecstasy, when the breathing stops, the whole mind remains absolutely fixed upon the Supreme. All nerve currents run upward with tremendous force and the result is Samâdhi or God-consciousness. Those who are mere scholars (Pandits) and have not attained Divine Love, confound the minds of others.

Some people are proud of their wealth, their **Pride.** fame and social position, but these things are transitory. None can take them away after death. It is not good to be proud of wealth. You may say, "I am wealthy," but then there are millionaires, multimillionaires, and so on. In the evening fireflies think that they are lighting the world; but when the stars begin to shine, their pride is subdued. The stars in turn think that they are lighting the world, but when the moon shines, the stars are put to shame. The moon, too, believes that her light illumines everything; but lo! the dawn appears and the rising sun effaces the light of the moon. If wealthy people thought of these things, they would no longer be proud of their wealth.

A householder: Revered Sir, we are householders; please give us some further instructions.

Srî Râmakrishna: First know God, then perform the duties of a householder.

Householder: Revered Sir, is this world unreal?

Srî Râmakrishna: So long as a man does not realize God, so long it is real; because at that time he makes mistakes and through self-delusion says: "Me and mine." Being fettered by this self-delusion, he drowns in the sea of lust and worldliness, and becomes so blinded by ignorance that he cannot see the way out. You yourself can notice how transitory the world is. Look at this house; how many people have come and gone; how many people have been born and have died in it! Now it exists, now it does not; it is ephemeral. Those whom you call your own will vanish when your eyes are closed. If you have no one in the household, still you are bound and cannot go anywhere because of some distant relative. The way is open, but the fish cannot escape from the net. The silkworm makes its own cocoon, but does not know how to get out and consequently dies in it.

A householder should take care of his children,

GOSPEL OF RAMAKRISHNA

but at the same time he should think of them as Baby Krishna, or as children of God. Serve your father as God, and your mother as Divine Mother. After realizing God, if a man lives with his wife, he has no physical relation with her. Both live like Bhaktas or true devotees. They talk of spiritual subjects and spend their time in thinking of God and in caring for His Bhaktas. They serve God who dwells in all beings.

How a householder should live in the world.

Householder: But, Revered Sir, we do not find any such husbands and wives.

Râmakrishna: Yes, there are some, but they are very rare. Worldly people do not easily recognize them. But in order to live like this both must be spiritual. If both enjoy Divine Love, then such a life is possible; otherwise there will be no harmony, but discord and trouble between husband and wife. Perhaps the wife will complain, saying: "Why did I marry this man! What pleasure does he give me? He simply sits quietly and thinks of God. He is losing his mind."

A devotee: These are some of the obstacles; but there may be others. The children may be disobedient or may be diseased. Then, Revered Sir, what is to be done?

Râmakrishna: It is very difficult for a householder to practise devotion. There are many obstacles. You all know them very well,—disease, sorrow, poverty, disharmony with the wife, disobedience and evil tendencies in the children; but there is a way out of it. One should occasionally live in solitude and pray and struggle hard to attain to God.

A householder: Revered Sir, is it necessary to leave one's home?

Râmakrishna: Not for good; but occasionally when you find opportunity, for a day or two, leaving behind responsibility, care and anxiety. But during this time you should not mix with worldly people or think of worldly affairs. Either live alone, or in the company of some saint or holy man.

Householder: Revered Sir, how can we know or recognize a saint?

Râmakrishna: He is a saint whose heart, soul, and inner nature have turned towards God; *How to recognize a saint.* he who has renounced woman and wealth. <u>A saint does not look at women with the eye of desire; if he comes near a woman, he sees the Divine Mother in her and worships her. His thoughts are always on God and his words are of Him.</u> He sees God every-

GOSPEL OF RAMAKRISHNA

where and <u>knows that by serving others, he serves Him</u>. These are some of the outward signs of a saint.

Householder: Revered Sir, is it necessary to remain long in solitude?

Râmakrishna: Until right discrimination is acquired.

Householder: Revered Sir, what is right discrimination?

Râmakrishna: <u>God is Truth, the world is untruth; this is discrimination.</u> <u>Truth means that</u> **Right discrimi-** <u>which is unchangeable and perma-</u> **nation.** <u>nent, and untruth is that which is changeable and transitory.</u> He who has right discrimination knows that God alone is the Reality; <u>all other things are unreal</u>. When right discrimination comes, then rises intense desire to know God. As long as one loves untruth, such as the pleasures and comforts of the body, fame, honor and wealth, so long one does not desire to know God, the Truth. Right discrimination between Truth and untruth leads one to search after God.

Another householder devotee: Bhagavan, we have heard that Thou hast attained to ecstasy and God-consciousness; wilt Thou please explain when and how such a state comes?

Râmakrishna: Ecstasy does not come to one who has not realized God. When a fish rises from deep water, it disturbs the surface of the water, and the larger the fish, the greater the disturbance. Therefore, a person in the state of ecstasy sometimes laughs, sometimes weeps, sometimes sings, sometimes dances, but one cannot remain in that state of ecstasy for a long time.

Ecstasy.

Householder devotee: Bhagavan, we have heard that Thou hast seen God. If this be true, please make us see Him also.

Râmakrishna: Everything depends upon the will of the Lord. What can man do? One may repeat His Holy Name, but sometimes tears flow and sometimes not. At the time of meditation, one day you may have perfect concentration and another day you will not be able to fix your mind at all. Work is necessary for God-vision. Once I was passing by a pool, the surface of which was covered by a thick scum; I saw a poor man pushing the scum to one side to look at the water. This showed me that if you wish to see the water, you must push aside the scum. That act of pushing is like the work which removes all the impurities of the heart. Then

Work necessary for God-vision.

GOSPEL OF RAMAKRISHNA

God is visible. Concentration, meditation, repetition of the Name of the Lord, charitable works, self-sacrifice, these works will remove the scum of ignorance which covers the water of Divinity in the pool of the heart.

Mahima,* who had joined the group of devotees, exclaimed: Oh yes, Bhagavan, such works are absolutely necessary. Tireless labor is needed to attain great results. How much we must study! Innumerable are the sciences, Scriptures and philosophies.

Râmakrishna: How much can you study? What results can you get by mere discrimination? First try to realize God. Have faith in the words of your Guru, and perform some good work. If you have not found a Guru, a true spiritual master, earnestly pray to God. He will show you what He is like. What can you know by reading books? Before you enter a market-place, you can hear only a loud confused uproar; but when you go near, all confusion will vanish and you will distinguish what each

---

* Mahima was the first name of a Brâhmin Zemindar and a scholar who was known as Mahima Charan Chuckravarti. He lived the life of a pure and spiritual householder and regarded Râmakrishna as the greatest Hindu sage of the age.

one is calling. Before you reach the shore, you hear the roar of the waves; but when you come near, you see vessels, sea-gulls, birds, and you can count the waves. One cannot realize Divinity by reading books. **There is a vast difference between book knowledge and realization.** After realization,

<small>Book knowledge and realization.</small>

all books, sciences and Scriptures seem to be like worthless straw. It is necessary first to make acquaintance with the landlord. Why are you so anxious to know beforehand how many houses, how many gardens, how many stocks and bonds he possesses? If you ask the servants, they will not tell you; nor will they notice you. But if you can once become acquainted with the landlord, by whatever means, you will learn about his possessions in a moment, and the servants then will bow down to you and honor you.

A devotee: Bhagavan, how can one make acquaintance with the Landlord?

Râmakrishna: For that, I say, work is necessary. What is the use of sitting quietly and saying, "God exists"? If you merely sit on the shore of a lake and say: "There are fish in this lake," will you catch any? Go and get the things necessary for fishing, get a rod and line and bait and throw some lure in the water. Then from the deep water the fish will rise and come nearer, and you will be able to see and catch them. You wish me to show you God while you sit quietly by, without making the least effort. How unreasonable! You would have me set the curds, churn the butter, and hold it before your mouths. You ask me to catch the fish and place it in your hands. How unreasonable! If a man desires to see the King in his palace, he will have to go to the palace and pass through all the gates; but if after entering the outermost gate he exclaims, "Where is the King?" he will not find him. He must go on through the seven gates, then he will see the King.

Mahima: Bhagavan, by what kind of work can God be attained?

Râmakrishna: There is no difference in work. Do not think that this work will lead to God and that will not. Everything depends upon His Grace. Whatever work you perform with **Work and grace.** sincerity and earnest longing will attract His Grace and help towards realization. Through His Grace the conditions for realization will become perfect. These conditions are association with the holy, right discrimination of the Real from the unreal, and the finding of the real Guru, or true spiritual master. If your family depends upon you, perhaps your brother will assume its responsibility for you. Perhaps your wife will not hinder you in your spiritual life, but will rather help you; or perhaps you will not marry at all and will not be attached to the world in any way. When such conditions become absolutely favorable, the realization of God becomes easy.

Once a man's son lay at the point of death and none could help him. Some one, however, **Parable of the father and his dying son.** said: "There is but one hope. If you can get the venom of a cobra mixed with a few drops of rain-water fallen under the constellation of *Swâti* in a human skull, by it your son's life will be saved." The father looked and found that the constellation of *Swâti* would be in the ascendant on the morrow; so he prayed, saying: "O Lord, do Thou make possible all these conditions and spare the life of my son." With extreme earnestness and longing in his heart he set out on the following evening and searched diligently in a deserted spot for a human skull. At last he found one under a tree and watched, praying. Suddenly a shower came up and a few drops of rain lodged in the upturned skull. He said to himself: "Now I have the water in the skull under the right constellation." Then he prayed earnestly: "Grant, Lord, that the rest may also come." In a short time he discovered a toad not far from the skull, and he prayed again. Then from the grass sprang a cobra to snatch the toad, but at that moment the toad jumped over the skull and the venom of the cobra fell into it. With overwhelming gratitude the anxious father cried out: "Lord, by Thy Grace all impossible things are possible. Now I know that my son's life will be saved." Therefore I say, if you have true faith and earnest longing, you will get everything by the Grace of the Lord.

God cannot be obtained so long as the mind is not absolutely free from all worldly attachment. A true sage is one who cannot hoard anything for himself. There is a saying: "A fowl of the air and a true sage do not gather stores; they do not keep anything for the morrow." As regards myself, I cannot keep anything even for my personal needs. I cannot put away any object, even a clove, for the future. At one time I thought of going to Benares, but afterwards I discovered that I had to carry clothes and take money with

Non-attachment necessary.

GOSPEL OF RAMAKRISHNA

me, so it was impossible for me to go. (Turning to Mahima) But you are householders, you can have both this and that, both the world and the spiritual life.

Mahima: Bhagavan, "this" cannot remain long.

Râmakrishna: When I was practising renunciation, one day I went to the Ganges near the *Panchavati* and took up a handful of earth and a handful of coins; then I began to discriminate, saying that earth and gold are one and the same; earth is gold and gold is earth; and after realizing the sameness, I threw both into the river. I prayed to my Divine Mother, saying: "O Mother, I do not desire material wealth or earthly prosperity, but only that Thou dwell within my heart." When the mind renounces attachment to lust and wealth, it turns towards God and ultimately becomes attached to Him. Then that which was bound becomes free. To be turned away from God is bondage. The mind is like the needle of a scale and God is the central point of balance. When the weight of worldly attachment is in the heart, the scale drops to one side and the needle of the mind is deflected from the central point or God. The heavier the weight, the

GOSPEL OF RAMAKRISHNA

greater is the deflection. Why does a child cry after its birth? It thinks, as it were: "I was enjoying Divine Communion, but now I have lost it. Where have I come and where is my God, where is my God?" For you (to Mahima) the renunciation should be in the mind only. You should remain in the world, but unattached to it.

Mahima: Revered Sir, can the world exist for the mind which is fixed on God?

Râmakrishna: Of course it will exist; otherwise where will it go? I see that wherever I remain, I am in the kingdom of God. Verily I say unto you, this world is the kingdom of God. Râmachandra, the Divine Incarnation and the Hero of the epic Râmâyana, said to his father that he would renounce the world and go to a spiritual Guru in order to attain spiritual wisdom. The father summoned the great sage Vashishta to reason with his son. Vashishta saw that Râma had intense dispassion for the world; he then said to him· "O Râma, first discriminate with me, then renounce the world." By right discrimination Râma realized that God manifests Himself in the form of Jiva, or the individual soul and the world. Everything lives and exists

The kingdom of God is everywhere.

in and through His Being. Then Râma kept silent.

Some time ago Vaishnava Charan said that perfect knowledge of God is attained when one perceives Him in all human beings. I have now come to a stage of realization in which I see that God is walking in every human form and manifesting Himself alike through the sage and the sinner, the virtuous and the vicious. Therefore when I meet different people, I say to myself: "God in the form of the saint, God in the form of the sinner, God in the form of the unrighteous and God in the form of the righteous." He who has attained to such realization goes beyond good and evil, above virtue and vice, and realizes that the Divine will is working everywhere.

There was a Hindu monastery in a certain village. The monks of the monastery went out every day with begging bowls to gather food. One day, a monk, passing by, saw a Zemindar severely beating a poor man. The holy man, being very kind-hearted, entreated the Zemindar to stop beating the man. The Zemindar, blind with rage, immediately turned on the monk and poured upon him the venom of his anger. He

Parable of the monk and the Zemindar.

GOSPEL OF RAMAKRISHNA

beat him until he was knocked unconscious on the ground. Another man, seeing his condition, went to the monastery and told what had happened. His brother monks ran to the spot where the holy man was lying. They lifted him and brought him to the monastery and laid him in a room; but the holy man still remained unconscious for a long time. Sorrowful and anxious, his brothers fanned him, bathed his face, put milk into his mouth and tried to nurse him back to life. Gradually they brought him back to consciousness. The holy man opened his eyes and looked at his fellow-brethren. One of them, desiring to know whether he could recognize his friends, asked him in a loud voice: "Mahârâj, dost thou recognize him who is feeding thee with milk?" The holy man answered in a feeble voice: "Brother, he who beat me is now feeding me." And Râmakrishna added: But one cannot realize this oneness of the Spirit unless one has reached God-consciousness.

Live in the world like a dead leaf. As a dead leaf is carried by the wind into a house or on the roadside and has no choice of its own, so let the wind of Divine Will blow you wherever it chooses. Now it has placed you in the world, be contented.

Resignation.

89

Again when it will carry you to a better place, be equally resigned. The Lord has kept you in the world, what can you do? Resign everything to Him, even your own dear self; then all trouble will be over. You will see then that He is doing everything; everywhere is the will of Râma * (God).

In a certain village there lived a weaver. He was very spiritual; everyone trusted and **Parable of the pious weaver.** loved him. The weaver went to the market to sell his cloth. If a customer asked the price of it, he would say: "By the will of Râma the thread cost one Rupee, by the will of Râma the labor cost four Annas, by the will of Râma the profit is two Annas, by the will of Râma the price of the cloth as it stands is one Rupee and six Annas." People had such confidence in him that they would immediately pay the price and take the cloth. This man was a true devotee. At night after dinner he would sit for a long time and meditate on God and repeat His Holy Name. Once it was late into the night; he could not sleep;

---

* The word Râma refers to the Divine Hero described in the Hindu epic called "Râmâyana." It is also a name which the Hindu Bhaktas use for the Supreme Lord of the universe.

he was sitting alone in the courtyard near the entrance, smoking. A gang of robbers was passing that way. They wanted a carrier, and seeing this man, they dragged him away with them. Then they broke into a house and stole a great many things, some of which they piled on the poor weaver's head. At this moment the watchman came up, the robbers ran away and the poor weaver with his load was caught. He had to spend that night in confinement. Next morning he was brought before the judge. The people of the village, hearing what had happened, came to see the weaver. They unanimously declared: "My lord, this man has not stolen anything." The judge then asked the weaver to describe what had occurred. The weaver said: "My lord, by the will of Râma, I was sitting in the courtyard; by the will of Râma it was very late in the night; I, by the will of Râma, was meditating upon God and repeating His Holy Name; when, by the will of Râma, a band of robbers passed that way; by the will of Râma they dragged me away with them; by the will of Râma they broke into a house; by the will of Râma they piled a load on my head; when, by the will of Râma, the watchman came up and, by the will of Râma, I was caught.

Then, by the will of Râma, I was kept in prison, and this morning the will of Râma has brought me before thee." The judge, seeing the innocence and spirituality of the man, ordered him to be released. Coming out, the weaver said to his friends, "The will of Râma has released me."

Everything depends on God's will. Whether you live in the world or renounce it, everything depends upon the will of Râma. Throwing your whole responsibility upon God, do your work in the world. If you cannot do this, what else can you do?

If a clerk be imprisoned, when the term of his sentence is over and he comes out, tell me, will he pass his time in dancing for joy over his release or resume his work as clerk? So when the householder is liberated from the prison of the world, will he spend his life in rejoicing over his liberation? He may continue to perform his duties as householder, if he so desires. He who has attained wisdom makes no distinction between this place and that place; to him all positions are equal. He who has found God here has also found Him there. When the tail of a tadpole drops off, it can live both in water and on land. When the tail of ignorance drops off, man becomes free. He can then live both in God and in the world equally well.

Those who follow monistic (Advaita) Vedânta, however, look upon this world as unreal, **The world like a dream.** like a dream. According to them Paramâtman, or the Over-Soul, is the witness of the three states of consciousness,—waking, dream and dreamless sleep. All these are ideas. The dream state is just as real as the waking state. Let me tell you a story.

There was a farmer who was a monist; he had attained to some realization. He lived like **Parable of the farmer and his only child.** any other farmer with his family, and he had a child. He and his wife had extreme love for this son because he was their only child. The farmer himself was a very spiritual man. He was respected and loved by everyone in the village. Once he was working in the field, when suddenly a man brought the news of his son's severe illness. He went home, called physicians, took great care, but could not save the child's life. Everybody in the household was overwhelmed with grief, but the farmer looked as if nothing had happened. He consoled others by saying, "What can be gained by mourning over the child?" The next day he went to the field as

GOSPEL OF RAMAKRISHNA

usual, and after finishing his work he came home and found his wife and the other members of the family still weeping and wailing and plunged in deep sorrow. The wife reproached him, saying: "How heartless you are! you have not shed a single tear for your only child." The farmer then calmly replied: "Shall I tell you why I do not weep? Last night I had a wonderful dream. I saw that I was a king, and the father of eight beautiful children, and that I was enjoying all the pleasures and comforts of life. Suddenly I woke up and the dream passed away. Now I am in great confusion,—whether I shall weep and wail for my eight children or for this only one." The farmer was an Advaita Jnâni, therefore he realized that the waking state was as unreal as the dream state, and that the one permanent Reality was Atman. But I accept all states as true,—the state of Samâdhi, which is the fourth state, and again, the waking, dream and dreamless sleep state. I accept Brahman the Absolute and Mâyâ, Jiva (the individual soul) and the world. If I do not take all, a portion will be missing and the weight will be less.

A devotee: How could the weight be less?

Râmakrishna: Brahman the Absolute is with

the individual souls and the phenomenal world. First, when a person is discriminating by saying: "Not this, not this," he leaves the individual egos and the phenomenal world aside; then after reaching the Absolute, when he returns, he realizes that the Absolute appears as the phenomenal world.

The Absolute and the phenomenal.

In a wood-apple there are seeds, pulp and the shell. When I take the pulp, I leave out the seeds and the shell; but when I speak of the weight of the wood-apple, the weight of the pulp alone would not be equal to it. You will have to weigh the pulp, seeds, shell and everything. That which has pulp has also seeds and shell. Similarly, that which is the Absolute has also all phenomena. Therefore I take both the Absolute Reality and the phenomenal reality. I do not blow away the phenomenal world by calling it a dream, because then the weight will be less.

Mahima: This is a wonderful harmony. From the Absolute to the phenomenal and from the phenomenal to the Absolute.

Râmakrishna: Those who are Jnânis (monists) look at the world as a dream, but the realistic Bhaktas take every state as real. There are some cows who pick only certain tufts of grass and give very little milk; but there are other cows who eat all kinds of grass and give plenty of milk. The Jnânis may be compared to the former, and the Bhaktas to the latter. <u>The highest of the Bhaktas take both the Absolute and the phenomenal</u>; therefore when they come down from the Absolute to the plane of relativity, they continue to enjoy the Absolute through the phenomenal. (To Mahima) You explain *Om* as containing three letters, *A-u-m*.

Mahima: Revered Sir, A-u-m means creation, preservation and destruction.

Râmakrishna: But for me it is like the sound d-o-n-g of a big bell, which is at first audible, then inaudible, and ultimately melts away into infinite space. So the phenomenal melts away in the Absolute; the gross, subtle and causal states lose themselves in the Great Cause, the Absolute; the waking, dream and dreamless sleep states become merged in the fourth state, Samâdhi. When the bell sounds, it creates waves like those in the ocean when a heavy stone is thrown into it. From the Absolute phenomena come out, from the same Absolute, which is the great First Cause, have also evolved the gross, subtle and causal bodies.

From the same Absolute, again, which is the fourth state, come the other three states of consciousness. The waves of the ocean are once more dissolved in the ocean. By this illustration of d-o-n-g I show that <u>the eternal word *Om* is symbolic of the evolution and involution of phenomena from and into the Absolute. I have *seen* all these things</u>. My Divine Mother has shown me that in the infinite ocean of the Absolute, waves rise and again merge into it. In that infinite spiritual space millions of planets and worlds rise and are dissolved. <u>I do not know what is written in your books; I have *seen* all this</u>.

Mahima: <u>Those who had realized, did not write the books. They were intoxicated by their own realization. They forgot everything, how could they write?</u> To write something is to have a calculating intellect. Others having learned from them, have written and their writings are known as Scriptures.

Râmakrishna: Worldly people say that it is impossible to be free from attachment to world-

When God is attained worldly attachment vanishes.

liness. But when God is attained, all worldly attachment vanishes. After realizing the absolute bliss of God-consciousness one cannot enjoy sense-pleasures or run after fame, honor or any worldly object. Moths after once seeing the light do not return to the darkness. As much as one thinks of God and meditates on Him, by so much will one lose one's taste for worldly pleasures. As much as one's love and devotion for God increases, by so much will diminish worldly desires and care for the body. Then one will look upon every woman as mother, upon his own wife as a spiritual helpmate; all animal passions will disappear; Divine spirituality will come, and non-attachment to the world; then one will become absolutely emancipated even in this life.

CHAPTER IV

VISIT TO THE PANDIT VIDYÂSÂGARA *

Srî Râmakrishna desired to meet Pandit Iswara Chandra Vidyâsâgara. One afternoon he was seen coming in a carriage with some of his disciples all the way from Dakshineswara, a distance of about six miles, to pay a visit to the Pandit at Bâdurbagan in Calcutta. As the carriage passed before Râjâ Râmmohun Roy's †

---

* Pandit Iswara Chandra Vidyâsâgara was the greatest Hindu scholar of his time in Calcutta. He was a true philanthropist, a patriot, an educationalist, and the founder of the Metropolitan Institution in Calcutta. The word Vidyâsâgara is a Sanskrit title which he acquired on account of his vast erudition. It means "ocean of knowledge."

† Râjâ Râmmohun Roy was a great Hindu reformer who lived between 1774 and 1833 A.D. He was the first earnestminded investigator of the science of comparative religion that the world has produced. He studied the Vedas in Sanskrit and the Buddhist Scriptures in the original Pâli

GOSPEL OF RAMAKRISHNA

house, the Bhagavân suddenly grew silent. <u>His mind was absorbed in meditation on the Divine Mother.</u> One of his disciples, not perceiving the sudden change that had come over him, said: "This is Râmmohun Roy's house." The Bhagavân replied: "Ah! Now my mind is not on such things"; and <u>immediately he entered into the ecstatic state (Bhâva)</u>.

The carriage, a short while after, drew up in front of the Pandit's house. Srî Râmakrishna alighted, supported by one of His disciples. Before reaching the staircase which led to the Pandit's study, which was also the drawing-room, the Bhagavân, putting his hand on His shirt, asked a disciple with some concern: "My shirt is unbuttoned; is it necessary to button it?" The disciple answered: "Do not trouble Thyself, Lord; none will find fault with Thee on that

Râmakrishna's childlike nature.

---

the Koran in Arabic, the Old Testament in Hebrew, and the New Testament in Greek. He denounced the practice of Suttee which was abolished in 1829. He established the Hindu Unitarian Theistic movement known as the "Brâhmo Samâj." He was the first Hindu Brâhmin of rank and influence who visited Paris and England. After nearly two years' stay in England Râjâ Râmmohun Roy died at Bristol in 1833.

account." The Bhagavân, like a child, seemed to be satisfied and did not think about it again. The party was then led upstairs into a room where the Pandit was seated in a chair facing the south. A table after the European fashion, with books and papers lying about on it, was before him, and he was talking with some of his friends. As the Bhagavân Srî Râmakrishna entered the room, the Pandit rose to receive Him. The Lord stood with His face to the west and with one hand resting upon the table. He looked upon the Pandit intently as if he was an old acquaintance, and <u>with a smile on His sweet, childlike radiant face, lost all sense-consciousness, and went into the ecstatic Samâdhi</u>.

After a while, taking his seat on a bench, the Bhagavân in his semiconscious state uttered, "I wish some water to drink." Thereupon Vidyâsâgara inquired of a disciple whether the Bhagavân would also like some delicious sweetmeats which he had just received from Burdwân.* Finding no objection, the Pandit went into his inner apartments and returned with water and the sweetmeats. He placed them

---

* Burdwân, an old city in Bengal, famous for delicious sweetmeats.

before the Lord. The disciples partook of the sweetmeats, but when they were offered to one young man, Vidyâsâgara said: "Oh, he is a child of the house; do not trouble about him."

The Bhagavân then said, referring to a young man who was sitting before him: "Yes, this young man is good. He is like the river Falgu,* covered with dry sand, but if you dig a little you will find a strong invisible current underneath. He has a spiritual current inside, although he does not show it on the outside."

Then addressing Vidyâsâgara he continued: "To-day I have at last reached the ocean (referring to the literal meaning of the word Vidyâsâgara,—the ocean of knowledge). So long I have seen only canals, lakes, or, at most, rivers, but now I see the ocean itself.

Râmakrishna's love of humor.

Vidyâsâgara: Then, Sir, Thou art welcome to take some salt water from it.

Bhagavân: No, my dear sir, why salt water? You are not the ocean of Avidyâ (ignorance),

---

* Falgu is the name of a sacred river near the holy city of Gayâ in India. It was on the bank of this river that Buddha attained to the highest enlightenment. Its bed is covered with sand like a desert, but a strong current of pure water flows underneath.

which leads away from God, but you are the ocean of milk, the ocean of Vidyâ, or true knowledge leading Godward.

Vidyâsâgara: Revered Sir, Thou mayest say *that*.

Bhagavân: Your Karma proceeds from the Sattwa element of nature. From it rises compassion. Whatever work is done for the good of others is absolutely free from fault. It may be called Râjasika, but it is the activity of Sattwa.

Good works and compassion for all.

There is no harm in such works. Sukadeva and others like him had compassion for all. They worked for humanity and helped mankind in the path of Divinity. You are giving free education and doing charitable works; that is good. He who performs good works through love, without seeking results, attains to God. But he who works for name, fame or any other selfish purpose remains bound. Further, I may say that you have already become *Siddha* (perfected).

Vidyâsâgara: Sir, how is that?

Bhagavân: You know that *Siddha*, or well-boiled potato, becomes soft and tender. Have you not become tender-hearted by your compassion for all?

GOSPEL OF RAMAKRISHNA

Vidyâsâgara: But the paste of Kalai (a kind of pulse) when boiled (Siddha) becomes harder. Is it not so?

Bhagavân, laughing: Yes, but you are not like that. Mere book-learned Pandits (scholars) are hard-hearted. They do good neither to themselves nor to others. They are like vultures who soar high in the sky, but always search after carrion-pits. They may talk about Divine truths, but their minds are attached to woman and wealth. Their attachment is to worldly things (Avidyâ). <u>Compassion, Devotion (Bhakti), Dispassion (Vairâgya)—these are the manifestations of Vidyâ</u>.

Book-learned Pandits like vultures.

Vidyâsâgara was listening to the words of wisdom with whole attention, while the eyes of other gentlemen present were fixed upon the blissful face of Râmakrishna radiant with Divine glory.

The Bhagavân continued: The Absolute Brahman is beyond the reach of Vidyâ (knowledge) as well as of Avidyâ (ignorance), which keeps one away from the realization of the Absolute.

Vidyâ and Avidyâ.

The absolute Brahman is beyond the reach of Mâyâ, while Mâyâ is either Vidyâ or Avidyâ.

Vidyâ-Mâyâ and Avidyâ-Mâyâ both exist in this world. As there are knowledge (Jnâna) and Devotion (Bhakti), so also there are lust and greed for wealth. Good and evil, virtue and vice, are to be found in this world of relativity; but Brahman is unaffected by them. They exist in relation to Jiva (individual ego), but cannot touch the Absolute Brahman.

Brahman may be compared to the light of a lamp. As by the same light one may read **Brahman untouched by good and evil.** the Holy Scriptures and another may forge a document, while the light remains unaffected by the good and evil deeds, so is the Absolute Brahman untouched by the good and evil of the world. He is like the Sun who shines equally upon the virtuous and the wicked.

If you ask, misery, sin, suffering, unhappiness,—whose are these? I should answer, they are for the Jiva. They do not affect the Brahman. Evil to Jiva is not evil to Brahman any more than the venom in the fangs of a snake is poison to the snake. Others may die of snake-bite, but as the poison does not hurt the snake, so indeed is the existence of sin and evil in relation to Jiva alone. Who can describe what the absolute Brahman is? Whatever can be uttered by the mouth has become defiled as it were, like the leavings of food. <u>The Revealed Scriptures, Vedas, Tantras, Purânas and all Holy Books, have become defiled as it were, like leavings of food, for they have</u> been uttered by human mouths.

Brahman indescribable.

But there is one thing that is never defiled in this manner and that is the Absolute Brahman. No one has ever succeeded in describing the Absolute by words of mouth. <u>Brahman is unspeakable, indescribable, unthinkable.</u>

Vidyâsâgara, interrupting, said to his friends: This is a grand idea. To-day I have learned this truth, that the Brahman is the one substance that has never been defiled by the mouth.

Bhagavân: Yes, that is so.

A certain father had two sons. To instruct them in the knowledge of Brahman he sent

Parable of the Vedic father and his two sons.

them to an Âchârya (preceptor). After a few years they returned home and saluted their father. The father was anxious to know how far they had learned about Brahman, so he asked his eldest son: "My dear son, you have studied all the Scriptures and philosophies, tell me what is Brahman like?" The eldest son then tried to describe

GOSPEL OF RAMAKRISHNA

the Absolute Brahman by quoting various passages from the Vedas. The father kept silent.

Turning to his younger son he asked the same question. The younger son did not answer in words, but remained motionless and communed with the Brahman in silence. The father then exclaimed: "My dear child, thou hast approached the realization of the Brahman. Thy silence is a better answer than the recitation of a hundred texts of the Vedas, for Brahman is indescribable by words. It is indeed the Absolute Silence." The knowledge of the Absolute Brahman is attained in the state of *Samâdhi*. In that superconscious state Brahman is realized. Then all thoughts cease to rise and perfect silence prevails in the soul. Even the power of speech remains unmanifested. How can one describe Brahman by words of mouth? Man thinks that he has known the Absolute Brahman.

An ant went to a mount of sugar. The ant did not realize how high was the mountain, but ate a small particle of sugar and was satisfied. It carried home another particle in its mouth. On its way it thought: "Next time I will carry the whole mountain." Such, alas, is the thought of

Parable of the ant and the mount of sugar.

107

small minds. They think that they have known the Absolute, not realizing that Brahman is beyond the reach of mind and thought. However great the mind may be it cannot fully comprehend the Absolute Brahman. Sukadeva * and other great spiritual teachers may be compared to large ants. They could carry in their mouth at utmost eight or ten grains from the mountain of sugar. It is as absurd to say that Brahman has been fully comprehended by a great man as it is absurd to say that the whole mountain of sugar was carried away by a large ant.

<u>What the Vedas and other Scriptures have said about the Absolute is like the description of the ocean given by a man who saw the vast ocean.</u> When asked what the ocean was like, he exclaimed in utter amazement: "Oh! what I have seen; how vast is the expanse! How big are the waves! What a thundering roar!"

Like unto this is the talk about the Absolute Brahman. The Vedas declare that Brahman is

---

* Sukadeva was the son of Vyâsâ, the author of the Vedanta Sutras and many of the Purânas. He was born with the *Brahma Jnâna*, or the knowledge of the Absolute. He, in his childhood, renounced the world with all its pleasures and attractions. He is regarded by the Hindus as **the Ideal Jnâni,** or Knower of Brahman.

the ocean of the Absolute Existence, Intelligence and Bliss. Sukadeva and other great spiritual teachers stood on the shore of that Infinite Ocean, saw it and touched its waters.

Some believe that even those great souls did not go into the Ocean, for whoever enters into that ocean of Brahman does not return to this mundane existence.

A doll made of salt once went to the ocean to measure its depth. It had a desire to tell others **Parable of a salt doll.** how deep was the ocean. Alas! Its desire was never satisfied. No sooner had it plunged into the ocean than it melted away and became one with the ocean. Who would bring the news regarding the depth? Similar is the condition of the Jiva (individual ego) who enters into the Infinite Ocean of the Absolute Brahman.

Some one asked: Bhagavan, is it true that the man who has entered into Samâdhi, or who has acquired *Brahma Jnânam*, does not speak?

Râmakrishna to Vidyâsâgara: Yes, he who has realized Brahman becomes silent. Discus-
Brahman is silence. sions and argumentations exist so long as the realization of the Absolute does not come. If you melt butter in a pan over fire, how long does it make a noise?

109

So long as there is water in it. When the water is evaporated it ceases to make further noise. Again if you throw a piece of dough in that hot clarified butter (Ghee) there will be noise until the cake is thoroughly fried. The soul of a seeker after Brahman may be compared to fresh butter. It is mixed with the water of egoism and worldliness. Discussions and argumentations (Vichâra) of a seeker are like the noise caused during the process of purification by the fire of knowledge. As the water of egoism and worldliness is evaporated and the soul becomes purer, all noise of debates and discussions ceases and absolute silence reigns in the state of Samâdhi.

<u>Thus realizing the Absolute Brahman in silence, the soul comes down on the plane of</u> *Egoism of a saint.* <u>relativity to help others and to teach mankind the highest wisdom of Brahman. Then he talks again and makes a noise again</u>, as the hot Ghee does when in contact with a piece of dough. Such a soul retains the sense of "I" simply to help mankind. Sankarâchârya and other spiritual teachers kept the purified sense of "I" without which all teaching is impossible.

The bee buzzes so long as it is outside the

GOSPEL OF RAMAKRISHNA

lotus and does not settle down in its heart to
Sages teach drink of the honey. As soon as it
for the good tastes of the honey all buzzing is at
of others. an end. Similarly all noise of discussion ceases when the soul of the neophyte begins to drink the nectar of Divine Love in the Lotus Feet of the Almighty. Sometimes, however, the bee after being intoxicated by the honey makes a sweet humming sound. So the God-intoxicated soul sometimes speaks for the good of others.

A pitcher makes a noise when it is being filled with water in a tank. But all noise stops as soon as the pitcher is full to the brim. The noise will be heard again if some water of the pitcher be poured into another pitcher. (Here water means the water of the Divine Wisdom, and the soul of a wise man is the pitcher.)

The question now arises, how do we explain the relation between a perfect Guru and his
Relation be- disciples? The Guru must talk in
tween Guru order to drive away the ignorance of
and disciples. his disciples. This kind of discrimination, however, does no harm. The boiling butter after it is clarified ceases to make any noise; but if the raw cake made of flour is thrown into it, it will produce much noise be-

GOSPEL OF RAMAKRISHNA

cause of the water in the cake. The noise will continue until the cake is properly fried. The unfried cake may be compared to the disciple, and the boiling butter to the Guru, the spiritual teacher. The sound of teaching is heard so long as the disciple is not perfectly enlightened.

Srî Râmakrishna continued: So long as the individual soul has the slightest attachment to the world of senses and desires it cannot attain to Brahma-Jnâna. He is a Jnâni who relinquishes all worldly desires and sense-pleasures by saying, "not this, not this," and then realizes the Supreme Brahman in Samâdhi.

Non-attachment.

A Jnâni knows that all phenomena of the universe which are subject to evolution, whether physical or mental, are within the realm of Mâyâ; they are unreal and transitory like the objects of vision in a dream. Therefore as one climbs the stairway step by step until the roof is reached, so he rises above them step by step, saying "not this," until he reaches the Absolute Brahman, which is the roof of the phenomenal universe.

A Jnâni goes so far as to realize that Brahman is the Absolute Reality and all phenomena unreal. A Vijnâni, however, goes farther and

GOSPEL OF RAMAKRISHNA

realizes more. He sees that the roof and the steps are all made of the same substance. Few

All phenomena unreal. can stay long on the roof (the realm of the Absolute). All those who reach this state of Samâdhi must return to lower planes, just as no one can sing on "Si," the highest note of the gamut, for a long time. The sense of "I" drags one down. But when a Vijnâni returns from Samâdhi to a lower plane of consciousness and perceives the world of relativity, he sees the Brahman everywhere, and that the same Absolute Being appears as Jiva and all the phenomena of the universe. He realizes, "I am Brahman," "I am He."

There are various paths which lead to the realization of the Absolute Brahman. The

Jnâna-Yoga and Bhakti-Yoga. path of a Jnâni is as good as that of a Bhakta. Jnâna-Yoga is true; so is Bhakti-Yoga. There is another path of Bhakti mixed with Jnâna which is equally true. So long as the sense of "I, me, mine" remains in the devotee, the path of Bhakti is easier for him.

A Vijnâni, however, realizes the Absolute Brahman as the unchangeable Reality of the universe, firm and immutable like the Mount *Sumeru*. It is beyond all activity of Mâyâ.

He also sees that the world has evolved out of the three *Gunas* (Sattwa, Rajas and Tamas) of the Prakriti or Cosmic energy.

Mâyâ or Prakriti consists of Vidyâ and Avidyâ. Vidyâ is that energy which leads Godward.

Mâyâ. It manifests itself as discrimination (Viveka), non-attachment (Vairâgya), devotion and love of God (Bhakti, Prema). But Avidyâ leads to worldliness. This energy expresses itself as various passions, desire for wealth and honor, ambition, work with attachment, selfishness. All these Vidyâ and Avidyâ forces rise from the Divine Energy of Brahman—they cannot affect the Brahman. The Vijnâni

Vijnâni and Bhakta. realizes that the same Absolute Brahman appears as the Personal God (Iswara), that He who is beyond all attributes is also the Personal God with all attributes and blessed qualities. The Vijnâni sees that Jiva (individual ego), phenomenal world, mind, intellect, Bhakti, dispassion, knowledge—all these are the glory of the supreme Personal Deity. If these manifestations of the Divine Glory did not exist, who would have worshipped Him as the Lord of the universe? If a rich man does not possess wealth and property, but becomes bankrupt, nobody will call him rich.

GOSPEL OF RAMAKRISHNA

Do you not see how beautiful is this world? How many varieties of phenomena—the Sun, moon, stars, various kinds of animals and vegetables, things large and small, good and bad, some men with great powers, others with few.

Vidyâsâgara: Is it then true, Revered Sir, that God has given to some greater powers than to others? Is the Lord partial?

Bhagavân: <u>The Lord dwells as the all-pervading Being (Vibhu) equally within all living creatures great or small, nay, even in the smallest ant or animalcule. The difference lies in the manifestation of powers (Sakti)</u>, otherwise how will it be possible for one strong man to defeat ten men in a hand-to-hand fight, while a weakling will run away from the presence of an ordinary mortal?

Unity in diversity.

If there were no difference in powers, why should people respect and honor you? You have no monstrosity, like two horns on the forehead, that people will come to see you out of curiosity. You have more compassion, more wisdom than others, therefore people come to see you and pay respects to you. Do you not think so?

There is nothing in mere book-learning.

GOSPEL OF RAMAKRISHNA

Book-learning. One should study books simply to find out the ways by which He (the Absolute Brahman) can be realized.

A holy man had a manuscript with him. Some one asked what it contained. The saint opened it and showed that on every page was written the sacred formula "Om Râma," the holy name of the Lord.

True meaning of Gitâ. Take the sacred book of Bhagavad Gitâ. What does it teach? If you wish to know it repeat the name "Gitâ" ten times in quick succession—"Gi-tâ, gi-tâ, gi-," etc. It will sound like "tâgi, tâgi," which has the same meaning as the Sanskrit word "Tyâgi," that is, one who has renounced everything of the world for the sake of the Lord. One truth which Bhagavad Gitâ teaches is this: "O Jiva, giving up attachment to objects and pleasures of the world, struggle to realize God." The mind of a man (whether a saint or a householder) must be free from all attachment to the world. Then and then alone the heart will be purified and the Absolute will be realized.

Chaitanya Deva * (God Incarnate of Nuddea),

---

* Chaitanya Deva, see note page 7.

when travelling on a pilgrimage in the Deccan (Southern India), saw in one place a man reading aloud the texts of the Gîtâ. At a little distance another man, with unrestrainable tears running down his cheeks, was listening. Chaitanya Deva asked him whether he understood the meaning of the texts. The poor man replied: "My Lord, I do not understand one word of what the Pandit is reading." Chaitanya Deva questioned him: "Why are you weeping, then?" The devotee answered: "I see the chariot of Arjuna, and the Blessed Lord Krishna is speaking before him. This Divine vision brings tears of love to my eyes."

Srî Râmakrishna continued: You may ask why does a Vijnâni prefer to have Bhakti (love and devotion)? The answer is—Because it is difficult for one to be free from the sense of "I." In the state of *Nirvikalpa Samâdhi,** it may vanish for the time being, but it comes back again; while for ordinary individuals it is almost impossible to eliminate this sense of "I, me and mine." However many times you may cut

---

* Nirvikalpa Samâdhi is described in the Râja Yoga as the highest state of Samâdhi in which the soul rises above the sense of "I" and the plane of all thoughts, ideas and emotions, and reaches the realm of the Absolute.

off the branches of the *Aswatthwa* tree, so long as the root is alive new branches will sprout; **Sense of "I."** similarly you may try to get rid of the sense of "I," but so long as the root is alive it will sprout up again and again. Even after acquiring Brahma-Jnâna the emancipated soul is forced back to the plane of this "Aham" sense of "I."

If you dream of a tiger you will tremble in every limb and your heart will throb violently. When you wake up you may realize that it was a mere dream, but still your heart will go on palpitating all the same. Similarly the sense of "I" remains even after the realization of the Absolute.

Thus, if the sense of "I" is the cause of all troubles and it is impossible to be free from it, let it stay on as "I," the servant of the Lord.

Râma Chandra (the God Incarnate) once asked his great devotee Hanumân: "My son, in what relation do you regard me?" The devotee replied: "When I think of myself as embodied, I am Thy servant and Thou art the Lord. When I think of myself as the Jiva (Ego) I am Thy part and Thou art the Universal Whole; but when I think of myself as the

Âtman, I am one with Thee. Then I realize 'I am Thou and Thou art I.'"

If the sense of "I" clings to one so persistently, let it remain like that of a true Bhakta who thinks of himself as the servant of the Lord.

"I" and "mine"—these two are the signs of *Ajnânam*, ignorance. My house, my wealth, my learning, my glory, all these are mine—this idea proceeds from ignorance of one's true Self, but *Jnânam* or divine knowledge means that state where Jiva realizes: "O Lord, Thou art the Master of all; house, family, children, friends, relatives, nay, whatever exists in the universe belongs to Thee." "Whatever is mine is Thine." "Nothing belongs to me"—such ideas rise from true knowledge.

<small>Ajnânam and Jnânam.</small>

It is good for everyone to remember that after death nothing of this world will remain with us. We have come here simply to perform certain Karma and gain some experience. Just as country people come to a big city like Calcutta to do some work, so we have come to fulfil our desires according to the tendencies with which we were born.

A rich man has given the charge of his beau-

GOSPEL OF RAMAKRISHNA

tiful garden to his *Sircar* (steward). When visitors come to see the garden the *Sircar* waits on them attentively. He shows them the beautiful parts of the garden with luxurious fruit-trees, flower-beds, palace-like buildings, lakes, etc., saying. "These are, gentlemen, our mango-trees. This is our orchard; this is our lake; how beautiful are our flowers! Here you see is our drawing-room with most expensive furniture, fine paintings by the best artists—all these belong to us." The same *Sircar* may be found fault with and dismissed by his master at any time with peremptory order to leave the garden at once. He will not be allowed sufficient time to pack up his trunk and take his own baggage with him. Such is the miserable plight of those who lay claim upon things which do not in reality belong to them.

Parable of the rich man and his Sircar.

Everything belongs to the Lord. It is ridiculous for man to say, "I am Kartâ" (the doer), "All these things are mine."

On two occasions the Lord cannot help smiling: A person is taken seriously ill and is about to die. The physician says to the mother of the patient: "Mother, there is no cause for fear. I shall save

The Lord smiles on two occasions.

your son's life." The physician forgets that <u>the will of the Lord is at the root of every event of life and death</u>. The Lord then smiles, thinking: "How foolish this man must be who boasts of saving the life of his patient when the latter is dying under My will." The Lord smiles again when two brothers are engaged in partitioning their estate. They take a measuring-tape and, putting it out across the land, say: "This portion is mine, and that is yours." The Lord smiles, thinking: "The whole Universe belongs to Me, but these foolish brothers say: 'This portion is mine and that is yours.'"

"O Lord, Thou makest everything and Thou art my nearest and dearest One. This house, this family, these relatives, these friends of mine, nay, this whole universe belongs to Thee, O Lord." Such is the nature of true Jnâna (knowledge). But "I do everything, I am the doer. My house, my family, my children, my friends, everything belongs to me"; all this proceeds from Ajnâna (ignorance).

A Guru was giving this instruction to his disciple: "The Lord alone is thine own and no one **The Lord alone** else belongs to thee." The disciple **is thine own.** replied: "But my mother and my wife, who take such good care of me, who love me and feel extremely unhappy when they do not see me, are also my own, are they not?" The Guru answered: "In this you are mistaken. I will show you that none of them truly cares for you. Never believe for a moment that your mother or wife will sacrifice her life for your sake. You can try and see. Go home and feign excruciating pain and I will come and show you." The disciple acted accordingly. Doctors were called in, but no one could afford relief. The mother of the patient was sorrowing and sighing. The wife and children were weeping. At this moment the Sannyâsin (Guru) appeared. "The disease is of a serious nature," he said, "and I do not see any chance of the patient's recovery unless some one come forward to give his or her life for the patient." At this all of them looked aghast. The Sannyâsin, addressing the old mother of the sick man, said: "To live or to die will be the same thing to you, if in your old age you lose your son who earns for himself and for you all. If you can give your life in exchange for his, I can save your son. If you, as mother, cannot make this sacrifice for him, who else in the world will care to do it?" The old woman stammered through her tears: "Revered father, I am ready to do

GOSPEL OF RAMAKRISHNA

anything you order for the sake of my son. But the thing is, my own life—and what is my life in comparison to that of my son? The thought—what will become of my little ones after my death, makes me a coward. Unfortunate that I am, these little ones are in my way!"

While listening to this dialogue between the Sannyâsin and her mother-in-law, the wife wept bitterly and, addressing her parents, said: "For your sake, dear father and mother, I cannot make the sacrifice." In this way everyone found an excuse. Then the Sannyâsin turned to the patient and said: "Do you see, no one here is ready to sacrifice his life for you. Do you understand now what I meant by saying that there was no depending on anybody?" When the disciple saw all this, he abandoned his so-called home and followed the Sannyâsin, his Guru.

Srî Râmakrishna continued: The Absolute Brahman cannot be known by reasoning. Be **Self-surrender** his servant and taking refuge with **and prayer.** Him pray to Him with earnestness and sincerity. He will surely reveal Himself unto you. Book-learning or intellectual discussions cannot reveal the Divinity.

Thus saying the Blessed One sang:

THE GLORY OF THE DIVINE MOTHER

1. Who knoweth what is Kâli (my Divine Mother)?
   Even the Six Schools of Philosophy get not a glimpse of Her.

2. The Yogi ever meditateth upon Her at the Mulâdhâra and the Sahasrâra.
   As the swans, male and female, commune with each other, so in this lotus (Lotus here is a symbol of Plexus) forest doth Kâli commune with Her consort (Shiva).

3. Kâli, the soul of Âtmârâma (Shiva), is as beloved as Sitâ is of Râma. The majesty of Kâli, Shiva (Kâla) alone can know, forsooth who else may know it?

4. For She giveth birth unto the universe; think how vast She is.
   She dwelleth within all things as the will omnipotent.

5. The Psalmist (Prasâd) * singeth: "Mortals

---

* Prasâd is the abbreviated form of the full name of the Hindu Psalmist, Râma Prasâd Sen. He was a great Yogi and a true devotee of the Divine Mother of the universe. His songs have deep spiritual meanings and Râmakrishna was very fond of them.

GOSPEL OF RAMAKRISHNA

may laugh at the thought of swimming across the mighty ocean," and this my mind perceiveth, but my heart enfoldeth it not; yet it still aspireth to touch the moon.

The Blessed One, referring to this song, said: See how Râmaprasâd describes that books and reasoning cannot reveal the Divine Mother. Faith is necessary.

The omnipotence of faith. Reason is weak. Faith is omnipotent. Reason cannot go far enough and must stop short of the goal. Faith will work wonders.

The parable of a Brâhmin priest and his boy. There was a certain Brâhmin priest who served in a household chapel. Once he went away leaving the charge of the service to his son. He told the boy to place the daily offering of food before the Deity and see that He ate it. The boy, following the instructions of his father, placed the offering before the image and silently waited. But the image neither spoke nor ate. The boy watched for a long time. He had firm faith that the Deity would come down from the altar, take the seat before the offering and eat it. Then he prayed: "O Lord, come and eat. It is getting very late; I cannot wait any longer." But the Lord did not speak. Then the boy began to cry, saying: "Lord, my father told me to see that Thou didst eat the offering. Why dost Thou not come. Thou comest to my father and eatest his offering. What have I done that Thou dost not come to me and eat my offering?" He cried bitterly and for a long time. Then as he looked up at the seat, he saw the Deity in a human form eating the offering. When the service was ended and the boy came out, the members of the household said to him, "If the service is over, bring out the offering." The boy replied: "Yes, but the Lord has eaten everything." In amazement they asked: "What did you say?" With absolute innocence the boy repeated: "Why, the Lord has eaten all that I offered." Then they entered the chapel and were dumbfounded at the sight of the empty dishes. Such is the power of true faith and true yearning!

Yes, faith will enable a man to cross the mighty ocean itself without the least difficulty. In the epic Râmâyana it is said: Râma Chandra (God Incarnate) worked hard to throw a bridge over the part of the sea separating Lankâ (Ceylon) from the mainland of India. But as if to prove the majesty, the omnipotence of faith, He gave it to His Bhakta, the great Hanumân,* to jump across the ocean by the unaided power of faith.

It is also told that once a Bhakta, a friend of Vibhishana,† wanted to go across the sea. Vibhishana, to whom he appealed for help, had the name of Râma (God) written on a leaf, without the knowledge of his friend. He then said to the Bhakta: "Take this and be careful that you have it tied to the end of your cloth. It will enable you to walk across the ocean in safety. But mind, never look inside, for you will go under the water if you open it." The Bhakta put faith in his friend's words and walked on the ocean in safety for some time, but unfortunately his curiosity became his enemy. He wanted to see what precious thing Vibhishana had given him that had the power

---

* Hanumân was a great devotee of Râma who, by the power of his absolute faith in the Lord, jumped across the ocean from India to Lankâ. He is regarded by the Hindus as the Ideal Bhakta of India.

† Vibhishana was the brother of Râvana, the King of Lankâ, (Ceylon) who was defeated by Râma, as described in the Hindu epic Râmâyana. He became a devoted disciple of Râma and followed His instructions as long as he lived.

of taking him unhurt over the mighty deep. When he opened it he discovered a leaf with the name of Râma written on it. He thought what a trifling thing it was; no sooner did that thought arise in his mind than he was drowned.

Those who belong to this class of Jivas cannot easily have faith in God, but those who are born with Divine qualities possess the highest faith naturally. When Prahlâda * tried to write the first letter of the Sanskrit alphabet, "K," it brought up before his mind the name Krishna, and he began to cry. <u>The natural tendency of a Jiva is to doubt and to become sceptical</u>. Hâzrâ † will not believe in the truth that Brahman and Divine Mother, the Absolute and His Energy, are one and the same. Yet, faith is omnipotent. Before it all the powers of nature shrink and give way. It carries one over seas and mountains with perfect ease. Sin and

---

* Prahlâda was a great Bhakta who, from his childhood, showed his extreme faith, love and devotion for the Supreme Lord of the universe. He is the Ideal Bhakta among the Hindus. His life is described in the Purânas.

† Hâzrâ was a moral householder who afterwards devoted his life in search after God. He became an ascetic and preferred to travel along the path of Jnâna.

GOSPEL OF RAMAKRISHNA

iniquity, worldliness and ignorance all vanish before true faith.

The Bhagavân sang:

The Name of the Lord

1. O my Divine Mother, if I die with Thy hallowed name (Durgâ, Durgâ) on my lips.
   Then in the end, O Giver of all Bliss, shall it be seen whether Thou savest Thy poor child drowning in the ocean of sin.

2. I might have slain a cow or a Brâhmin or an unborn child!
   I might be a drunkard, nay more, the slayer of a woman!
   But of all these dire sins I have not the slightest fear.
   Through faith in Thy Holy Name I can reach the highest bliss of Brahman.

Yes, faith is at the root of all spiritual progress. Thou canst do without all other things, only thou must have faith. Have but faith in the Lord and thou shalt become at once free from the vilest, the blackest, of all sins.

The one thing needed is faith and Bhakti—love, devotion, prayerfulness, self-surrender. It is exceedingly difficult, especially in this age, for a man with his limited faculties to come to my Mother through Vichâra (discriminatoin of the Real Brahman from the unreal phenomenal universe), unaided by the Divine Person. Verily has Prasâd, the "Sweet Psalmist" of Bengal, laid stress on this difficulty in his well-known song:

THE DIVINE MOTHER AND THE ABSOLUTE BRAHMAN

1. Like a mad man, O mind, what seekest thou in the dark room?
   He (Divine Being) cometh in deep meditation; without that, who can approach Him?

2. The moon of desire still shineth in thy secret chamber.
   First bring it under control with all thy might. It will hide itself at the dawn of Divine wisdom.

3. Holding this as the ideal, the great Yogi practiseth meditation for ages. When realization cometh it attracts the soul as a magnet draws unto itself a piece of iron.

4. Thou shalt not find It in the Six Schools of Philosophy, in the Vedas, Tantras or in the Holy Scriptures. It loveth the sweetness of true devotion (Bhakti) and abideth in the body with everlasting Bliss.

5. Prasâd says: O mind, shall I disclose in public (*Châtor*) the true nature of that which I worship as my Divine Mother? Guess and understand it from these hints.

There was a deep silence at the close of this song, which had been listened to with rapt attention. Everyone was moved.

At the end of this song the Bhagavân was once more found to be in that indescribable state of *Samâdhi*. His sweet divine voice became still. His eyes remained fixed and steadfast. But his spiritual eye was feasting on the beatific Vision of the Divine Glory! There was left just enough of self-consciousness to bring the soul face to face with the Divine Mother. This blessed Vision the Bhagavân enjoyed for a long time. His face was radiant with celestial light and expressed by sweet smiles the unbounded happiness which He was enjoying within Himself, and

Râmakrishna's Samâdhi.

in His semiconscious state He uttered these words:

Bhakti, or devotion, means whole-hearted love for the Lord. The Absolute Brahman is called "Divine Mother" by the Psalmist. Prasâd asks his mind to understand it by hints; He who is described in the Vedas as the Absolute Brahman is my Divine Mother; I am praying to Her.

What is Bhakti?

That which is the Absolute (Nirguna), impersonal beyond all attributes, is also the same as the Personal God who is with all attributes and blessed qualities. The Absolute Brahman again is inseparable from the Divine energy (Sakti).

Brahman impersonal and personal.

The term "Brahman" refers to that aspect of Divinity which is impersonal and which is beyond all activity. But when we think of Him as creating, preserving and destroying all phenomena, then we call Him the Personal God, Divine Mother or Kâli.

In reality there is no distinction between "Brahman," or the Impersonal Absolute, and "Sakti," the Divine Mother. The Brahman and the Sakti are one just as fire and its burning power are one. As by the word fire we understand its power of burn-

Brahman and Sakti are one.

ing, so by the latter we know that it is the same as fire. By realizing the one both are realized.

<u>They are one just as much as milk and its whiteness are one. We cannot conceive the milk without the whiteness.</u>

They are one just as a gem and its brightness are one. We cannot conceive a gem without the brightness.

They are one just as the serpent and its sinuous motion are one. We cannot conceive of the serpent without the serpentine movements.

He who knows what "light" is has the knowledge of darkness also. He who has the conception of the phenomenal world must have also some conception of the Absolute Noumenon. He who knows the Sakti, or the Personal aspect of the Absolute Being, knows also the Impersonal Brahman. Again, he who has realized the Absolute Noumenon has also realized the phenomenon. He who has realized Brahman has also realized the Personal God or Divine Mother (Sakti).

The power of the Divine Mother. <u>This Divine Mother bestows the highest knowledge of Brahman (Brahmajnâna) by bringing her devotee into the state of *Samâdhi*.</u> She it is who brings him down on the plane of sense-consciousness and allows him to retain the sense of "I" and "me."

By the power of my Divine Mother all mortals (Jiva) possess the sense of "I" and "mine." She again reveals to the soul of one who is in *Samâdhi*, that all living beings, nay, the whole universe, is but the manifestation of the Divine Energy.

It is She who makes one reach the Brahmajnâna, the highest knowledge of the Absolute, and She again makes another Her beloved devotee who surrenders himself to Her omnipotent Will. This truth is the great secret of all secrets. Therefore the Psalmist says: "Shall I disclose it in the *Châtor*?"

Vidyâsâgara asked his friend who was sitting near by: "Do you understand the meaning of *Châtor*?" The friend replied: "I know that '*Chattara*' means a courtyard within a house."

Vidyâsâgara: Exactly. It may also mean a public market-place. So Râma Prasâd does not want to make this secret known to the public.

Bhagavân with his smiling face spoke to Vidyâsâgara: "Oh, you are a Pandit, a great scholar, you must know all this." When I sing the praise of my Divine Mother I refer to the

GOSPEL OF RAMAKRISHNA

same Absolute Brahman. The term "Mother" is very sweet. Therefore I like to call Him "Mother." We must learn to love the Personal God (Iswara). Through love He can be easily attained. Love, devotion and faith are the most valuable. Listen to another song. The Bhagavân sang again:

LOVE FOR THE DIVINE MOTHER

1. Ecstasy dawneth when I meditate upon my Divine Mother.
   As is the ardor of thought so is the attainment; but the root must be perfect faith.

2. If the mind diveth into the sea of Bliss at the feet of my Mother, then is there no further need of worship, rituals, sacrifice or repetition of the Lord's name.

3. The devotee of the Divine Mother is free even in this life and doth enjoy everlasting Bliss.

He who can dive into the sea of Bliss becomes immortal. The Lord is described in the Vedas as the Ocean of Immortal Bliss. Whosoever enters into it becomes free from death. Some people have a wrong idea that too much meditation upon

The Lord, the Ocean of Immortality.

the Absolute will unbalance the mind. No one becomes unbalanced by meditating upon the Absolute.

Devotional exercises, rituals, ceremonials, sacrifices or the pouring of oblations into the sacred fire—such works are needless when true love for the Lord comes in the heart of the devotee. A fan is needed so long as there is no breeze. So when the breeze of Divine Love blows all ritualistic works become unnecessary.

Referring to Vidyâsâgara the Bhagavân continued: The works which you are doing are good works. **Selfless works purify the heart.** If you can perform them without seeking their result and without thinking that you are the "doer," then it will be still better. The highest result of works done in this selfless manner is the attainment of true love for God. Such works purify the heart and bring God-consciousness in the end. <u>But as your love for the Lord becomes more and more intense, your religious works will become less and less.</u> A married woman diligently performs the household duties, but she is not allowed to do any heavy work when she is about to give birth to her child. You are doing charitable works and other works for the good of humanity. In reality, however, they are of great help to yourself. They will purify your heart and bring unselfish love for God. Man has no power to **Doing good to the world.** do good to the world; the Lord doth everything. He who hath made the Sun and the moon, He who hath given affection in the hearts of parents, He who hath bestowed compassion upon the great souls, He who hath brought unselfish love and devotion in the hearts of saints and sages, doth everything for the good of His world; who else hath the power to perform any good act? Whosoever performeth good works without holding any desire for their fruits will do good for himself.

There is gold inside, under the cover of earth. You have not discovered it yet. If you once realize this secret treasure your worldly duties will vanish and you will not care for other works, just as a mother loves nothing better than to fondle and kiss her new-born baby. Go onward and do not stop in one place. Remember the parable * of the wood-cutter and stop not until the goal is reached. The goal is the realization of God. By His grace His true

---

* See page 243.

devotee can see Him and can talk with Him just as I am talking with you.

Absolute silence prevailed when the Blessed Lord spoke these words with fire and eloquence. Everyone's heart was moved by that divine love which was flowing with mighty force within the soul of Bhagavân Srî Râmakrishna.

With a smiling face the Bhagavân said: You know all that I have told, but you do not realize how much you possess, in the same manner as Varuna, the Lord of the ocean, does not care to know how many beautiful and valuable jewels there are in His boundless treasury of the deep.

Vidyâsâgara: Revered Sir, Thou canst say so.

Bhagavân: Yes; do you not know that very often a millionaire Bâbu does not know even the names of his own attendants? He does not remember in what places his valuable things are kept.

Everyone was listening to this interesting conversation when Bhagavân suddenly asked Vidyâsâgara: "Will you not come to the Temple garden? It is a beautiful place."

Vidyâsâgara: O yes; certainly. Thou hast been so kind as to come to me, shall I not return my visit to Thee?

Bhagavân: A visit to me! Oh, for shame! for shame!

Vidyâsâgara: My dear Sir, this from Thee! I wish to know why dost Thou say so?

Bhagavân: Well, we are like fishing-boats, **Humility of Râmakrishna.** small and light enough to row about on ponds, narrow canals or even on large rivers, but you are like a big steamer. Who can tell?—you might founder on the sand-bank if you venture too far up the stream; but now at this season steamers may go up without much danger.

Vidyâsâgara: Oh I see; this is the rainy season.

At about eight in the evening it was announced that the carriage was ready to take Srî Râmakrishna back to the Thâkurbâdi at Dakshineswara. The Bhagavân became absent-minded for a while; perhaps His mind was fixed upon the Divine Mother, or perhaps He was asking Her blessing upon His kind host. The Bhagavân then rose to bid him farewell and Vidyâsâgara, with a lighted candle in his hand, led the way down-stairs and through the compound of his house to the gate. Outside the gate a carriage was waiting to receive the honored guest and His devoted companions from the Thâkurbâdi. An unexpected sight greeted the eyes of the party as they came out. It was a man who might have been a little under forty standing before the gate with folded hands. He was dressed in white and wore a white turban on his head. He had a fair complexion and expressive eyes and a smile was on his face. No sooner did he see the Bhagavân than he fell at His feet with his head touching the ground.

The Bhagavân said: Is it you, Balarâm? How is it that I find you here?

Balarâm * replied, smiling: O Revered Sir, I have been waiting for some time here at the gate to see Thee.

Bhagavân: Why did you not come in?

Balarâm: I came late, so I would not interrupt Thee, but thought it better to stay here.

The Bhagavân then stepped into the carriage with His companions.

Vidyâsâgara asked a disciple: Shall I see the carriage hire paid?

The disciple replied: No, Sir, you need not

---

* Balarâm Basu was a Hindu Zemindar in Calcutta. He was a true householder disciple of Râmakrishna. His house was blessed many a time by a visit of Râmakrishna and His beloved disciples. His whole family regard Râmakrishna as the Divine Incarnation in a human form. See Chapter XII.

trouble yourself. It has already been paid by a friend.

The Pandit then folded his hands and bent his head and body to make his Pranâma (Salutation) to the Bhagavân. All assembled about the carriage did the same. The little group at the gate, with the venerable Vidyâsâgara at their head still holding the lighted candle in his hand, stood for a while looking in the direction of the carriage, wondering who this God-intoxicated Man might be, so wise yet so child-like, so full of joy, so sweet, so godly! Verily a Light come down to set ablaze the dry bones of a workaday world! Embodied Love, like the dew of heaven falling on the dry thirsty heart of man! A Voice crying unto sunken, self-weary man, "Thou must be born again and love!" A Healer from another clime of this strange disease of modern life! A Man among men, eager to solve for them the enigma of the universe!

Râmakrishna leaves Vidyâsâgara.

CHAPTER V

DAY ON THE RIVER WITH KESHAB CHUNDER SEN *

i

It was the day of the festival of Lakshmi.† Srî Râmakrishna was seated in His room talking with Bijoy aud Haralal, when a gentleman entered and announced that Keshab Sen had

---

* Keshab Chunder Sen was the third great Brâhmo Samâj leader after Râjâ Râmmohun Roy. He was born in 1838 and died in 1884 A.D.

In 1858 he became a member of the Âdi Brâhmo Samâj. In 1866 he founded a new branch under the name of Bhâratavarshiya Brâhmo Samâj, which was afterwards known as the church of the "New Dispensation."

In 1870 he came to England to propagate his mission. He was an eloquent preacher and orator. He accepted a great many of the teachings of Râmakrishna and regarded Him as one who had constant communion with Brahman.

† Lakshmi, the goddess of fortune and prosperity.

GOSPEL OF RAMAKRISHNA

come on board a steamer which had just landed and was lying at anchor before the Ghât. A short while after Keshab's disciples came in and bowed down before the Bhagavân, saying: "Keshab Bâbu has sent us to Thee with the request that Thou wilt kindly join him, if it so please Thy Holiness." Srî Râmakrishna consented and, accompanied by several of His devotees, was taken by Keshab's disciples to the steamer.

Râmakrishna goes on board the steamer.

As the small boat which carried the Bhagavân came alongside, everybody was eager to have a glimpse of the Blessed One and crowded to the gangway. Keshab was anxious to see that He got on board in safety. Mahendra,* who had been there for some time, looked at Him and noticed that He was in Samâdhi and as motionless as a statue. It was with great difficulty that He was brought back to sense-consciousness once more in order to be taken into the cabin on the upper deck. The state of Divine ecstasy had not entirely left Him even then. He leaned on a disciple as He was led to the cabin. His body moved

Râmakrishna's ecstasy.

---

* See note page 33.

GOSPEL OF RAMAKRISHNA

mechanically, but His mind was fixed on God. When He had entered the cabin, Keshab and others bowed at His feet. But what little sense-consciousness remained now began to leave Him. Inside the cabin were a bench, a table and a few chairs. The Bhagavân was seated on one of the chairs; Keshab also took a chair and Bijoy, another. Other devotees, most of them Brâhmos, sat on the bare floor. The cabin being a small one, many remained standing at the door or at the windows looking in eagerly. <u>The Bhagavân was absolutely devoid of outer consciousness.</u> Everybody was watching His face. Keshab noticed that so large a number of people had come together in the cabin that the Bhagavân was in need of air. The devotees all gazed with fixed eyes. <u>After a time the Bhagavân came down from His Samâdhi, but the consciousness of the Divine Presence was as intense as before</u>. He talked to the Mother of the universe in words that were scarcely articulate, saying: "O Mother, why hast Thou brought me here? They are hedged around and are not free! Is it indeed possible for me to save them out of their prison house?"

A Brâhmo said to the Bhagavân: Sir, these

GOSPEL OF RAMAKRISHNA

gentlemen have been fortunate enough to see
Powhâri Bâbâ of Gâzipur. Powhâri Bâbâ * at Gâzipur. The Bâbâ is another holy man like Thy revered self.

Srî Râmakrishna had not yet recovered the power of speech. His heart was full and He could not speak, but only smiled on the good man who talked of the Bâbâ. The Brahmo continued: Sir, Powhâri Bâbâ has Thy photograph, which he has put up in his room.

The Bhagavân smiled again, pointing to His body with His finger and in a subdued tone said:

Devotee's heart the temple of the Lord. A pillow-case! It is nothing but a pillow-case. But there is one thing to be borne in mind: the heart of the devotee is the temple of the Lord. It is indeed a fact that the Lord is more or less manifest in all things, but He is manifest in a special sense in the heart of a devotee (Bhakta). Thus a Zemindar may be met at any of the houses of which he is the owner;

---

* Powhâri Bâbâ was a great Vaishnava Saint who lived for many years in an underground cave near Gâzipur. The name "Powhâri," which literally means "one who lives on air," was given to him because he could live for months without eating or drinking anything. He was regarded by all as the greatest Vaishnava Saint of the age.

yet people will say that he is usually to be seen in some particular drawing-room. The heart of the devotee is the Lord's drawing-room. If one wishes to meet the Lord, one would better seek an audience in the drawing-room.

The same Being whom the followers of non-dualistic (Advaita) Vedânta call Brahman, the Absolute, is called Âtman (Self) by the Yogis, and Bhagavân, or the Personal God with Divine attributes, by the devotees, or Bhaktas (lovers of God). The high-caste Brâhmin is always the same person; but when he worships the Lord, he is called a priest; and when the same man is employed in the kitchen, he is called a cook.

Various aspects of the Brahman.

The follower of monistic (Advaita) Vedânta, who seeks to realize the Absolute Brahman, discriminates, saying: "Not this, not this." That is, the Absolute is not this, not that, not any finite object, not the individual soul, not the external world. When, as the result of this kind of reasoning, the heart ceases to be moved by desires; when, in fact, the mind is merged in superconsciousness, then Brâhma-jnâna is reached. One who has truly attained to this Brâhma-jnâna realizes that Brahman the Absolute alone is real, and the

Discrimination of an Advaitin.

world is unreal, and that all names and forms are like dreams. What Brahman is cannot be described by word of mouth nor can one even say that He is personal. Such is the point of view of a non-dualist.

The dualistic devotees and lovers of the Personal God (Bhaktas), on the contrary, accept all states as real. Unlike the non-dualists, they look upon the waking state as a reality and they do not hold that the external world is like a dream. They say that the external world is the glory of the Lord. The heavens, stars, moon, mountains, ocean, men, birds and beasts, all these He has created. He manifests His glory by these. He is both within and without. He dwells in our hearts. <u>The most advanced Bhaktas say that the Lord Himself manifests as the twenty-four categories of the Sânkhya philosophy, that He appears as the individual soul and the external world</u>. A Bhakta wishes to enjoy communion with his Lord and not to become one with Him. His desire is not to become sugar, but to taste of it. Do you know what are the innermost thoughts and feelings of a true devotee? He says: "O Lord! Thou art the Master, I am Thy servant.

Bhakta's attitude.

The innermost feelings of a true Bhakta.

Thou art my Mother, and I am Thy child"; or again: "Thou art my Child and I am Thy father or Thy mother"; or thus: "Thou art the Whole and I am Thy part." The dualistic devotee does not wish to say, "I am Brahman."

A Râja Yogi also seeks to realize the Universal Being. His object is to bring the finite human soul into communion with the infinite Spirit. He tries first to collect his mind which is scattered in the world of senses, and then seeks to fix it on the Universal Spirit; hence the necessity of meditating on Him in solitude and in a posture which causes no distraction.

Râja Yogi.

But all these various ideals are of one and the same Brahman, the difference being only in the names. It is the same Being whom men call by the name of the Absolute (Brahman), the Universal Spirit, the Impersonal God, or the Personal God with Divine attributes.

Different aspects of God.

ii

The steamer had already started and was on its way to Calcutta. Many there were who looked on Srî Râmakrishna with eyes that did not move, and who drank the nectar of the words that dropped from His hallowed lips. They did not perceive that the steamer was in motion. The Temple garden of Kâli had faded from sight. Beneath were the sacred waters which reflected the blue firmament above, but the murmur of the waves fell unheeded on the ears of the devotees. The magic of the blessed vision had thrown a charm over them. They beheld before them a wonderful Being, a God-in-Man and a Man-in-God, with smiles playing on His sweet face, radiant with the joy of the Lord, and with eyes enhanced in beauty by the collyrium of Divine Love. They gazed as if spell-bound, on One who had given up the world and its pleasures, on One intoxicated with the Love of the Lord and who looked not for anything except the Lord.

Srî Râmakrishna: The followers of Advaita Vedânta maintain that creation, preservation, **The world as** and dissolution, the individual ego, **a dream.** the external world, all these are manifestations of the Eternal Energy (Sakti). They also say that when these are properly analyzed, they appear as dreams, that the Absolute Brahman alone is the Reality, and all else is unreal. Even eternal Energy (Sakti) is like a dream, unreal; but you may analyze and discriminate thousands of times, you cannot transcend the realm of Divine Energy (Sakti) unless you have reached the highest state of Samâdhi, super-consciousness. <u>The very thoughts like: "I am meditating," "I am thinking on the Absolute," are within the realm of Sakti.</u> They are the manifested powers of that Eternal Energy. Therefore the Absolute Brahman and the Eternal Energy are inseparable and one. The existence of one implies that of the other, as fire and its burning power. If you admit the existence of fire, how can you deny its burning power? No one can think of fire without thinking of its burning power. Again, the power of burning cannot be conceived as separate from fire. In the same manner, we cannot think of the rays of the sun, without thinking of the sun himself. Again, we cannot think of the sun without thinking of his rays. Therefore, no one can think of Brahman as apart from Sakti, or Sakti as separate from Brahman. Likewise, no one can conceive of the phenomenal as independent of the Absolute, or of the Absolute as apart from the phenomenal. The same Eternal Energy, the Mother of all phenomena, is creating, preserving, and

The realm of the Divine Energy.

Relation between Brahman and Sakti.

destroying everything. She is called Kâli, the Divine Mother. Kâli is Brahman, Brahman is Kâli, one and the same Being. I call Him Brahman when He is absolutely inactive; that is, when He neither creates, nor preserves, nor destroys phenomena; but when He performs all such actions, I call Him Kâli, the Eternal Energy, the Divine Mother. They are one and the same Being, the difference is in name and form, just as the same substance water is called by different names in different languages, such as jal, aqua, pâni, etc. <u>Yes, the Being is the same,</u> **One God has** <u>only the names are different under</u> **many names.** <u>different aspects</u>—like the same substance expressed in different languages, such as jal, water and pâni. A tank may have four Ghâts (landing-places with steps). The Hindus drink at one Ghât and call it jal; the Mohammedans drink at another and call it pâni; while the English who drink at a third call it water. Similarly, God is One, only His names are different. <u>Some call Him by the name of Allah, some God, some Brahman, others Kâli, others again Râma, Hari, Jesus, Buddha</u>.

Keshab, smiling: Please tell us once more, Revered Sir, in what different ways Kâli, the

Mother of the Universe, is making Herself manifest in this world of Her sports.

Srî Râmakrishna, smiling: Oh, the Mother sports with the world, Her toy, under various aspects and names. Now She is the God Unconditioned, Absolute, Formless (Mahâ-Kâli): now the Everlasting as distinguished from Her works (Nitya-Kâli). Under another aspect She is the Goddess of burning Ghâts or crematories, the dreaded Being who presides over death (Smasân-Kâli); now again does She stand before us ready to bless, to preserve Her children (Rakshyâ-Kâli); under another aspect She appears pleasing to the eye of Her devotees as the Mother with the dark blue color, Consort of the God of Eternity and Infinity. Mahâ-Kâli and Nitya-Kâli are described in the sacred books, the Tantras: "When nothing was—neither sun, nor moon, nor planets, nothing but Darkness Deep, there was alone my Divine Mother, Formless, the Eternal Consort of the Infinite." As Mother with the dark blue color (Syâmâ), She is tender and loving. She is the bestower of all blessings and makes Her children fearless; She is worshipped in the Hindu household. As Preserver She appears in times of plague, famine, earth-

The Mother of the universe and Her sports.

GOSPEL OF RAMAKRISHNA

quake, drought or flood. At cemeteries, burning Ghâts or crematories She appears in the form of the Destroyer. The dead body, the jackal, the spirits of destruction are Her terrible companions. She lives in the midst of those horrible scenes, of those fearful environments. Streams of blood, a garland of skulls thrown round Her neck, a girdle made of the hands of those that are dead, are the symbols that mark Her as the dread Mother, as the All-Destroyer.

Now look at Her mode of creation. At the end of a cycle, upon the destruction of the **Creation of the world.** world, my Mother, good Matron that She is, puts together the seeds of creation. The mistress of a house has a hodgepodge pot of her own in which to keep sundry things for household use. (Râmakrishna, smiling) Yes, my friends, that is indeed so. The mistress of a house has such a pot in her possession. In it are kept the "sea-foam" in a solid state, small parcels containing seeds of the cucumber, gourd, and so on. She brings them out when wanted. In much the same way my Mother keeps the seeds of creation after the destruction of the world at the end of a cycle.

My Mother, the Primal Divine Energy, is both within and without this phenomenal world. Having given birth to the world, She lives within it. In the Vedas we find the illustration of a spider and its web. She is the spider and the world is the web that She has woven. The spider brings the phenomenal web out of herself and then lives on it. My Mother is both the Container and the Contained.

Divine Mother omnipresent.

Divine Mother, the material and the instrumental cause.

Is Kâli, the Divine Mother, black? She looks black from a distance, but when realized, She is not black. The sky looks blue from a distance, but look at it near you, it has no color. The water of the ocean is blue from a distance. Take a little up in the hand, and it has no color.

Kâli, why black?

Saying this, the Bhagavân became intoxicated with Divine Love, and began to sing:

"Is my Divine Mother black?
   O mind! What dost thou say?
Though black, She with Her flowing hair
   Illumines the lotus of the heart."

Bondage and freedom, of both She is the maker. Through Her inscrutable power of

GOSPEL OF RAMAKRISHNA

The power of the Divine Mother. Mâyâ a man of the world becomes bound by woman and gold. Again, through Her grace he becomes free. She breaks all fetters and takes Her children across the ocean of the world; and the Bhagavân sang in His divine voice:

THE DIVINE MOTHER AND THE LIBERATED SOUL

1. O Mother, Thou art flying the paper kite (of the human being) in the market-place of this world.
   It flies on the wind of hope, tied to the string of Mâyâ.

2. Ribs, nerves and bones make up its frame,
   Of Thine own qualities hast Thou made the Kite, to display Thine art.

3. Thou hast rubbed the string with the Mânjâ (paste with powdered glass) of worldliness, and it has become sharp.
   Among hundred thousand Kites one or two have their strings cut, and are freed;
   Then with a laugh Thou clappest Thy hands.

4. Prasâd says, The Kite thus set free will fly swiftly on fair winds and drop beyond the ocean of this world.

Srî Râmakrishna continuing: My Divine Mother is playful. <u>The world indeed is Her sport</u>. She does what She will and is blissful. It is Her pleasure to give freedom to one among a hundred thousand of Her children.

Divine Mother's will.

A Brâhmo: Sir, She can, if She pleases, set every body free. Why is it then that She has bound us hand and foot with the chains of the world?

Srî Râmakrishna: Well, I suppose it is Her will. Her will is to play with all these things. In the game of Hide-and-Seek, whoever touches the Grand-dame is out. He no longer runs about. If all the players touch the Grand-dame at the same time, how can there be any game? The Grand-dame would not like it; for she is pleased to have the play go on.

And the Bhagavân, placing Himself in the position of a man of the world laying the trouble of his heart before the Mother, sang:

The Divine Mother and Her Children

1. This is the grief for which I grieve.
   When Thou, O Mother, art here, thieves (passions) rob me though I am wide awake.

GOSPEL OF RAMAKRISHNA

2. I promise to repeat Thy Holy Name, but at the proper hour I forget.
   Now I have learnt and felt that all this is Thy trick.

3. Thou hast not given, so Thou hast not received aught to eat or to keep. Am I to be blamed for this?
   Hadst Thou given, Thou wouldst surely have received; and I would have offered Thy gifts to Thee.

4. Fame or calumny, sweet or bitter—all is Thine.
   O Ruler of all feelings, abiding in them, why dost Thou hinder when I enjoy sweet ecstasy?

5. Prasâd says: Thou hast given me a mind, but by a glance of Thine eye Thou hast so bent it, that I roam through this world, Thy creation, seeking joy but mistaking bitter for sweet (unreal for Real).

Delusive power of Mâyâ.
Man has forgotten his true Self and has become worldly by the delusive power of Mâyâ. Therefore Prasâd says: "Thou hast given me a mind, but by a glance of Thine eye Thou hast so bent it that

I roam through this world, Thy creation, seeking joy but mistaking bitter for sweet."

A Brâhmo: Revered Sir, is it true that God cannot be realized without giving up the world?

The Bhagavân, smiling: Oh no! You do not have to give up everything. You are better off **Renunciation not necessary for all.** where you are. By living in the world you are enjoying the taste both of the pure crystallized sugar and of the molasses with all its impurities. You are indeed better off. Verily I say unto you, you are living in the world, there is no harm in that; but you will have to fix your mind on God, otherwise you cannot realize Him. Work with one hand and hold the Feet of the Lord with the other. When you have finished your work, fold His feet to your heart with both your hands.

<u>Everything is in the mind. Bondage and freedom are in the mind</u>. You can dye the **Power of the mind.** mind with any color you wish. It is like a piece of clean white linen; dip it in red and it will be red, in blue it will be blue, in green it will be green, or any other color. Do you not see that if you study English, English words will come readily to you? Again,

if a Pandit studies Sanskrit, he will readily quote verses from Sacred Books. If you keep your mind in evil company, your thoughts, ideas and words will be colored with evil; but keep in the company of Bhaktas, then your thoughts, ideas and words will be of God. The mind is everything On one side is the wife, on the other side is the child; it loves the wife in one way and the child in another way, yet the mind is the same.

By the mind one is bound; by the mind one is freed. If I think I am absolutely free, whether I live in the world or in the forest, where is my bondage? I am the child of God, the son of the King of kings; who can bind me? When bitten by a snake, if you assert with firmness, "There is no venom in me," you will be cured. In the same way, he who asserts with strong conviction "I am not bound, I am free," becomes free.

Some one gave me a book of the Christians. I asked him to read it to me. In it there was only one theme—sin and sin, from the **Sense of sin.** beginning to the end. (To Keshab) In your Brâhmo-Samâj the main topic is also sin. The fool who repeats again and again, "I am bound, I am bound," remains in bondage.

He who repeats day and night, "I am a sinner, I am a sinner," becomes a sinner indeed.

It is necessary to have absolute faith in the Name of the Lord. "What! I have uttered His Holy Name, can there still be sin in me? Can I still be in bondage?" Kristo Kishore was a pious Hindu, a Brâhmin of Brâhmins, who worshipped the Lord with single-minded devotion. He went to Vrindâvan. One day, while visiting the shrines, he felt very thirsty. He went to a well, and finding a man standing there, he asked him: "My man, can you draw some water for me?" The man replied: "O holy sir, I belong to a low class, that of a cobbler." Kristo Kishore thereupon said to him: "It matters not. You say 'Shiva' (the Holy Name of the Lord) and draw the water for me."

Saving power of God's name.

By repeating the blessed Name of God, man's body, mind and soul become absolutely pure. Why talk of sin and hell-fire? Repeat but once, "I shall never again do the evil deeds that I have committed in the past," and by thy faith in His Hallowed Name thou shalt be freed from all sins.

I used to pray to my Divine Mother for true

devotion (Bhakti) alone. With flowers in my clasped hands, I prayed: "Do Thou, O Mother, grant that I may have pure and unalloyed devotion. Here is sin, here again is virtue; I lay them at Thy feet; Oh take them both. Here is knowledge (of many things), here again is ignorance; Oh take them both and grant that I may have devotion alone. Here is purity and here again is impurity; I desire neither of them. Here are good works, here are bad; both I lay at Thy feet; Oh grant that I may have devotion alone and love for Thee."

Prayer to the Divine Mother.

One living in the world may also see God. It was the case with Râjâ Janaka, the great royal devotee, who realized while on the throne that the world was a structure of dreams. For a lover of God, however, such is not the feeling. And the Bhagavân sang:

Example of Janaka.

He who has attained to Bhakti or true devotion to the Lord says:

"This world is the abode of happiness;
  I eat, drink and enjoy its pleasures.
Janaka Râjâ was a great potentate;
  In what was he lacking?
He harmonized God and the world
  And tasted the joys of both."

No one can suddenly become like Janaka. Râjâ Janaka performed great penances and austerities in solitude for many long years. Even when living in the world one should occasionally go into solitude. It will bring great good to one who can sincerely and earnestly cry for God three days and three nights in solitude, alone. Indeed, one day passed in that way would be a great gain. People will shed a jarful of tears for wives and children, but who weeps one tear for the Lord? It is necessary to practise every now and then devotional exercises in solitude. A worldly-minded aspirant absorbed in various works and duties finds in the first stage of his spiritual life a great number of obstacles in the path of self-control and devotion. As a young tree planted on the foot-path needs a fence around it that it may not be eaten up by sheep and cattle, so in the first stage of a spiritual aspirant, a fence is necessary, but when the tree grows large and the trunk and roots are thicker and stronger, no fence is required. Then it is not injured even if an elephant be tied to it.

Value of solitude.

The disease of a worldly man is of a serious type; his organs with their functions are entirely out of order. Would you keep a large

GOSPEL OF RAMAKRISHNA

water-jar and savory pickles in the same room in
Solitude a remedy for worldliness. which a patient with typhoid fever was lying? If you wish to cure such a patient, you must have him removed from that room, in case it is impossible to send away the jar and the pickles. A man of the world is like unto such a thirsty patient; worldly attractions are like the jar of water; sense objects are like the savory pickles; desire to enjoy those things is the patient's thirst. The mouth waters at the mere thought of the pickles. We should not therefore remain near them all the time. Hence solitude is the best remedy for worldliness. First acquire right discrimination and true dispassion and then live in the world. In the sea of the world there are crocodiles of passions and desires. Rub the body with *turmeric-paste* if you wish to bathe in the sea, for then crocodiles will do no harm to you. The turmeric is discrimination (of the Real from the unreal) and true dispassion. God is the only Reality, the phenomenal universe is unreal.

Along with this another thing is needed, that is intense devotion to God. The Gopis[*] of

---

[*] The milkmaids of Vrindâvan who loved the Lord Sri

Vrindâvan had such devotion. They had an **Intense devotion necessary.** intense love for Srî Krishna, God Incarnate.

The Bhagavân then said to Keshab and other devotees with great feeling: You are Brâhmos; you believe that God is formless and you do not believe in God Incarnate. Well, it matters not. You need not accept Râdhâ and Srî Krishna as Incarnations of the Supreme Being; but the intense love and yearning which the Gopis felt for Srî Krishna is a thing which you may well make your own, for yearning is the next step leading to God-vision.

iii

It was ebb-tide. The steamer was going fast down-stream towards Calcutta. It had got to the other side of the Howrah Bridge within sight of the Botanical Gardens. The Captain had orders to go a little farther down. How

---

Krishna, then living among them as a shepherd-boy. When eleven years old He left Vrindâvan. Srî Krishna is looked upon as an Incarnation of God. He loved and was loved by everyone. He is the Impersonation of Divine Love. **Vrindâvan** is the sacred forest near Mathurâ in India where the shepherd Krishna played his boyish sports with boys and girls and performed many miracles.

GOSPEL OF RAMAKRISHNA

far the steamer had actually proceeded was not known to those who were listening to Srî Râmakrishna and watching His movements. They listened with such rapt attention that they had no idea either of time or of distance.

Keshab now offered the Bhagavân puffed rice with the kernel of the cocoanut. All present were invited to partake of these. They took them in the folds of their cloth, ate and were very happy. It seemed as if a festival were being held on board the steamer. The Bhagavân noticed that Bijoy and Keshab were not quite at home in each other's presence. He wished to see them make up their difference, for was not His mission to bring peace and goodwill among men? He said to Keshab:

Look, my dear sir, here is Bijoy. As to your quarrels, well, do not worry yourselves on their account. There was fighting even between Shiva and Râma. Shiva was Râma's spiritual Guru. After a little fighting, they made it up and became once more as good friends as ever. But the fighting went on among their followers. The gibbering of the ghosts and the chattering of the monkeys could not so easily be quieted down. You too will be very good friends, once again. But your followers, I dare say, will follow your example. These differences, you know, are things that cannot be avoided. There was the tug of war even between father and son. Take the case of Râma and his sons Laba and Kusha. Take another case: The mother fasts on Tuesday for the welfare of her daughter, but the daughter, quarrelling with the mother, fasts on Tuesday for her own welfare, as if her welfare were different from that gained by her mother's fasting. In the same way, you, Keshab, have a religious society (Samâj) of your own, and Bijoy, too, must have a separate society of his own. Well, there is room for all kinds of things under Providence—even for quarrels and differences. When God-Incarnate (Krishna) Himself appeared at Vrindâvan, the question may well be asked: Why did Jatilla and Kutilla stand in the way of His mission of love? I suppose His sport as a Divine Lover would have died a natural death from want of nourishment but for these obstructions, the *Jatillas* and *Kutillas*. Opposition adds zest to a thing. Râmânuja* held the doctrine of Vishishtâdvaita (qualified non-dualism). His Guru (spiritual guide), how-

---

* See note page 370.

ever, was an Advaitist (non-dualist without any qualification). They had their differences. Master and disciple disputed and refuted each other's opinions. This is natural. Be it so; still to the master the disciple is always his own

They all rejoiced. Srî Râmakrishna said to Keshab: You do not study and examine the nature of your disciples. For that reason they drop away. All men look alike, but they differ in their nature. In some the Sattwa quality is predominant, in others Rajas, and in the rest Tamas. *Pooli* (cakes) all look alike on the outside, but the contents vary; some may contain sweet thickened cream, others cocoanut sweetened with sugar, while others may have boiled *Kalai* (pulse) with no sweetening.

The nature of disciples must be examined.

Do you know how I feel about it? Like a child I eat, drink and play, depending on my Divine Mother, who knows everything. These three words prick me: Guru (spiritual master), Kartâ (the Lord), and Bâbâ (father). I cannot bear them. The infinite Existence-Intelligence-Bliss is the one Guru for all. He will teach everybody. I am only His child.

God the one master.

It is a difficult task to teach others. One

can become a true spiritual teacher only when one has realized God and received a Divine commission from Him. So commissioned were Nârada,* Sukadeva and Sankarâchârya:† If you are not commissioned, who will listen to you? You know Calcutta and her fondness for the latest sensation. Milk puffs up so long as it is over burning wood; but when the wood is withdrawn, the puffing ceases instantly. The people of Calcutta are fond of new sensations. They say they want water and they begin to dig a well at one place; but they give it up as soon as they find that the earth is hard and stony. They then set to work to dig at another place. Suppose the soil is sandy there; they will as readily give up digging at that spot. They will look about for another locality. That is the way with these people. Their good opinion is by no means worth having.

Who is a true spiritual teacher?

---

* Nârada. In the Hindu Scriptures Nârada is described as the Ideal lover of God. He communed with the Lord under all conditions. The Lord Vishnu selected him as His most beloved messenger.

† Sankarâchârya was the commentator of the "Vedânta Sutras" and the greatest exponent of the Advaita (monistic) Vedânta. He lived in India in the eighth century A.D.

GOSPEL OF RAMAKRISHNA

Divine commission cannot be obtained by mere imagination. Verily I say, the Lord can be realized and He will speak to thee. Then thou mayest receive His commission. What great power lies in such Divine command! By it mountains may be shaken to their foundation. What can a mere ordinary lecture do? People may listen to it for a time, but they will soon forget it. It will not produce a lasting impression and they will not live according to it.

Divine commission.

For the teaching of Divine truths a badge of authority is indispensable. A man who tries to teach others without it will be laughed at. He cannot get realization himself and he tries to show the way to others. It is like the blind leading the blind. In this way more harm is done than good. When God is realized the inner spiritual sight opens and it is then that the true teacher can perceive the sickness of the soul and can prescribe the proper remedy. Without God's command a man easily becomes egotistic and thinks, "I have the power to teach others." Such egotism is the result of ignorance. In ignorance one feels, "I am the doer;" but when one realizes that "God is the Lord and doer of all, I cannot

Ordinary spiritual teachers are blind.

GOSPEL OF RAMAKRISHNA

do anything," then one becomes absolutely free even in this life. All misery and restlessness proceed from the sense of "I" and "me," "I am the doer," "I am the actor."

You talk glibly of doing good to the world. Is the world contained in a nutshell? Besides, who are you to do good to the world? First practice devotional exercises and realize God. Attain to Him. If He graciously gives you His powers (Sakti), then you can help others, and not till then.

First see God, then help the world.

A Brâhmo devotee: Revered Sir, are we to give up all works until we have seen God?

Srî Râmakrishna: No, why will you give up all works? Meditation upon God, chanting His Holy Name, and other devotional exercises are daily works which you should have to perform.

The devotee: But what about household works and business affairs?

Srî Râmakrishna: Oh! you will also perform those, but only so far as is absolutely necessary for living in the world; and you should at the same time pray in solitude unto the Lord with tears in your eyes for His grace, and for strength to do your duties without seeking any reward. Say when you pray: "Lord, grant that my work in

Pray that worldly work may grow less.

… the world and for the world may grow less and less day by day, for I see that my work growing manifold only makes me lose sight of Thee. Sometimes I think that I do my duties unattached to the world, but I know not how I deceive myself and do them through attachment instead. I give alms to the poor, and behold, I seek for fame, Oh I know not how!"

Shambhu (Mullik) * talked of founding hospitals and dispensaries, schools and colleges, of *God-vision and philanthropic works.* building roads, sinking wells and digging tanks for the good of all. I said to him: "Yes, whatever comes in your way and is absolutely necessary you will do; even that, without seeking any reward. Do not seek more work than you can well perform. If you do you will forget the Lord. A man desired to see the shrine of the Divine Mother. On his way he stopped and spent all

---

* Bâbu Shambhu Charan Mullik was a Hindu multi-millionaire of Calcutta. He had a large garden-house near the Temple of Dakshineswara where many a time he entertained Bhagavân Râmakrishna. It was in this garden-house Râmakrishna had the vision of Christ who entered into His body and remained with Him for three days and three nights. Râmakrishna said to His disciples that during that time He was not conscious of His being a Hindu and that He could not enter into the Temple compound.

GOSPEL OF RAMAKRISHNA

the day in distributing alms to the poor. When he went to the shrine, the door was closed and he could not see the Holy of Holies. The wise ones should first see the Holy Mother, by pushing their way through the crowd assembled at the gate of the Temple, and after seeing Her, they may then turn their attention to alms-giving and other good works, if they so desire."

All good works are for the realization of God. Works are the means and God-vision is the end.

God-vision the end of all performance of duty.
Therefore I said to Shambhu: "Suppose you see God, or that God manifests Himself to you, will you say to Him: 'Lord, do Thou grant that I may have lots of dispensaries and hospitals, schools and colleges!'" A true devotee shall rather pray in this wise: "Grant, O good Lord, that I may have a niche in the Lotus of Thy Feet, that it may be my privilege to live always in Thy Holy Presence and that I may have deep and unalloyed devotion unto Thee."

Karma Yoga is very difficult. It is difficult in this materialistic age (Kali-yuga) to get through *Path of Bhakti* all the works, all the duties laid upon *Yoga best for* us by the Sacred Books. Verily in *this age.* this age, earthly life depends entirely upon material food. Works and duties, there is scarcely time enough for them. It will be all over with the patient suffering from the burning fever of this world if he is allowed to go through the slow process of treatment practised by the old-fashioned Hindu physicians. People are short-lived and the malaria carries one off in a few days. The specific for the present day is Dr. D. Gupta's patent fever mixture, which produces a miraculous effect at once. <u>Yes, in this age the one means of realizing God is Bhakti or sincere devotion and love for Him, and earnest prayer and the chanting of His Holy Name and Divine attributes</u>. (To Keshab and other devotees) Your path, too, lies through devotion and self-surrender to the Lord (Bhakti Yoga). Blessed are ye who sing the Name of Hari and chant the praises of my Divine Mother. Your path is right. Unlike the non-dualists, you do not believe that this world is only a dream. You are not Jnânis, but Bhaktas; you believe in a Personal God, that is good. You are Bhaktas. If you can sincerely and earnestly cry for Him, you will surely obtain Him.

(To Keshab) You talk against child marriage and the caste system, about female emancipation and female education. I say one thing is needful,—the realization of God and devotion to Him. <u>First realize God and all other things shall be added unto you.</u> Jadu Mullik is a rich man. If you wish to cultivate his acquaintance, do not trouble yourself as to how much wealth he has, how many houses he owns, how many country-houses and gardens. First, be introduced to him and he will furnish you with all the necessary information afterwards.

There was a young man named Podo in a certain village. In that village was an old **Parable of the deserted temple.** dilapidated temple. The holy image of God once worshipped there had disappeared and it was now the home of small bats. One day at nightfall the villagers were surprised to hear the sound of bells, gongs, and conch-shells issuing from the deserted temple. Men, women and children all flocked to the place. They thought that some devotee must be worshipping some image of God newly set up within the temple by performing the Ârati, the evening ceremony of waving the lights and offering flowers, fruits and holy water. With folded hands they all stood listening to the sacred sounds before the temple. One of them, more curious than the rest, had the courage to go inside. To his surprise he saw that Podo was ringing the bell and blowing the shell; but the floor was as dirty as before with impurities of all kinds and there was no image of God on the altar! He then called out, saying: "O Podo, thou hast no Mâdhava (Srî Krishna, God-Incarnate) in the temple; how is it, then, that thou hast raised all this clamor by blowing the conch-shell? And behold! thou hast not even taken the trouble to cleanse the temple by removing the impurities and dirt of years and washing the floor with the holy water of the Ganges!"

First realize God in the temple of your heart. With that in view, you must cleanse it of all **First cleanse** impurities, all sin and iniquity, all **the heart.** attachment to the world caused by the power of the senses. It is then that the time comes for blowing the shell, if need be. Talk of social reforms! You may well do so after realizing God. Remember, the Rishis of old gave up the world in order to attain to God. This is the one thing needful. All other things shall be granted unto you.

iv

The steamer had come back to Koylâghât (Calcutta). All on board held themselves in readiness to land. As they came out of the cabin they saw that the full moon had bathed the bosom of the Holy Ganges and the adjoining banks with her mellow light. The Bhagavân with two or three disciples got into a cab which had been kept waiting for Him on the shore. Nandalâl, Keshab's nephew, also got in. He wished to go with the Bhagavân for some distance. When all had seated themselves in the cab, Srî Râmakrishna asked: "Where is Keshab?" In a few moments Keshab came up smiling and inquired who were going with Him. Being satisfied with the answer, he bowed down to the ground before the Bhagavân, who affectionately bade him adièu.

The cab set out. The Bhagavân was filled with supreme joy as the carriage drove along. Suddenly He said: "I am thirsty; what is to be done?" Nandalâl stopped the carriage before the gates of the India Club and went upstairs to bring water. It was brought in a glass tumbler. The Bhagavân, smiling, asked, "Is the glass well washed?" Nandalâl replied, "Yes." The Bhagavân drank the water. He was childlike in His simplicity. He put forward His face to look at the various objects on both sides. His joy knew no bounds as He saw men, animals, carriages, houses, the moonlight, the lighted streets!

Nandalâl got out at Colutolâ. The cab came to a stop before the door of Suresh Mitra's* house. Suresh was very much attached to the Bhagavân, but he was not at home. He had gone to visit a newly-purchased garden at Kânkurgâchi. His people opened a room on the ground floor and invited the party to be seated there. The cab-fare was to be paid. Who was there to pay it? Had Suresh been at home, he would have done so. The Bhagavân said to a disciple: "Ask the ladies of the house for the fare. I suppose they know well enough that their husbands are in the habit of coming to our place."

Narendra (Vivekânanda) lived in the same neighborhood, so the Bhagavân sent for him. Meanwhile the inmates of the house led Him upstairs into the drawing-room. The matting of the floor was covered with a carpet and a white sheet. Three or four pillows were lying about. On the walls there hung a beautiful oil-painting which Suresh intended to be a representation of the harmony of all religions.

---

* Bâbu Suresh Chunder Mitra was a devoted householder disciple of Râmakrishna. The Bhagavân used to call him Surendra. See Chapter VIII.

In the painting Srî Râmakrishna was represented as pointing to Keshab that all religions lead to one goal—be it Hinduism, Mahometanism, Buddhism, Christianity, or their various sects.

The Bhagavân was conversing with smiles on His lips when Narendra came up. His joy redoubled. He said to Narendra as He talked: We enjoyed such a pleasant trip on board the steamer with Keshab Sen. Bijoy also was there, and many of those present here. You may ask Mahendra how I talked to Keshab and Bijoy about the mother and her daughter both observing fast on Tuesday each for her own welfare, and how God's Sports in this world would suffer for want of nourishment in the absence of obstructions like Jatilla and Kutilla.

It was getting late. But Suresh had not come home as yet. The Bhagavân asked to go back to the Temple at Dakshineswara. It was about half-past ten and He wished to leave for the garden. The streets were flooded with moonlight. The cab was at the door. The Bhagavân got in. Narendra and Mahendra bowed low to the Master and started for their homes.

CHAPTER VI

SUNDAY AT THE TEMPLE

i

THE nineteenth of August, 1883, fell on Sunday and was the first day after the full moon, so the devotees had leisure to come and see their beloved Master at Dakshineswara. Everyone had free access. He talked with everybody who came. His visitors were from all classes of people,—Sannyâsins * and Paramahamsas,† Hindus, Christians and Brâhmos, Sâktas, Vaishnavas and Shaivas,—women as well as men. It was noon. Srî Râmakrishna was seated in His usual place in His room. A disciple came and saluted Him, falling at His

---

* Sannyâsins are those who have renounced the world and its pleasures for the sake of the Lord.

† Paramahamsas are those who have attained to *Nirvikalpa Samâdhi*, or Brahma-Jnâna.

hallowed feet. The Bhagavân made him sit down and kindly inquired after the welfare of himself and of his family. A short while after the Bhagavân began to talk to him upon the Vedânta. He said:

The Astâvakara Samhitâ * deals with the knowledge of the Âtman (Self). The knowers **Non-dualistic** of the Self declare: "I am He, I am **Vedântins.** that Supreme Self." This is the view of all the Sannyâsins belonging to the non-dualistic (Advaita) school of Vedânta. But it is not meet that a man of the world should hold such a view. He is doing all kinds of work; how at the same time can he be that Highest Self, the Absolute Brahman, who is beyond all actions? The Non-dualistic Vedantins hold that the Self has no attachment to anything. Pleasure, pain, virtue, vice, can never affect the Self in any way; but they do affect men who think that their soul is the same as the body. Smoke can blacken only the wall, but not the space through which it moves. There was a certain devotee named Krishna Kisore, who used to say that he was *Kha*, or empty space. He

---

* Astâvakra Samhitâ is a work containing the highest exposition of the Advaita Vedânta, written by the ancient sage Astâvakra, who was the preceptor of King Janaka.

meant that he was the same as the Highest Self, Brahman the Absolute, who is sometimes likened to Âkâsa (infinite space) because nothing can be predicated of It. A true philosopher has some right to say this. As for others, such a sentiment is altogether out of place.

But it is good for everyone to cherish the idea that he is free. "I am free," "I am free"; if a man constantly says this, he is sure to be free. On the other hand, he who always thinks that he is in bondage brings bondage on himself in the end. The weak-minded man who always says, "I am a sinner," "I am a sinner," is sure to have a fall. A man should rather say: "I repeat the Holy Name of God; how can there be any sin in me, or bondage of the world?"

Thought of freedom brings freedom.

Then turning towards the disciple, the Bhagavân said:

To-day my mind is not at ease. I hear from Hridai * that he has been ailing much. Is this

---

* Hridâya Mukerji was an old servant of Srî Râmakrishna and served Him for nearly thirty years in the Temple of Dakshineswara—till 1881. He was a remote nephew of Srî Râmakrishna. His birthplace was in the village of Siore, in the district of Hughly. He breathed his last towards the end of April, 1889. "Hridai" was a pet abbreviation of his name used by Srî Râmakrishna.

181

anxiety due to Mâyâ (attachment) or Dayâ (compassion) towards him?

Mâyâ and Dayâ.

The disciple did not know what to reply and remained silent.

Srî Râmakrishna: Do you know what is Mâyâ? <u>Love towards one's own father, brother, sister, wife, child, nephew, niece, is called Mâyâ, and compassion means loving all beings equally.</u> Now what is this, my anxiety, due to—Mâyâ or compassion? But Hridai did a great deal for me. He served me much. He never hesitated to do all sorts of menial services for me. My mind will be set at rest if he can get the money he needs. Now whom am I to ask for money? And how can I ask, being a Sannyâsin?

At two or three o'clock in the afternoon two great devotees, Adhar * and Balarâm, came and prostrated themselves before Him and took their seats. They asked Him how He was doing. The Bhagavân replied: "Well, my body is all right, but not so is the mind." He did not mention anything about Hridâya's illness.

---

* Adhar was the first name of Bâbu Adhar lâl Sen, a rich Hindu Deputy Magistrate of Calcutta. He was a devoted householder disciple of Râmakrishna, who often sanctified his home by His holy visits.

GOSPEL OF RAMAKRISHNA

ii

In the course of the conversation, when the talk was about the Goddess *Simhavâhini** (seated upon a lion) belonging to the Mullik family of Barabâzâr, He said: Once I went to see the Simhavâhini. She was then staying in one Mullik's house at Châshâdhopâpârâ. The house was almost a deserted one. The family had become very poor. In some places there was filth, in other places mosses were growing undisturbed. The cement upon the wall was crumbling down, and brick-dust and sand were slowly falling. Other houses belonging to the Mulliks are very neat and clean, but this was not so. Can you explain why this was the case? <u>The truth is that everyone must reap the fruit of his past actions. We should believe in the law of Karma.</u> One thing, however, I saw in that deserted house,—that the face of the Goddess was beaming with glory. <u>We should believe in the Divine Presence infilling the images of the Deity.</u>

Law of Karma.

The Divine Presence in images.

---

* In Hindu mythology the Goddess Durgâ destroyed the Demons, riding upon a wild lion. Hence Her name is "Simhavâhini."

I went to Vishnupura.* The Râjâ has several good temples. In one of the temples there is the image of a Goddess named Mrinmayi. A big tank is before the temple. But how was it that I smelled in the tank the spices that women use to perfume their hair? I did not know that they offered such spices to the Goddess when they went to worship her. I had not seen her image near the tank, but in Samâdhi I saw her Divine form down to her waist. The Divine Mother of the universe appeared to me in the form of Mrinmayi.

By this time other devotees had arrived. The talk then turned on the Kabul war and the civil war that came after. One gave the news that Yâkub Khân † had been deposed from his throne, adding: Sir, Yâkub Khân is a great devotee.

Srî Râmakrishna: Well, pleasure and pain, happiness and misery, are things one cannot **Trials of a devotee.** separate from the body. We read in Kavi Kankana's ‡ "Chandi" that Kâluvira, a great devotee, was shut up in prison.

---

* The name of an ancient city in Bengal.

† Yâkub Khân was the Amir of Afghanistan who was deposed by the British after the Kabul war of 1879.

‡ Kavi Kankana was a great poet of Bengal, whose famous

They placed a heavy stone upon his breast. Yet Kâlu was the favorite child of the Mother of the universe. Pleasure and pain, happiness and misery, come with the body. How great a devotee was Srimanta! How fondly the goddess loved his mother Khullanâ! But what an amount of trouble he had to go through! They took him to the scaffold to be executed. A certain woodman, a great devotee, was fortunate enough to see the goddess, and the goddess loved him very much and showed her kindness towards him; but he had to go on with the trade of woodcutter all the same. He had to sell firewood to get his livelihood. It does not follow that a devoted lover of God must be very well off in the world. But he is rich in spirit, though he may be poor in worldly things. Devaki in prison saw God in the form of a human being holding the conch-shell, discus, mace and lotus in His four hands; but she could not get out of the prison for all her God-vision.

A devotee is rich in spirit.

Disciple: But she should have got rid, not only of imprisonment, but of her body, that being the source of all her troubles.

---

work is entitled "Chandi," or the exploits of the Divine Mother. Kâluvira and Srimanta were the heroes of this poem.

Bhagavân: One's body is the result of one's past actions. Therefore one must bear with it so long as the past actions are not cleared up. A blind man taking a bath in the holy water of the Ganges has his sins washed off, but his blindness continues all the same. It is the result of the actions of his previous life. But however the body may be under the influence of pleasure and pain, however the body may be happy or miserable, the true devotee is all the same rich in spirit, rich in knowledge (Jnâna) and the love of God (Bhakti). Take for instance the Pândavas. How many dangers and difficulties they had to face! What wants and miseries to bear! But amidst all these they never lost their wisdom. Can you find others equally wise and devoted to God?

Body result of past actions.

At this time Narendra (Swâmi Vivekânanda) and Visvanâtha Upâdhyâya,* the Nepaulese Resident in Calcutta, entered. Bowing down to Srî Râmakrishna, they took their seats. Srî Râmakrishna asked Narendra to sing. There

---

* Visvanâtha Upâdhyâya was a Brâhmin scholar and a devotee of Srî Râmakrishna. He was like a consul of the Nepaul Government to the British.

GOSPEL OF RAMAKRISHNA

was hanging on the western wall of the room a Tânpurâ (a stringed musical instrument). Narendra took it down and began to tune it. Everyone was intently looking upon his face, eager to listen to his songs.

Bhagavân to Narendra: This instrument no longer sounds as before.

Visvanâtha: It is filled, therefore there is no sound, as with a vessel filled with water.

Srî Râmakrishna: But how do you explain the life of Nârada and of other Divine Teachers? They had realized God, but still spoke. They were filled, but they gave forth sounds.

Visvanâtha: They spoke for the good of mankind.

Bhagavân: <u>Yes, Nârada and Sukadeva came down from the highest state of Samâdhi. Their hearts went out to those who were weary and heavy-laden and knew not God. They spoke for the good of others.</u>

Narendra began to sing:

1. In the temple of the heart dwelleth the Eternal Truth.
   Ever beholding His glorious and lovely form, when shall we dive in the sea of His Beauty?

2. In the form of Infinite Wisdom the Lord will enter my soul.
   The restless mind filled with wonder will take refuge at His Blessed Feet.
   Immortal Bliss, like embodied nectar, will rise in the firmament of the soul.

3. At Thy sight we shall be mad with joy even as the *Chakora** is maddened at the sight of the moon.

4. O King of kings, there is none like Thee, all good and all peaceful.
   At Thy feet, O Beloved, I shall offer myself and thus fulfil the aim of my life.

5. Even here shall I enjoy heavenly bliss, so great a privilege where could I find?

6. O Lord, beholding Thy pure and perfect form, all sins will take flight, even as darkness vanishes before light.

7. O kindle in my heart the light of burning faith, fixed firm like the polar star, and thus, O Friend of the meek, fulfil my one desire. Day and night merged in the

---

* *Chakora* is the name of a kind of aquatic bird.

Bliss of Thy Love. O I shall forget myself having attained to Thee.
(O when will this come?)

Srî Râmakrishna had lost Himself in deep Samâdhi as soon as He had heard the words **Samâdhi of Râmakrishna.** "Immortal bliss like embodied nectar." There He sat with clasped hands, turning His face toward the East. He was diving deep into the Ocean of Beauty of the All-Blissful One. No external consciousness, no sign of breathing, no motion in any of His limbs, no quiver of the eye,—like one drawn in a picture! He had gone away somewhere from this kingdom, from this world of the senses.

Returning from Samâdhi, the Bhagavân murmured in an indistinct voice: "Thou art I, I am Thou. Thou eatest, Thou and I eat. What is this? Have I jaundiced eyes? I see Thee everywhere. Wherever I cast my eyes, I see Thy form." Then He repeated the holy name of Krishna: "O Friend of the meek and gentle! O Lord of my heart! O Divine Shepherd!" After repeating this a few times, He again went into Samâdhi. Coming back to sense-consciousness, He opened His eyes and found that the room was full of people of every

GOSPEL OF RAMAKRISHNA

class. Narendra, seeing that the Bhagavân was in Samâdhi, had left the room and gone to the eastern veranda, where Hâzrâ* was seated on a blanket telling his beads. Narendra began to talk with him. In the meanwhile the Bhagavân looked for Narendra in the room, but he was not there. The *Tânpurâ* (musical instrument) was lying on the ground. The devotees all had their eyes fixed upon the Bhagavân, who began thus, referring to Narendra: He has lighted the fire. It matters not whether he remains in the room or leaves it!

Then turning towards Visvanâtha and His numerous devotees, He said: Meditate upon **Bliss comes in meditation.** God, the sole Existence, Knowledge and Bliss Eternal, and you also shall have bliss. That Being of Knowledge and Bliss is always here and everywhere, only It is covered and obscured by ignorance. The less is your attachment towards the senses, the more will be your love for God.

Visvanâtha: The more we near our home at Calcutta, the farther we are from Benares, and the more we near Benares, the farther we are away from our home.

---

* See note page 128.

Bhagavân: As Srimati (Râdhâ) * neared Srî Krishna, she perceived more and more the charming fragrance of His sweet person. The more one approaches God, the more does one's love toward Him increase. The more the river nears the sea, the more it is subject to ebb and flow. The Ganges of knowledge flowing in the soul of a wise man runs only in one direction. To him the whole universe is a dream. He always lives in His own True Self (Âtman). But the Ganges of love in a devotee's heart does not run in one direction. It has its ebb and flow. A devotee laughs, weeps, dances, sings. He wants sometimes to enjoy his Beloved, to merge into his Beloved! He swims in Him, dives, rises up in his joy as merrily as a lump of ice floats upon the water.

Lover of God.

But in fact God the Absolute and God the Creator are one and the same Being. The Absolute Existence-Intelligence-Bliss is the All-knowing, All-intelligent and All-blissful Mother of the Universe. The precious stone (*Mani*) and its brightness cannot be separated in thought, for

God the Absolute and God the Creator one.

---

* Srimati Râdhâ was the beloved consort of Srî Krishna, the greatest of the Saviours among the Hindus.

191

we cannot think of the stone without its brightness, nor can we think of the brightness apart from the stone. <u>The Absolute Existence-Intelligence-Bliss, the Undifferentiated, appears as differentiated into many.</u> He has various names applied to Him according to the various powers manifested. That is the reason of His having many forms. Hence a devotee has sung: "O my Mother Târâ,* Thou art even all that." Wherever there is action, such as creation, preservation and destruction, there is Sakti or Intelligent Energy. But water is water whether it is calm or disturbed. That One Absolute Existence-Intelligence-Bliss is also the eternally Intelligent Energy which creates, preserves and destroys the universe. Thus it is the same Visvanâtha whether he does nothing or performs his worship or visits the Governor-General. In all cases it is the same Visvanâtha, only these are his different Upâdhis or states.

Visvanâtha: Yes, Sir, that is so.

Bhagavân: I said this to Keshab Chandra Sen.

---

*Târâ is another name of the Divine Mother of the universe.

GOSPEL OF RAMAKRISHNA

Visvanâtha: Well, Sir, Keshab Chandra Sen does not respect our orthodox Hindu manners, customs and laws. How can he be a real saint?

The Bhagavân (turning towards His devotees): Visvanâtha never wants me to go to see Keshab Sen.

Visvanâtha: But Thy Holiness will go. What can I do?

Bhagavân: You go to see the Governor-General, who according to your Shâstras* is a Mleccha (unclean), and for money, too; and may I not go to see Keshab Sen? It does not become you to speak in this way. You often say: "It is God who has manifested Himself as the human soul and the world itself." What you say you must mean; what you mean you must say!

After this Râmakrishna abruptly left the room and went to the northeastern veranda. Visvanâtha and other devotees remained waiting for Him in the room. Narendra was found talking with Hâzrâ on the veranda. Srî Râmakrishna knew that Hâzrâ was an out-and-out non-dualist and a dry logician. He upheld that all the universe was a mere dream; that all

---

* Hindu Sacred Books are called Shâstras.

GOSPEL OF RAMAKRISHNA

kinds of worship and offerings were mental delusions; that God was the one changeless Entity; and that a man should only meditate upon his Âtman (Self), and do nothing else.

Bhagavân (laughing): What are you talking about?

Narendra: We are discussing themes all too big for ordinary mortals.

Bhagavân (laughing): But however you may talk, know that pure selfless devotion (Bhakti) and pure selfless knowledge (Jnâna) are both one; their goal is the same. Smooth and easy is the path of devotion leading to God.

Pure Bhakti and pure Jnâna one.

Narendra: There is no use in reasoning like a philosopher; make me, O Mother, mad with Thy love. I have been reading Hamilton's Philosophy, and he writes: "A learned ignorance is the end of philosophy and the beginning of religion."

Bhagavân: What does that mean?

Narendra explained it in Bengali. Srî Râmakrishna laughed and thanked him in English, saying, "Thank you!" Everyone laughed at this, for the Bhagavân's knowledge of English was confined to a few such expressions.

iii

Soon twilight began to fall. The devotees one after another took leave of the Bhagavân, and so did Narendra.

The day was drawing to a close. The Temple-servant was arranging the lights. The priests were busy saying their prayers as they stood waist-deep in the sacred waters of the Ganges, purifying themselves body and soul. They were shortly to go to their respective temples to perform the *Ârati*, the evening ceremony. The young men of Dakshineswara had come with their friends to take a walk in the garden. They were strolling about the rampart, enjoying the sweet evening breeze made fragrant by the flowers and watching the slightly undulating breast of the swiftly-flowing Ganges. Some of them, perhaps the more thoughtful, could be found going about by themselves in the solitude of the sacred trees called the *Panchavati*.

Evening at the Temple.

Bhagavân Srî Râmakrishna also looked at the Ganges for some time from the western veranda.

It was evening. The lamp-lighter had lighted all the lamps of the big temple. The old maid-servant came and lit the lamp in the Bhagavân's room and burned incense there. In the meantime the Ârati ceremony had begun in the twelve shrines dedicated to Shiva. It began soon after in the temples of Kâli, Mother of the Universe, and of Srî Vishnu. The united and solemn sound of gongs, bells, cymbals, grew more solemn and sweet as it was echoed back by the murmuring Ganges below.

It was the first lunar day after the full moon. A short while after nightfall the moon rose. Gradually the tops of the trees in the garden, as well as the big temple compound, were bathed in her balmy light. At the magic touch of her radiance the waters of the Ganges shone bright like silver and flowed on dancing with great joy.

When at nightfall Srî Râmakrishna bowed down to the Divine Mother, He repeated the Holy Names of God, keeping time all the while by clapping his hands. In His room there were pictures of various Incarnations of God. He bowed before each picture, repeating the Holy Name of each. He also repeated His favorite *mantrams*, each having some lofty, unifying principle running through it, such as:

(1) Brahma-Âtmâ-Bhagavân. (The Absolute Brahman of the Vedânta, True Self and the

Personal God of the Bhakta are three in one and one in three.)

(2) Bhâgavata - Bhakta - Bhagavân. (The Word, the devotee and the Personal God are three in one and one in three.)

(3) Brahma-Sakti, Sakti-Brahma. (God the Absolute and the Creative Energy are one and the same.)

(4) Veda-Purâna-Tantra-Gitâ-Gâyatri. (God of the Scriptures and Holy texts.)

(5) Saranâgata, Saranâgata. (I take refuge in Thee. I am Thine, I am Thine.)

(6) Nâham-Nâham, Tuhu-Tuhu. (Not I, not I, but Thou, but Thou.)

(7) Ami Yantra, tumi yantri. (I am the machine; Thou art the One who runs the machine.)

After all these repetitions were ended, He meditated upon the Mother Divine with clasped hands.

A few of the devotees had been walking about in the garden during the evening. When the Ârati ceremonies were over in the temples, one after another they came together in Srî Râmakrishna's room.

He was sitting on His seat with devotees before Him on the floor. He said: Narendra,

Râkhâl and Bhavanâtha—these are Nityasiddhas (perfect even from their birth). They need no training. What training they go through is more than they need. You see that Narendra never cares for anyone. He was with me in Visvanâtha's carriage the other day. When he was requested to sit upon the better seat, he paid no heed at all. Moreover, he never shows to me that he knows anything, lest I praise him before men. He has no Mâyâ, no attachment. He looks as if he were free from all bondage. For a single individual he has many gifts and many noble qualities. He is also very courteous in his manners. He knows how to control his senses; he has said that he will not marry, but will live a pure life. That is good. I always go into Samâdhi when I see him.

We mould our character according to the company we keep; and we keep such company **Character and** as is in harmony with our character. **associations.** For this reason the Paramahamsas (perfected souls) like to keep the company of innocent children because their minds are pure, simple and unstained by worldliness.

As Srî Râmakrishna was speaking these words, a worthy Brâhmin entered the room and bowed

GOSPEL OF RAMAKRISHNA

down at His feet. The Bhagavân had known him before and loved him because he was sincere and simple. He had studied Vedânta in Benares, the seat of great learning. Râmakrishna said to him: Well, you have not been here for a long time. How are you?

The Brâhmin, smiling, replied: "Revered Sir, the duties of the world, as Thou knowest, take most of my time."

He then took his seat and Râmakrishna continued: You remained in Benares for a long time. Tell us what you saw there. Let us hear something about Dayânanda.*

Brâhmin: Yes, I met Dayânanda. Thou hast also seen him.

Râmakrishna: Yes, I went to see him once. He was staying in a garden-house not very far from here. That day he had an appointment with Keshab Sen. He was a great scholar; he also believed in the Devas (perfected spirits), but Keshab did not, whereupon he said: "If

---

*Dayânanda Saraswati was a Sannyâsin of the Advaita Vedânta School. He was a great Vedic scholar, speaker and a Hindu reformer of the nineteenth century. He wrote Sanskrit Commentaries on the Vedas and was the founder of a reformed Hindu Sect known as the "Ârya Samâj," which is now in a flourishing condition. He died in 1883 A.D.

God created all these phenomena, could He not create Devas?" He believed in one God, but without form. Visvanâtha was repeating the Holy Name of the Lord, "Râma, Râma"; at this he said: "Better repeat the name 'Sandesha, Sandesha' (sweetmeat, sweetmeat)."

Brâhmin: In Benares, Dayânanda had long theological discussions with the other pandits. In the end all the pandits unanimously stood on one side, while he stood alone on the other; and then the pandits drove him from the city by raising the outcry: "Dayânanda's position is false and must not be accepted!" I also saw Colonel Olcott, the Theosophist. The theosophists believe in the existence of the Mahâtmâs, the realm of the moon, the realm of the sun and the astral realms. They believe that the astral bodies go to these places and so on. Revered Sir, what dost Thou think of Theosophy?

Râmakrishna: <u>Bhakti, devotion to the Supreme, is the only thing worth having.</u> Do they **Devotion to the Supreme.** seek Bhakti? Then it is good. If their aim be the realization of God, then they are all right; but by simply dwelling upon these realms and Mahâtmâs one cannot search after God. <u>One should practise Sâdhana (devotional exercises) to attain true Bhakti.</u>

One should have extreme longing for realization. One should gather up all the mental activities and concentrate them upon Him. Realization of God does not come so easily; it requires a great deal of Sâdhana. A man asked: "Why can I not see God?" I replied: "If you wish to catch a big fish, which lives in deep water, you will have to make many preparations to attract him. You must get the line, rod, hook and float; you must put on savory bait; then when you see bubbles in the water, you may know that he has come near. Similarly, if you wish to see God, devote yourself to the practice of true Bhakti."

Bhakti and Jnâna. A devotee: Which is better, Bhakti or Jnâna?

Râmakrishna: <u>The highest form of Bhakti comes through extreme love for God.</u> Three friends were walking through a forest. A tiger appeared. One of them cried out: "Brother, we shall be devoured by the tiger"; the second said: "Why shall we be devoured? Come, let us pray to the Lord." Hearing this, the third one replied: "Oh no, why trouble the Lord? Let us climb this tree." The man who said, "We shall be devoured," did not know that the Lord is the protector of all; he who wished to pray to the Lord was a Jnâni; he knew that the Lord is the Creator, Protector and Destroyer of all phenomena; but the third man, who said, "Why trouble the Lord, let us climb the tree," was a true lover of God. He had had the taste of Divine Love, the highest form of Bhakti. In one aspect of Divine Love (Prema) the lover thinks of himself as greater than the object of love; he has the constant desire to protect the Beloved and make Him happy by removing all troubles and anxieties. The Gopis had true Prema, or Divine Love.

In Divine Love the sense of "I" and "mine" exists, as was shown by the mother of the Divine Incarnation, Krishna. For her, Krishna was only a son and not the Lord of the universe. She loved to nurse Him and take care of Him, always calling Him "my Krishna," and feeling the same anxiety about Him that an earthly mother would feel about her son. When a certain saint spoke to her, saying: "Your Krishna is the absolute Master of the world; He is not human"; Yasodâ, the mother of Krishna, replied: "Oh no, He is not the Lord of the universe; He is my child. I cannot think of Him as other than my child." Divine Love is mani-

Divine Love and its various aspects.

fested by various relations; the closer the relation, the stronger the tie of love. The relation of a servant to his master was manifested by Hanumân; the relation of a friend to his friend was shown by Arjuna to Krishna; while the Gopis were devoted to the Lord as their Divine husband.

Some people think that they are bound (Baddha), that they will never attain to Divine Wisdom, or to Divine Love. But all this fear vanishes from the heart of a true disciple if his Guru, or spiritual guide, be gracious to him.

Parable of the tiger. There was a flock of sheep in the woods; suddenly a tigress jumped into their midst. At that moment she gave birth to a cub and died on the spot. The kind-hearted sheep took care of the cub, and brought it up among them. They ate grass, the cub followed their example; they bleated, the cub also learned to bleat. In this manner the cub grew up not as a young tiger but like a sheep. One day a full-grown tiger came that way and watched with wonder the grass-eating tiger. The real tiger drew nearer, but the cub began to bleat. Then the real tiger dragged him to the edge of a lake and said: "Look here! Compare your face with mine. Is there any difference? You are a tiger like me; grass is not your food; your food is animal flesh." But the grass-eating tiger could not believe it. After a long time the real tiger convinced him that he was of the same species. Then he gave him a piece of flesh to eat, but he would not touch it; he began once more to bleat and to seek for grass. At last, however, the real tiger forced him to eat animal flesh; at once he liked the taste of the blood, gave up his grass-eating and bleating, and realized that he was not a sheep but a tiger. He then followed the real tiger and became like him.

The human soul is the child of God, but it does not know it, and therefore it lives like an ordinary mortal (sheep); but when, by the grace of the Guru, he realizes his true nature, he becomes free from all fear and attains to perfection. Therefore I say, when the grace of the Guru comes, all fear vanishes. He will make you know who you are and what you are in reality. You will have to do very little for yourself after you have received that grace. You will then be able to distinguish between the Real and the unreal and to realize that God is Truth and the world is unreal.

Human soul, the child of God.

A fisherman came to a garden at night and threw his net in the pond to catch some fish. **Parable of the false Sâdhu.** Hearing the noise, the owner sent his men to capture him. The men came with torches in their hands to discover the thief. In the meantime the fisherman dropped his net, covered his face with ashes and sat under a tree, pretending to be a holy man absorbed in meditation. The men could not find the thief; they simply noticed that a holy man was meditating under a tree, so they returned to the owner and told him what they had seen. Everybody then brought flowers, fruits, and sweets to the holy man and paid him great honor and respect. Next morning crowds of people came to see the Sâdhu and offered to him money and various other things. The fisherman thought: "How strange it is! I am not a holy man, still people have so much respect for me and I have received so many gifts. If I become a genuine Sâdhu (Anchoret), how much more I shall get! Undoubtedly I shall see God." If merely feigning to be a holy man could so far awaken him, what can be said of him who has practised all virtues in order to become a true holy man! He will realize what is Real and what is unreal, that God is Truth and the world is unreal.

A devotee: Where shall I meditate on God?

Râmakrishna: The heart is the best place. Meditate on Him in your heart.

CHAPTER VII

SOME INCIDENTS IN THE LIFE OF SRÎ RÂMAKRISHNA (AS TOLD BY HIMSELF)

i

I practised austerities for a long time. I cared very little for the body. My longing for
Days of struggle. the Divine Mother was so great that I would not eat or sleep. I would lie on the bare ground, placing my head on a lump of earth, and cry out loudly: "Mother, Mother, why dost Thou not come to me?" I did not know how the days and nights passed away. I used to have ecstasy all the time. I saw my disciples as my own people, like children and relations, long before they came to me. I used to cry before my Mother, saying: "O Mother! I am dying for my beloved ones (Bhaktas); do Thou bring them to me as quickly as possible."

At that time whatever I desired came to pass. Once I desired to build a small hut in the Panchavati * for meditation and to put a fence around it. Immediately after I saw a huge bundle of bamboo sticks, rope, strings and even a knife, all brought by the tide in front of the Panchavati. A servant of the Temple, seeing these things, ran to me with great delight and told me of them. There was the exact quantity of material necessary for the hut and the fence. When they were built, nothing remained over. Everyone was amazed to see this wonderful sight.

All desires fulfilled.

When I reached the state of continuous ecstasy, I gave up all external forms of worship; I could no longer perform them. Then I prayed to my Divine Mother: "Mother, who will now take care of me? I have no power to take care of myself. I like to hear Thy name and feed Thy Bhaktas and help the poor. Who will make it possible for me to do these things? Send me someone who will be able to do these for me." As the answer to this prayer came Mathura Bâbu,† who served me so long and

---

* Five sacred trees planted together to form a grove to be used for contemplation.

† Mathura Bâbu was the son-in-law of Râni Râshmoni,

with such intense devotion and faith! Again at another time I said to the Mother: "I shall have no child of my own, but I wish to have as my child a pure Bhakta, who will stay with me all the time. Send me such an one." Then came Râkhâl (Brahmânanda).

Those who are my own are parts of my very Self.

ii

In referring to the time of joyous illumination which immediately followed His enlightenment, He exclaimed:

What a state it was! The slightest cause aroused in me the thought of the Divine Ideal. **Visit to Zoological Garden.** One day I went to the Zoological Garden in Calcutta. I desired especially to see the lion, but when I beheld him, I lost all sense-consciousness and went into Samâdhi. Those who were with me wished to show me the other animals, but I replied: "I saw everything when I saw the king of beasts. Take me home." The strength of the lion had aroused in me the consciousness of the

---

the founder of the Temple garden at Dakshineswara. He recognized the Divine powers and superhuman character of Srî Râmakrishna and became His devoted disciple.

omnipotence of God and had lifted me above the world of phenomena.

Another day I went to the parade-ground to see the ascension of a balloon. Suddenly my eyes fell upon a young English boy leaning against a tree. The very posture of his body brought before me the vision of the form of Krishna and I went into Samâdhi.

Divinity everywhere.

Again I saw a woman wearing a blue garment under a tree. She was a harlot. As I looked at her, instantly the ideal of Sitâ* appeared before me! I forgot the existence of the harlot, but saw before me pure and spotless Sitâ, approaching Râma, the Incarnation of Divinity, and for a long time I remained motionless. I worshipped all women as representatives of the Divine Mother. I realized the Mother of the universe in every woman's form.

Mathura Bâbu, the son-in-law of Râshmoni, invited me to stay in his house for a few days. At that time I felt so strongly that I was the maid-servant of my Divine Mother that I thought of myself as a woman. The ladies of the house had the same feeling; they did not

---

* Sitâ was the consort of Râma, the Divine Incarnation and the Hero of Râmâyana. She was the perfect type of womanhood according to the Hindus.

GOSPEL OF RAMAKRISHNA

look upon me as a man. As women are free before a young girl, so were they before me. <u>My mind was above the consciousness of sex</u>.

What a Divine state it was! I could not eat here in the Temple. I would walk from place to place and enter into the house of strangers after their meal hour. I would sit there quietly, without uttering a word. When questioned, I would say, "I wish to eat here." Immediately they would feed me with the best things they had.

iii

Once I heard of a poor Brâhmin who was a true devotee and who lived in a small hut in Bâghbâzâr. I desired to see him, so I asked Mathura Bâbu to take me to him. He consented, immediately ordered a large carriage and drove me there. The Brâhmin's house was so small that he scarcely had room to receive us, and he was much surprised to see me coming with such a rich man in such a carriage!

Visit to a poor Brâhmin.

At another time I wished to meet <u>Devendra Nâth Tâgore</u>.* He is a very rich man, but in

---

* Devendra Nâth Tâgore was a Hindu multimillionaire of Calcutta. He was born in 1818 A.D. In 1841 he became

GOSPEL OF RAMAKRISHNA

spite of his enormous wealth he is devoted to God and repeats His Holy Name. For this reason I desired to know him.

Visit to Devendra Nâth Tâgore.

I spoke about him to Mathura Bâbu. He replied: "Very well, Bâbâ, I will take Thee to him; he was my classmate." So he took me and introduced me to him, saying: "This holy man has come to see you. He is mad after God." I saw in him a little pride and egotism. It is natural for a man who has so much wealth, culture, fame and social position. I said to Mathura Bâbu: "Tell me, does pride spring from true wisdom or from ignorance? He who has attained to the highest knowledge of Brahman cannot possess pride or egotism, such as 'I am learned,' 'I am wise,' 'I am rich,' and so on." While I was speaking with Devendra Nâth Tâgore, I went into a state from where I could see the true character of every individual. In this state the most

---

a follower of Râjâ Râmmohun Roy, the founder of the Âdi Brâhmo Samâj, and in 1844 he became the Âchârya, or the spiritual leader of this Theistic Hindu Church. During the latter part of his life he retired from the world and devoted his time entirely to spiritual studies. He was regarded by the Hindus as the "Maharshi," or the holy man of his age.

learned pandits and scholars appear to me like blades of grass. When I see that scholars have neither true discrimination nor dispassion, then I feel that they are like straws; or they seem like vultures who soar high in the heavens, but keep their minds on the charnel-pits below on the earth. In Devendra I found both spiritual knowledge and worldly desire. He has a number of children, some of whom are quite young. A doctor was present. I said: "When you have so much spiritual knowledge, how can you live constantly in the midst of so much worldliness? You are like Râjâ Janaka; you can keep your mind on God, remaining amid worldly pleasures and luxury. Therefore I have come to see you. Tell me something of the Divine Being." Devendra then read some passages from the Vedas and said: "This world is like a chandelier, and each Jiva (individual soul) is like a light in it." Long ago, when I spent nearly all my time meditating at the Panchavati, I saw the same thing. When Devendra's words harmonized with my experience, I knew that he must have attained to some true knowledge. I asked him to explain. He said: "Who would have known this world? God has created man to manifest His glory. If there were no light in the chandelier, it would be all dark. The chandelier itself would not be visible." After a long conversation Devendra Nâth Tâgore begged me to come to the anniversary of the Brâhmo-Samâj. I answered: "If it be the will of the Lord. I go wherever He takes me."

iv

Padmalochana was the most eminent scholar in the court of the Râjâ of Burdwan. He came **Visit to Padmalochana.** to a garden-house near Dakshineswara, and as I had a desire to meet him, I sent Hridai to find out whether he had pride or not. I learned that he was simple and absolutely free from scholarly pride, so I went to see him. He was indeed a great scholar and a true Jnâni. He defeated all the great pandits and theologians. He said that when he was in the court of the Râjâ a theological discussion arose regarding the Hindu Trinity,—whether the first person of the Trinity, Brahmâ, was greater than the third person of the Trinity, Shiva. The pandits referred to him for the final decision and Padmalochana replied: "I have seen neither Brahmâ nor Shiva; how can I decide?" He wished to hear me sing the praises of my Divine Mother. I had a long conversation with him. He became truly devoted to me and said: "I have never found so much happiness anywhere." He revered me although I used to cry for my Divine Mother like a child.

V

Nothing but discourses on God appealed to me at this period. If I heard worldly conversation, I would sit in a corner and weep bitterly. When I went with Mathura Bâbu to Benares, I was sitting with him in the drawing-room when some friends came in to see him and began to discuss worldly affairs. "So much we have gained, so much we have lost." Hearing this I was in tears and cried aloud: "Mother, why hast Thou brought me here? I was much better off in the Temple. I have come to the Holy City to hear only of lust and gold; but there in the Temple I did not have to listen to such conversation."

Distaste for worldly conversation.

I was at this time like a young boy and so Mathura Bâbu fulfilled all the desires that arose in my mind. My heart and soul, however, were constantly longing to hear about the

Supreme Being. I searched for the places where

Longing to hear about the Supreme. the Holy Scriptures, were expounded. There was a Brâhmin in the neighborhood who was a great pandit and who had true faith. I used to go to hear him very often. A saint lived near by on the bank of the Ganges and I wished to go with this Brâhmin to see him; but a priest who looked upon the world as a dream discouraged me by saying: "The body of a saint is an earthly cage; what good can one obtain by visiting such a cage?" I spoke of this to the Brâhmin and he replied: "He who thinks of God, he who repeats His Holy Name and has renounced everything for the sake of the Lord, must not be regarded as an earthly cage. The priest does not know that the form of a devotee is a spiritual form full of Divine intelligence." This Brâhmin once asked me why I had thrown away my Brâhminical thread. I replied: "When the storm of Divine ecstasy overtook my heart and soul, it blew away all signs of caste and creed. If you once become mad after God, then you will understand me." But after some time this Brâhmin himself caught the madness of Divine ecstasy. He would utter nothing but "Om, Om," and sit in silence in his own room. He would not mix with or speak to anyone. His friends and relatives called in physicians. He told one of them: "You can cure my disease, but do not take my 'Om' from me." Once I went to see him when he was in this state. I asked him what was the matter and he answered: "The tax-collectors have been here and I am wondering what I shall do. They said that they would seize my belongings." I replied: "What will you gain by thinking in this way? Let them sell your belongings. If they put you in jail, they cannot harm you, because you say that you are nothing but (Kha) infinite space." I would often repeat this, his own statement, to him and say: "As you are infinite space, no tax can be drawn out of you."

vi

During this period I was absolutely outspoken. I observed no formality or etiquette;
Absolute frankness. I was fearless. Once I met a rich Zemindar and asked him: "What is our highest duty? Is not the attainment of God our highest duty?" He replied: "We are men of the world; salvation is not for us. When

even Yudhisthira,* the purest and most perfect of mortals, had to see purgatory in a vision because he had once wavered for half a second from absolute Truth, what can we expect for ourselves?" I could not bear his words and rebuked him sharply, saying: "What kind of man are you, that you think of the momentary vision of purgatory? You must not think of that, but of Yudhisthira's truthfulness, forgiveness, patience, right discrimination, renunciation, devotion and love for God."

At another time I went to see a Zemindar who had the title of Râjâ, and I told him plainly that I could not call him Râjâ because he was not really one.

One day I saw a pious Brâhmin who was counting his beads on the bank of the Ganges. I stood near him and knew that his mind was not fixed on God but on earthly things. Immediately I roused him by striking him on the shoulder. At another time Râshmoni, the founder of the Temple, was praying in the Temple while I was singing the holy song of the Divine Mother. I perceived that her mind was

---

* Yudhisthira was the Hero of the Mahâbhârata and the Hindu emperor of ancient India.

on worldly objects and instantly I roused her in the same manner. In amazement she folded her hands and remained motionless before me.

vii

Keshab Chunder Sen was suffering from a serious illness. Bhagavân Srî Râmakrishna **Visit to Keshab Sen.** was very anxious to see him, so He came one day with a few of His disciples to Keshab's home, where He was received by some of Keshab's disciples. They led Him to the drawing-room and seated Him on a couch. The room was fitted up with modern furniture. The Bhagavân looked at it for a moment; then His mind turned within and He went into Samâdhi. After recovering sense-consciousness, He spoke thus:

There are two, the physical body and the Âtman; the body is born, so it must die, but **Body and Âtman.** Âtman is deathless. It is separate from the body, like a nut in the shell; but when the nut is unripe, it is difficult to separate the kernel from the shell; so it is with worldly people who have not realized God. Their Âtman remains attached to the body; but in true knowledge the Âtman appears as separate from the body.

At this moment Keshab entered the room. He was extremely thin and looked almost like a skeleton. He could hardly stand on his feet. With great difficulty he walked to the couch and sat at the feet of Bhagavân Srî Râmakrishna. The Bhagavân came down from the couch and sat on the floor. Keshab touched his forehead to the floor and remained prostrate before Him for some time. Râmakrishna held Keshab's hand and said:

So long as there is knowledge of variety, so long there is bondage. When perfect knowledge comes, man realizes one Spirit in all. In that state he also sees that the same One has become the individual soul, and the phenomenal world with its various states and elements. It is true that the Universal Spirit dwells everywhere, but His manifestation varies. In some places there is greater manifestation and in others less. Wherever there is greater manifestation of the Spirit, there is also greater manifestation of Divine Powers.

Perfect knowledge brings realization of oneness.

First you will have to realize unity by discrimination: "Not this, not this." Then after reaching this state of realization, when you come down to phenomena, you will discover that variety has come from unity and the same unity is the goal of variety. The difference in the manifestation of Sakti or power makes the variety. When the flood of spiritual realization comes in the soul, like a sheet of water the Universal Spirit covers everything. All distinctions vanish. Then a boat can pass over a field and the way from one place to another becomes straight across the water.

Unity and variety.

Keshab was listening with rapt attention. Although the room was crowded, absolute silence prevailed. The Bhagavân, looking at Keshab, then asked:

How are you? How do you feel? You are suffering; but your illness has a deep meaning. In this body you have gone through various stages of spiritual development; the body is now suffering from the reaction. When the spiritual waves arise, the consciousness of the body vanishes; but it tells upon the body in the end. When a big steamer plies in the waters of the Ganges, I have seen the waves dash against the shore for some time after; the larger the boat, the stronger the waves; sometimes they break down the banks. If an elephant enters a small hut,

Meaning of Keshab's illness.

it shakes it and breaks it to pieces; so when the elephant of the spiritual Ideal enters into the body, it shakes and sometimes shatters it. What happens; do you know? If there be a fire in the house, it burns up many things. Similarly, the fire of Divine Wisdom burns all passion, anger and other enemies, and in the end destroys the sense of "I, me and mine." The body is then wrenched and shattered. You may think that everything is finished, but so long as there is the least sign of illness, so long He will not make you free. If you enroll yourself as a patient in a hospital, you cannot come out before you are absolutely cured.

Keshab began to smile. The Bhagavân continued: Hridai used to say, after seeing the condition of my body: "I have never seen so much spirituality with such a state of body!" But although my body was weak, still I never stopped talking of God with others. At one time, I remember, I was thin like a skeleton, yet I would continue discussions on spiritual subjects for hours.

Then shedding tears of sympathy for Keshab, the Bhagavân said: It is His will. Everything happens by Thy will O Lord! Thou doest Thy work; by mistake people say, "I do." The gardener sometimes uncovers the roots of rose-bushes that the dew may fall upon them. Sometimes he trims off some of the roots so that the flowers will become larger. Perhaps the Lord is preparing you to do greater work. But I feel very unhappy when you are ill. Last time when you were ill, I was so anxious about you that I would cry at night and pray to my Divine Mother for your recovery. Sometimes I said to my Mother: "If Keshab passes away, with whom shall I talk about God?" But this time I do not feel the same way.

Everything the will of God.

At this moment Keshab's aged mother came near the door and addressed the Bhagavân, saying: "May Keshab be cured of his illness?"

The Bhagavân replied: Pray to my blissful Divine Mother. She will remove all pain and trouble. (To Keshab) Do not spend so much time with your family and children. Their company will drag you to worldliness. You will feel better if you think of God and talk about Him.

Keshab's mother said: Do Thou bless my Keshab.

Râmakrishna: What power have I? God

will bless him. Thou doest Thy work, O Divine Mother! People say by mistake, "I do it." Two are the occasions when the Lord smiles. First, when brothers remove the chains which partition off the family property, saying: "This is mine and that is thine"; and secondly, when the physician of a dying patient declares: "I shall make him live."

Keshab then began to cough and could not remain longer, so he bowed down before the Bhagavân, saluted Him, and with great difficulty walked out of the room. Keshab's eldest son was there. A Brâhmo devotee said: Bhagavan, lay Thy hand on his head and bless him.

Râmakrishna replied: It is not for me to bless anyone.

He then gently touched him on his arm and said to the Brâhmo devotee: I cannot say to anyone, "Be thou cured." I never asked my Divine Mother for that power. I simply ask for pure love and nothing else.

Srî Râmakrishna then rose to leave. Keshab's disciples accompanied Him to the door with great reverence, and He passed from the house with His disciples.

CHAPTER VIII

FEAST AT THE GARDEN-HOUSE OF SURENDRA *

i

Srî Râmakrishna was invited by one of His beloved disciples, Surendra, a householder, to a feast made in his garden-house at Kânkurgâchi near Calcutta.

These feasts were invariably occasions for the gathering of His disciples, devotees and admirers. They were times of real festivity and rejoicing, during which the Holy Name of God was chanted to the accompaniment of *Mridangas* and other musical instruments. All the while the Bhagavân could be seen at His best, singing, dancing with the joy of the Lord, and frequently lost in that blessed state of ecstasy or Samâdhi. When the singing of devotional

---

* See note page 177.

hymns and the spiritual excitement which came with it were over, the company present would be treated by the Bhagavân to one of those celestial conversations, so laden with sermons for the spiritual welfare of humanity, which will never die in the memory of those who had the rare privilege of listening to Him.

The first part of the day was given to Sankirtan (singing forth the Name of the Lord). They were singing the songs telling of the separation of the Gopis from the Lord Srî Krishna, who had gone to Mathurâ. In the course of the songs, the Bhagavân was frequently in a state of Samâdhi. They were singing. Suddenly He rose to His feet, saying: "O my friend, do thou bring my beloved Krishna to me or take me over to the place where He is." The Bhagavân, it would appear, had merged His personality in that of Râdhâ,* the chief of the Gopis. He realized that He and Râdhâ were one. With those words He stood **Râmakrishna's ecstasy.** speechless and motionless, with fixed half-closed eyes that moved not, evidently having lost all sense-consciousness. Coming to Himself, He again, in a voice that

---

* See note page 191.

drew tears from the eyes of those who heard Him, cried out: "O my friend, do me this favor and I shall be thy most devoted servant. Remember it was thou that taughtest me my love for the Beloved."

The chorus went on singing. Râdhâ was made in the song to say: "O! I will not go to the bank of the Jamuna to draw water, for coming up to the Kadamba tree I am put in mind of my own, my Beloved." Râmakrishna, heaving a sigh, said, "Ah, me!" As the chorus chanted aloud the name of the Lord, the Bhagavân was again on His feet and in Samâdhi. Recovering His sense-consciousness, He could only repeat inarticulately: "Kitma, Kitma," for "Krishna, Krishna."

The Sankirtan was brought to a close by the Bhagavân Himself leading the chorus in the well-known piece: "Victory to Râdhâ, Victory to Govinda," and dancing with His disciples, who formed a ring around Him.

The dancing and singing had all taken place in the reception-hall. The Bhagavân then with-

The madness of love for the Lord.

drew into one of the adjoining rooms to the west. To a disciple He said, talking of the Gopis: How wonderful was their devotion! At the sight of the

Tamâl tree they were seized with the very madness of love.

Disciple: This was also the case with Chaitanya. Looking at the forest he thought it was Vrindâvan, the sacred birthplace of Srî Krishna, that was before him!

Bhagavân: Oh! if anyone is but favored with a single particle of this ecstatic love! What devotion! What intense love! Of this devotion they not only had the full complement (sixteen Annas) but a great deal more than the full complement—five Sikâs and five Annas! This is called the madness of Divine Love. The chief thing is to have intense love and sincere and earnest longing for God. On whatever path you may travel, whether you believe in the Divinity with or without form, whether you have faith in God-incarnate in a human form or not,—if you have intense love and sincere longing for Him, you are sure to attain to Him. He alone knows what He is like. He Himself will make you realize His Divine Nature. Why should you be mad after the things of the world? If you must be mad, be mad for God. There is a madness of Divine Love, a madness of Bhakti, or ecstasy, and a madness of Jnâna. Râdhâ had the madness of

Divine Love. Hanumân showed the madness of true devotion. When Sitâ was forced by Râma to prove her chastity by going through the ordeal of fire, Hanumân, although a devotee of Râma, was so maddened that he wished to kill his Lord, the Divine Incarnation. I saw a true Jnâni, who wandered like a madman. He came to the Temple garden. He had so realized the oneness of the Spirit in every living creature that when he saw a dog eating the remains of a dish, he held him by the ears and said: "Brother, wilt thou eat all?" He then took a portion and ate with the dog. He said to Hridrai: "When the holy waters of the Ganges and the water of the gutter appear the same, then will come the realization of Divine oneness."

At one time I had this madness. I used to walk like a madman, seeing the same Spirit everywhere and recognizing neither high nor low in caste or creed. I could eat even with a Pariah. I had the constant realization that Brahman is Truth and the world is unreal like a dream. Once Mathura Bâbu took me in a boat. The Mohammedan crew were cooking and I was about to eat with them, but Mathura Bâbu would not let me. In that state I used to bow down before everybody and would ask them to repeat the Holy Name of the Lord. As in a violent storm a screen of dust rises, hiding the trees of different kinds and making all trees appear alike, so in that storm of spiritual vision I could not distinguish one man from another as high or low.

A devotee: Bhagavan, how can a man live in the world and experience any of these kinds of madness?

Srî Râmakrishna: These states are not for those who are living in the world and performing the duties of the world, but for those who have absolutely renounced internally and externally. External renunciation is not for those who live in the world. They should practise internal renunciation or mental non-attachment.

(To a disciple) A man brought a bottle of wine; I went to touch it but could not.

Disciple: Why, Bhagavan?

Râmakrishna: When Divine bliss is attained, one becomes intoxicated with it, he does not need to drink wine. When I see the feet of my Divine Mother, I feel as intoxicated as if I had drunk five bottles of wine. In this state one cannot eat anything and everything.

Divine intoxication.

GOSPEL OF RAMAKRISHNA

Disciple: As regards eating, one should eat what one gets.

Râmakrishna: That depends upon the spiritual state. In the path of Jnâna that produces no harm; when a Jnâni eats, he pours the food as an offering in the fire of Kundalini. But for a Bhakta it is different. A Bhakta should eat only pure food, such food as he can freely offer to his Beloved Lord. Animal food is not for a Bhakta. But at the same time, I must say, if a man loves God after eating the flesh of a pig, he is blessed, and wretched is the man who lives on milk and rice, but whose mind is absorbed in lust and gold. Once I took as *mantram* the name of Allah from a Mohammedan teacher and repeated the name for several days and ate their food.

Food for a Bhakta.

ii

The Bhagavân then came back into the hall followed by His disciples and seated Himself. A pillow was placed for Him to recline upon. Before touching it, He said, "*Om tat sat*" (Brahman is the only Reality). The pillow was, of course, one which had been used by the unholy men of the world, and the Bhagavân was purity itself. It was getting late, but no dinner was

GOSPEL OF RAMAKRISHNA

being served and the Bhagavân became a little impatient like a child. Surendra, the host, was a beloved disciple of the Lord. The Bhagavân said: Surendra's disposition has grown admirable. He is very generous; those who go to him for help never come away disappointed. Then he is very outspoken. He is bold enough to speak the truth.

In this age truthfulness is the best of all ascetic practices. He who is firm in truthful-
Truthfulness. ness attains to God. Lack of truthfulness destroys all virtue. For this reason, when I say anything even inadvertently, such as, "I shall go there. I shall do that," I must go, because I have said it. I may lose my firmness in truthfulness if I do not keep my word to the very letter. Openness as opposed to dissimulation is the fruit of the practice of many religious austerities in one's previous incarnations. In a well-known song by Tulsi Dâs * it is said: "Give up dissimulation and

---

* Tulsi Dâs was a great Hindu poet who lived between 1544 and 1624 A.D. He was a devoted worshipper of Râma. His *Hindi* poem, "Râmâyana," or history of Râma, as well as Proverbs and other verses, are to this day household words in every town and rural district where the *Hindi* lan-

cunning." Do you not see that whenever God has taken a human form, this great virtue of guilelessness has never failed to come to view? Look at Dasaratha, the father of Râma, and Nanda Ghosh, the father of Srî Krishna. They were both free from guile. (To a young disciple) Like men of the world, you have accepted a position, but you are working for your mother. Otherwise I should have said: "For shame! For shame! You must serve only the Lord." (To Mani Mullik) This young man is open and guileless to a degree; only nowadays he occasionally tells untruths, that is all. The other day he said that he would come to see me, but he did not. (To Mahendra) You went to see Bhagavân Dâs; how did you like him?

Mahendra: Yes, Revered Sir, I went to see him. The great Vaishnava sage has become very old. He was lying down when I saw him; a disciple put some food into his mouth. He can hear only when addressed in loud tones. After hearing Thy name, he said to me: "You need not fear anything. Râmakrishna is a

---

guage is spoken. He is regarded by the people as a Hindu saint of the Vaishnava sect.

Divine Manifestation. To worship His name is to worship God."

Here Mahima came in and the Bhagavân exclaimed: This is a visit quite unexpected! We expect at most a shallop in this poor river of ours, yet here comes a ship! But then it is the rainy season!

The conversation next turned on the spiritual aspect of feasts and the Bhagavân said to Mahima: Why is it that people are fed at a feast? Do you not think that it is the same as offering a sacrifice to God who is the Living Fire in all creatures? But bad men, not God-fearing, guilty of adultery and fornication, should on no account be entertained at a feast. Their sins are so great that several cubits of earth beneath the place where they eat become polluted.

iii

Protâp Chunder Mozoomdâr,* a member of the Brâhmo-Samâj, entered and saluted Srî

---

* Protâp Chunder Mozoomdâr is well known in America as Mr. Mozoomdar. He was a co-worker of Keshab Chunder Sen and became a leader of the "New Dispensation" sect of the Brâhmo-Samâj. He came to the Parliament of Religions at Chicago in 1893 A.D., and delivered addresses in

Râmakrishna. The Bhagavân, as usual, returned his salutation with His well-known modesty, bowing very low. Mozoomdâr said: Revered Sir, I have recently been to Darjeeling.

Srî Râmakrishna: But you do not appear to be much the better for the change. What is the matter with you?

Mozoomdâr: The same complaint to which Keshab Chunder Sen succumbed.

A certain Mahratta lady was then spoken of. Mozoomdâr said that she had been to England and had embraced Christianity. He asked the Bhagavân whether He had ever heard of the woman. The Bhagavân replied: No, but from what I hear from you, I should think she must be a person who wishes to make a name for herself. Egotism of this kind is not good. Those who seek for fame are under a delusion. "I do this or that," this sense arises from ignorance. But "O Lord, Thou art doing everything" is true

Egotism rises from ignorance.

---

many principal cities of America. He was the author of the "Oriental Christ." In 1879 he wrote his celebrated article on "Râmakrishna," which was published in the *Theistic Quarterly Review* of India; and which was incorporated with "My Master" by Swâmi Vivekânanda.

knowledge. <u>God is the real Actor, others are actors in name only.</u>

The calf says, "Hâmmâ" or "Aham" (I). Now look at the troubles caused by the self which says "I, I." In the first place, the calf is sometimes taken into the field where it is yoked to the plough. It is there made to work on from morning till evening, alike in the sun and in the rain. Its troubles are not yet over. It is very often killed by the butcher. Its flesh is eaten as meat. Its skin is tanned into hides which are then made into shoes. The sufferings of the calf in this state know no bounds. But that is not all. Drums are made with the skin which is thus mercilessly beaten, sometimes with the hand and sometimes with the drumstick. It is only when out of its entrails are made strings for the bows used for carding cotton that the troubles of the poor creature are over. And that is because it no longer says, "Hâmmâ, Hâmmâ" (I, I), but "Tuhum, Tuhum" (It is Thou, O Lord! It is Thou!). Similarly, when Jiva (ego) says, "O Lord! Not I but Thou art the doer and actor, I am merely an instrument in Thy hand," it becomes free from all the world's troubles and attains to absolute freedom from birth and rebirth in this world of sorrow and suffering.

A devotee: How can Jiva become free from egoism (Ahamkâra)?

Bhagavân: Egoism does not leave until one has realized God. If anyone has become absolutely free from egoism (Ahamkâra) you must know that that person has seen and realized Divinity.

Devotee: Revered Sir, what are the signs of one who has seen and realized God?

Bhagavân: The signs of one who has seen God are thus described in Bhâgavatam. There are four kinds. First, His conduct is like that of a child. A truly wise man who has seen the Lord becomes like a child. A child has no real egoism. He is not bound by any custom. The self of the child is nothing at all like the self of the grown-up man. The second sign is that one who has seen God does not care for his body or his dress. Purity and impurity seem to him the same. Third, Such an one sometimes acts like a madman, now laughing, now weeping, and the next moment talking to himself; now dressed like a Bâbu (gentleman) and now taking his one garment under his arm and going quite naked like

Signs of one who has realized God.

a child. Lastly, he may remain inert and motionless for a long time in the state of Samâdhi.

Devotee: After God-vision does egoism (Ahamkâra) disappear entirely?

Bhagavân: Sometimes the Lord wipes out the last stain of egoism, as in the state of Samâdhi. Again, sometimes He leaves a faint trace of egoism, but that is harmless. It is like that of an innocent child, who knows not the doing of injury to anyone. The steel sword is turned into gold by the touch of the Philosopher's Stone. It still retains its shape but it does not injure anyone.

Bhagavân to Mozoomdâr: You have been to England and America. Tell me all about what you saw there.

Mozoomdâr: Sir, people in England mostly worship what Thou callest Kânchan (gold), but there are some good men and women who are not so attached to worldliness. Generally speaking, one sees nothing but worldly activity (Rajas) everywhere from beginning to end.

Bhagavân: I have seen the same thing too. Why in England and America alone? Attachment to work is to be found in every country. That worldly activity is the first chapter of life. So long

Attachment to work.

as the Rajas quality predominates, attachment to work increases. One cares more for one's own worldly good,—riches, honor, fame. It gradually leads to ignorance which makes one forget God, the Reality of the universe. God cannot be realized until the Sattwa qualities, such as devotion, right discrimination, dispassion and compassion for all, prevail. All attachment to lust and gold proceeds from Rajas and Tamas qualities, but work cannot be renounced entirely. Propelled by nature (Prakriti) you plunge into work even against your wish. Therefore I say you should work with non-attachment; in other words, you should work without seeking the fruit.

In a great religious ceremony we give alms to the poor and do various other charitable works and may think that we are absolutely unattached to the results of such works, but in the end we find that the desire for name and fame has crept up in the heart, we do not know how. But he alone who has seen and realized God can become absolutely unattached to work and its result.

A devotee: What is the path for those who have not realized God? Is it necessary for them to give up all work and worldly activity?

GOSPEL OF RAMAKRISHNA

Râmakrishna: In this age (Kali-Yuga) the path of devotion and love (Bhakti-Yoga) is easy for all. The practice of Nârada's Bhakti is better adapted to this Yuga. One should repeat the Holy Name of the Lord and chant His praises and with earnest and sincere heart, pray to Him, saying: "O Lord, grant me Thy divine Wisdom, Thy divine Love. Do Thou open my eyes and make me realize Thee."

Path of devotion.

When Karma Yoga is so difficult to practice, one should pray to the Lord in this manner: "O Lord! Do Thou reduce our Karma to a minimum, and the little work that we daily perform, may we do it with non-attachment by Thy grace. O Lord! Do not let our desire for work increase in number and bind us to worldliness."

Devotee: People of the West (in England and America) always say, "Work, work, work." Is not work (Karma) then the end and aim of life?

Is work the aim of life?

Râmakrishna: The end and aim of life is the attainment of God. Work (Karma) is nothing but the first chapter of life; how can it be its end and aim? But work, without seeking the result, is a means, not the end.

No one, however, can avoid work (Karma). Every mental action is a Karma. "I am thinking," "I meditate," "I feel," each of these is a Karma. The more one attains to true devotion the less becomes one's worldly work. The pleasures of the world do not satisfy such a soul. They lose their charm. How can one who has tasted the *Sherbet* made with pure crystallized sugar be pleased with the taste of a drink made with molasses or treacle? On one occasion a Karma Yogi (Sambhu) said to me: "May Thy blessing be that my wealth be spent in building hospitals and dispensaries, in making roads, in sinking wells for travelers, in establishing schools, colleges, and in other good works." Whereupon I replied: "Sambhu, all these works are good when they are performed with non-attachment. But that is very difficult. In any case you should always keep in mind that the end and aim of your human existence is the attainment of God and not hospitals and dispensaries. Suppose the Lord appears before you and graciously offers to fulfill your desires. Will you then pray for dispensaries and hospitals, tanks and wells, roads and serais, or will you say: 'O Lord! Grant that I may have pure and unalloyed love for Thee and unswerving devotion to Thy feet, that I may always feel Thy presence and realize Thee under all conditions'?" Hospitals, dispensaries and all these things are transitory; God alone is the Reality, all else is unreal. Once placed face to face with the Vision Divine, we see them as no better than dreams and then we pray for more light, more wisdom, more Divine Love, the love which lifts a man to God, the love which makes us realize that we are really sons of the Supreme Being, of whom all that can be said is that He exists, that He is Knowledge itself in the highest sense, and that He is the Eternal Fountain of Love and Bliss.

Attainment of God-vision. Again, when one attains to God-vision, one feels that God alone is the real Actor in the universe, the Doer of all things, and that we can do nothing. If God does everything, then why, instead of realizing Him, shall we get entangled in the meshes of worldly works? First realize God; then, if it be His will, many hospitals and dispensaries may be established. Therefore, I say, never lose sight of this goal of life that I have pointed out for you, but move onward through the practices of devotion and love. When you have advanced far enough you will know that God alone is the Reality, that all the things of the world are unreal and that the highest end and aim of life is the attainment of God.

There was a wood-cutter who led a very miserable life with the small means he could **Parable of a wood-cutter.** procure by daily selling a load of wood brought from a neighboring forest. Once a Sannyâsin, who was passing that way, saw him at work and advised him to go further into the forest, saying: "Move onward, my child, move onward." The wood-cutter obeyed the injunction and proceeded onward until he came to a sandalwood-tree, and being much pleased, he took away with him as many sandal logs as he could carry, sold them in the market and derived much profit. Then he began to wonder within himself why the good Sannyâsin had not told him anything about the wood of the sandal-tree, but had simply advised him to move onward. So the next day he went on beyond the place of the sandalwood until he came upon a copper-mine, and he took with him all the copper that he could carry, and selling it in the market, got more money by it. Next day, without stopping at the copper-mine, he proceeded further still, as the Sâdhu had advised him to do, and he came upon a silver-mine and took with him as much of it as he could carry, sold it and got even more money, and so daily proceeding further and further, he found gold-mines and diamond-mines and at last became exceedingly rich. Such is also the case with the man who aspires after true Knowledge. If he does not stop in his progress after attaining a few extraordinary and supernatural powers, he at last becomes really rich in the eternal knowledge of Truth.

So go on, my children, and never lose sight of your ideal! Go onward and never stop until you have reached the goal. Arriving at a particular stage, do not get the idea that you have reached your journey's end. Work is only the first stage of the journey. Bear in mind that doing works *unattached* is exceedingly difficult, that therefore Bhakti Yoga, the path of love, is better suited to this age, and that work, even if unattached, is not the end of your life, but only a means to an end. So march on and never halt till you have come up to the great Ideal of your life—the realization of God.

Referring to lectures given by members of religious bodies like the Brâhmo Samâj and

GOSPEL OF RAMAKRISHNA

Harisabhâ,* the Bhagavân said: One can form an estimate of a man from the lectures he delivers. A pandit was lecturing as the preceptor (Âchârya) of a certain Harisabhâ. In the course of his sermon he said: "The Lord has not *Rasa* (sweetness). Let us make Him sweet by giving Him our love and devotion." By sweetness he meant love and tenderness.

Lectures and sermons of preachers.

It reminded me of the story in which a boy was trying to convince his friends that his uncle had a great many horses by saying he had a whole cow-house full of horses. Of course any intelligent person could at once see that a cow-house was not the same as a stable and that horses are never kept in a cow-house. What would people think after hearing such absurd statements? They would laugh and come to the conclusion that the uncle had no horses at all. See how absurd it is to say that God is devoid of sweetness, God who is the Fountain-head of all sweet and tender qualities!

Story of a boy and the cow-house.

Then turning to Mozoomdâr the Bhagavân said: You are an educated and intelligent man,

---

* Harisabhâ is an orthodox Hindu Society.

you are a deep thinker. Keshab and yourself were like the brothers Gour * (Chaitanya) and Netâi.† You have had enough of this world—enough of lectures, controversies, schisms and the rest. Do you still care for them? Now, it is high time for you to collect your scattered mind and turn towards God. Plunge into the ocean of Divinity.

Mozoomdâr: Yes, Revered Sir, that I ought to do. There is no doubt about it. But all this I do simply to preserve Keshab's name and reputation.

Râmakrishna (smiling): You believe that you are doing all this, as you say, for Keshab, but after a while this idea will change and you will think differently. Let me tell you a story. A man built a cottage on a mountain-top. It cost him hard labor and much money. After a few days there arose a cyclone and the cottage began to rock to and fro. He was very anxious to save

Story of a man and his cottage.

---

* "Gour" is the abbreviated form of "Gourânga," another name of Chaitanya. See note page 7.

† "Netâi" is also the abbreviated form of "Nityânanda," the most powerful preacher among the followers of Chaitanya. He is regarded by the Vaishnavas of this sect as the spiritual brother of Gourânga.

GOSPEL OF RAMAKRISHNA

it, so he prayed to the Wind-god, saying: "Lord, I beseech thee, do not destroy this cottage"; but the Wind-god did not listen. He prayed again, but the cottage kept on rocking. Then he thought out a plan to save it. He remembered that in the mythology Hanumân was the son of the Wind-god. Instantly he cried out: "Lord, I beg of Thee, spare this cottage, for it belongs to Hanumân, Thy son." But the Wind-god did not listen. Then he said, "Lord, I pray Thee, spare this cottage, for it belongs to Hanumân's Lord, Râma." Still the Wind-god did not listen. Then, as the cottage was about to topple over, the man, to save his life, ran out of it and began to swear, saying: "Let it go to destruction! What is that to me?" You may now be anxious to preserve Keshab's name; but console yourself with the thought that it was after all owing to God's will that the religious movement connected with his name was set on foot, and that if the movement has had its day, it is also owing to that same Divine will. Therefore dive deep into the sea. And the Bhagavân sang:

1 Dive deep, dive deep, dive deep, O my mind! into the sea of Beauty.

Make a search in the regions lower, still lower
   below the bottom of the sea:
Thou wilt surely find the jewel of *Prema* (intense love of God).

2. Within thy heart Vrindâvan (the abode of the God of Love).
Search, search, search; searching Thou wilt find it.
Then in the heart shall burn, burn, burn the Lamp of Wisdom without ceasing.

3. Who is it that steers the boat on land, on land, on land?
Says Kuvir: Listen, listen, listen; meditate on the Lotus feet of Guru.

Do you hear the song? You have finished your lectures, quarrels and fights. Now dive in this ocean. There is no fear of death in this sea. It is the sea of Immortality. Do not fear that one becomes unbalanced by meditating on God. I once said to Narendra (Vivekânanda)—

Mozoomdâr (interrupting): Who is this Narendra?

Bhagavân: Oh, there is a young man of that

name. Well, I said to Narendra: "God is like a sea of immortal syrup. Would you not dive deep into this sea? Suppose, my boy, there is a basin containing the syrup of sugar and that you are a fly anxious to drink of the sweet liquid. Where would you sit and drink?" Narendra said in reply: "Why! from the edge of the basin! If I go far from the edge I may be drowned and lose my life." Thereupon I said to him: "My boy, in the sea of Divinity there is no fear of that kind. Do you not know that it is the sea of Immortality? Whosoever dives into this sea does not die but obtains everlasting life." He who is mad after God can never become unbalanced or insane. (To the Bhaktas)

God, the sea of Immortality.

Work without devotion (Bhakti) to God has in this age no ground to stand upon. First cultivate devotion (Bhakti); all other things — schools, dispensaries, and charitable works shall, if you wish, be added unto you. First devotion, then work. Work, apart from devotion or love of God, is helpless and cannot stand.

Work without devotion.

Mozoomdâr made inquiries about the disciples. He asked whether those who came to the Bhagavân were getting better in the spirit day by day. The Bhagavân said: I place before them the ideal of a wet-nurse as teaching them how to live in this world. The maid-servant referring to her master's house says, "This is our house." All the while she knows that her home is far away in a distant village, to which her thoughts are all sent forth. Again, referring to the master's child in her arms, she will say: "My Hari has grown very wicked," or "My Hari likes to eat this or that," and so on. But all the while she knows that Hari is not her own. I tell those who come to me to live a life unattached like this maid-servant. I tell them to live unattached to this world, to be in the world but not of the world, and at the same time to have their mind directed to God, the heavenly home from whence all come. I tell them to pray for love of God (Bhakti), which will help them so to live.

After a short time the conversation turned on the agnosticism of Europe and America, and Mozoomdâr said: Whatever people in the West may profess to be, none of them, as it seems to me, is an atheist at heart. The European thinkers all admit an unknown Power behind the universe.

Bhagavân: How can they be atheists when they believe in Sakti, the Eternal Energy?

Mozoomdâr: They also admit the moral government of the universe.

As Mozoomdâr rose to take leave, the Bhagavân said to him: What shall I say? It is better that you cease to have anything to do with all those things—schisms, controversies, etc. All quarrels and disputes spring from egotism and attachment to the world. These keep men away from God. Therefore abandon all earthly attachment and fix your mind on the Almighty.

V

Mozoomdâr then saluted the Bhagavân and withdrew. After he had gone, a devotee asked: Revered Sir, Thou didst go to see Vidyâsâgara, what dost Thou think of him?

Râmakrishna: Vidyâsâgara is a very learned scholar He is kind and charitable, but he has no spiritual consciousness. There is gold inside; if he had been aware of it, he could not have devoted so much of his time to external work. Eventually his work would have been finished. If he knew that God was dwelling within his heart, his mind would have been fixed in thinking and meditating on Him. Some people have to perform work without attachment for a long time before true dispassion for the world comes; then the mind runs towards God and becomes absorbed in Him. Whatever work Vidyâsâgara has done for others has been very good and helpful.

<small>Compassion and attachment.</small> To be kind and compassionate is also good; but there is a difference between compassion and attachment. Compassion is good, but attachment is not. Attachment is love for wife, children, brother, sister, father, mother and other relatives, while true compassion is equal love for all living creatures.

Mahendra: Is compassion also a bondage?

Râmakrishna: This question is not for ordinary mortals. Compassion is the result of the <small>Sattwa, Rajas, and Tamas.</small> Sattwa quality. The Sattwa quality is protective, the Rajas quality is creative, and Tamas is destructive: but Brahman the Absolute is beyond these three qualities, Sattwa, Rajas, and Tamas. It is also beyond Prakriti or nature. Where there is absolute Reality, no quality of nature can reach. As a thief cannot go to the exact spot where the treasure is, because he is afraid of being caught, so Sattwa, Rajas, and Tamas, like

252

GOSPEL OF RAMAKRISHNA

thieves, cannot go to the realm where is the treasure of the Absolute.

A man was going through the woods. On his way he was caught by a band of three **Parable of the three robbers.** robbers. They took away everything he had. Then the first robber asked: "What is the use of keeping this man alive?" And drawing his sword, he was about to kill him, when the second robber stopped him, saying: "What good will be done by killing him? Tie his hands and feet and throw him to one side." So they bound his hands and feet and went away leaving him by the roadside. After they had been gone for a while, the third robber returned and said to him: "Ah! are you hurt? Come, let me untie the cords and release you." Then when he had removed the cords, he said: "Now come with me. I will show you the road." After walking for a long distance, they found the road, and then the robber said: "Look, there is your home. Follow the road and you will soon reach it." The man, thanking him, replied: "Sir, you have done me a great service. I am greatly obliged to you. Will you not come with me to my house?" The robber answered: "No, I cannot go there; the guard would find me out."

This world is the wilderness. The three robbers are the three Gunas of nature,—Sattwa, Rajas, and Tamas. Jiva or the individual soul is the traveler; self-knowledge is his treasure. The Tamas quality tries to destroy the Jiva, the Rajas quality binds him with the fetters of the world, but the Sattwa quality protects him from the actions of Rajas and Tamas. By taking refuge with the Sattwa quality, Jiva becomes free from lust and anger, which are effects of Tamas; the Sattwa quality also emancipates the Jiva or the individual soul from the bondage of the world. But Sattwa quality itself is also a robber. It cannot give Divine wisdom or the knowledge of the Absolute. It leads one, however, up to the path of the Supreme Abode and then it says: "Behold, there is thy home!" Then it disappears. Even the Sattwa quality cannot go near the abode of the Absolute.

Three Gunas of nature.

What the Absolute is no one can tell. He who has attained the Absolute cannot give any information about it. Four travelers discovered a place enclosed by a high wall, with no opening anywhere. They were very anxious to see what

About the Absolute nothing can be told.

was inside. So one of them climbed to the top of the wall and as he looked in, he shouted with amazement and joy, "Ha! ha! ha!" and without giving any information to his fellow-travellers, he jumped inside. The others did likewise. Whoever climbs to the top of the wall jumps inside with extreme joy and never comes back to give the news of what he has found. Such is the realm of the Absolute. <u>The great souls who have realized the Absolute have not come back, because after attaining the highest knowledge of Brahman, one absolutely loses the sense of "I."</u> The mind ceases to be active, and all sense-consciousness vanishes. <u>This state is called Brahma-Jnâna or Divine wisdom</u>.

Parable of the four travelers.

A devotee: Revered Sir, did not the perfected soul Sukadeva attain to Brahma-Jnâna, the Knowledge of the Absolute?

Râmakrishna: Some say that Sukadeva saw the ocean of the Absolute Brahman and touched its waters, but he did not go into the water; therefore he was able to come back and teach mankind. Others believe that he attained to the Absolute Brahman and then returned to help humanity.

Devotee: Does sectarianism exist after the

knowledge of the Absolute (Brahma-Jnâna) has been attained?

Râmakrishna: I was talking with Keshab Sen of this Brahma-Jnâna. Keshab asked me to say more about the Absolute. I replied: "If I say more, your sect and creed will vanish." Keshab answered: "Revered Sir, then I do not wish to hear more." Still, I said to Keshab: "'I, me, mine,' this is ignorance; 'I am the doer,' 'I am the actor,' 'This is my wife, these are my children, my property, wealth, fame,' all these arise from ignorance." Keshab replied: "Revered Sir, nothing will be left, if the sense of 'I' be abandoned." I answered: "Keshab, I do not ask you to abandon the whole of the sense of 'I'; but leave out the unripe 'I'— 'I am the doer,' 'my wife, my children, I am the teacher,' abandoning this sense of 'I,' retain the ripe 'I'—'I am His servant, I am His devotee,' 'I am not the doer, but He is the Actor.'"

Devotee: Can the ripe "I" make a sect?

Râmakrishna: I said to Keshab: "I am the leader of a sect, I have founded a sect, I am teaching others, all these proceed from the sense of the unripe 'I.'" Therefore I asked

GOSPEL OF RAMAKRISHNA

Keshab to abandon this "I." I also said to him: "You talk of your sect, many members of your sect have resigned." Keshab replied: **Keshab and his disciples.** "Revered Sir, after remaining for three years under my instructions, they have now joined another sect, and at the time of leaving, they criticised and slandered me." I said to him: "You do not understand the inner nature of your disciples. You must study their predominant traits and you must not make disciples indiscriminately."

Râm Bâbu*: Bhagavan, I do not see what good has been done by the New Dispensation of Keshab Sen. If Keshab himself had realized God, the condition of his disciples and followers would have been different. In my opinion he has had no realization.

Srî Râmakrishna: Oh yes, he must have some realization; otherwise why should so many people honor and respect him? Why do they not honor and respect the leaders of other branches of the Brâhmo-Samâj in the same

---

* Râm Bâbu was a devoted householder disciple of Srî Râmakrishna. He was a scientist and a teacher of chemistry in the Medical College of Calcutta. He was a good speaker and a writer.

way? Without Divine will no one can command such respect from the masses. A man cannot become a true spiritual leader unless he practises absolute renunciation. Without this people will have no faith in him. They will say: "This man is worldly. He himself enjoys the pleasures of the flesh and wealth, yet he tells us that God is Truth while the world is unreal like a dream." The world will not receive his teachings unless he has renounced everything. A few people may listen to him and follow him. Keshab Sen was in the world and had his mind on worldly things. He tried to support his family by giving lectures and by marrying his daughter to a prince, thus protecting his worldly relations and social position. Once Keshab asked me: "Why can I not see God?" I answered: "Because you have absorbed yourself in seeking the honor and respect of people, in education and so on. So long as the child is absorbed in playing with its dolls, the mother does not come. But when the child throws away the doll and cries for the mother, the mother cannot stay away. You think that you are a leader, but the Divine Mother thinks: 'My child believes that he has become a leader and is happy; let him enjoy his belief.'" I also told him to believe in the Divine Mother, that the Absolute and the Divine Mother are one. The Divine Mother is the eternal Energy. They are inseparable. **The Absolute and the Divine Mother.** They appear as separate so long as we are conscious of the body and as we try to describe them by words. Eventually Keshab believed in the Divine Mother. Once he came with his disciples to see me. I asked him to give a lecture, so he delivered his lecture and after it I had a long talk with him. I said: "He who is the Personal God manifests in one form as His devotee and in another form as His word." **God, His devotee and His word one.** Then I went on to say to him: "You are living in the realm of Mâyâ (worldliness). This Mâyâ does not let anyone know God. It keeps all in ignorance."

How wonderful is its power! It entangles even a Divine Incarnation and makes Him suffer from hunger, thirst, sorrow, misery, like an ordinary mortal. **Delusive power of Mâyâ.** Do you not see how Râma, the Divine Incarnation, suffered for Sitâ? How with great sorrow, He wept bitterly when Sitâ was stolen away from Him? In the Hindu mythology there is a story that Vishnu incarnated in the form of a boar to destroy the demons; but after destroying the demons, He did not care to return to his Heaven, He wanted to live as a boar. He had some little ones and He was happy with them. The Devas of the heaven thought: "How is it that our Lord does not come back? What has happened?" Then they went to Shiva and asked Him to persuade Vishnu to return to His heaven. Shiva came and entreated Him, but He was taking care of His young ones and paid no heed. Then Shiva tore open His body with His triad and freed Him from His self-delusion. Vishnu then laughed and returned to His heavenly abode. Such is the power of Mâyâ! To go beyond its realm and rise above the Gunas (qualities) is extremely difficult. He who has attained to God has transcended Mâyâ with its qualities.

Vishnu as a boar.

CHAPTER IX

VISIT TO A HINDU PANDIT AND PREACHER

i

It was the day of the great car festival of Jagannâth. The streets of Calcutta were crowded with people. Boys and girls were playing along the way and amusing themselves by blowing horns and pipes made of palm-leaves. A light rain was falling and the roads were wet and muddy. About four o'clock in the afternoon the Bhagavân came out of Ishân's * house and entered a carriage which was waiting for Him at the door. Immediately after taking his seat He lost sense-consciousness and went into that state of pure God-consciousness which He had often called His *Âbesha*. The disciples followed their Divine

Âbesha of Râmakrishna.

---

* Ishân Chunder Mookerjee was a pious Brâhmin householder. He regarded Srî Râmakrishna as the Incarnation of Divine Wisdom.

Master on foot, for they were eager to be present at this memorable meeting with Pandit Sasadhar,* the great preacher of the Vedânta philosophy and religion.

The Pandit was visiting a friend in Calcutta. As Srî Râmakrishna's carriage drew up at the entrance-door, He was warmly welcomed by the host and his people. Coming upstairs the Bhagavân met Sasadhar advancing towards Him. He appeared to be a middle-aged man with a fair complexion and around his neck was thrown a rosary of Rudrâksha beads. He came forward with a reverential air, saluted the Bhagavân, and led Him to the parlor which was intended for His reception. The disciples and others went in after Him and seated themselves as near Him as they could. Among the many disciples present was Narendra. The Bhagavân, smiling in His semiconscious state,

---

* Pandit Sasadhar Tarkachurâmoni was a Sanskrit scholar of great renown and an eloquent preacher of the philosophy and religion of Vedânta. By his powerful speeches he succeeded in checking the materialistic tendency of the Hindu students of Bengal. He also gave rational explanations of the rituals and ceremonies described in the Hindu Scriptures.

said: "Very good, very good! Well, what kind of lectures do you give?"

Sasadhar: Revered Sir, I try to explain the truth taught by the Holy Scriptures.

Bhagavân: For this age Bhakti Yoga, communion with God by love, devotion and self-surrender, as practised by the Rishi Nârada, is enjoined. There is hardly time for Karma Yoga, for doing the works laid upon man by the Scriptures. Do you not see that the well-known decoction of the ten medicinal roots (Dasamul Pâchan) is not the medicine for fevers of the present day? The patient runs the risk of being carried off before the medicine has had time to take effect. "Fever-mixture" is therefore the order of the day. Teach them Karma if you like, but leave aside the head and tail of the fish. I tell people not to bother with the long ritual of Sandhyâ, but to repeat only the short Gâyatri.* You are welcome to talk of work to such people if you must.

---

* Gâyatri is the most sacred and the most universally used of all Vedic prayers among the Hindus. It is a Sanskrit *Mantram* or formula which means: "Let us meditate on that glorious self-effulgent light of the Divine Sun; may He enlighten our *Buddhi* or understanding." This is still the daily prayer of all the Hindus of the upper three castes.

GOSPEL OF RAMAKRISHNA

Give thousands of lectures, you cannot do anything with worldly men. Can you drive a nail into a stone wall? The head will be broken without making any impression on the wall. Strike the back of an alligator with a sword, it will receive no impression. The mendicant's bowl (of gourd-shell) may have been to the four great holy places of India but still be as bitter as ever. But you will learn this gradually. A calf cannot stand on its legs all at once. It falls down, gets up, falls again, and then it learns to stand and run. You do not know who is a Bhakta (godly) and who is worldly; but that is not your fault. When a heavy storm blows, one cannot distinguish Tamarind from Mango-tree.

Effect of lectures on worldly men.

It is true, however, that no one can absolutely renounce all works without realizing God. The question is, how long should Sandhyâ (ritua's) and other ceremonial works be practised? So long as the Holy Name of the Lord does not bring tears of love to the eyes and produce horripilation in the body. When you are uttering "Om Râma," if tears of love come to your eyes, you will know for certain that the term of your Karma (works and duties) is over. You are no longer obliged to perform Sandhyâ and other works. You have risen above Karma When the fruit appears, the blossom drops off. The true Bhakti is the fruit, while work is the blossom.

When the daughter-in-law of the house is with child, she cannot do much work; so the mother-in-law daily reduces the number of her duties. As the time of her delivery draws near, the mother-in-law seldom allows her to do anything; and when the child is born, she fondles and caresses it and ceases altogether to work.

Sandhyâ merges into Gâyatri; Gâyatri into Om, and Om ultimately loses itself in Samâdhi. **All rituals end in Samâdhi.** As the sound of a bell—Ding, dong—gradually fades away into the Infinite, so the soul of a Yogi gradually rises with the Nâda (the sound of Om) and becomes merged in the Absolute Brahman in Samâdhi. Into this Samâdhi eventually enter all Karma,—Sandhyâ, Gâyatri and other works. In this manner the Jnânis are freed from all rituals and religious exercises.

ii

As the Bhagavân was talking of Samâdhi, a strange heavenly expression came over His sweet, radiant face. He lost all outward consciousness.

After remaining speechless in this state for some time, He came down and like a child said, "Give me a little water." This call for water was the usual sign of His return to the plane of sense-consciousness. Then He murmured: "O Mother! The other day Thou didst show me Vidyâsâgara. Then I desired to see a Pandit and Thou hast brought me here."

Turning to Sasadhar, the Bhagavân said: My son, add to your spiritual strength, go **The necessity** through devotional exercises a little **of practice.** longer. You have hardly got up into the tree, how can you expect to lay your hand upon its fruit? But you are doing all this for the good of others. Saying this the Bhagavân bowed to Sasadhar and continued: When I first heard your name, I inquired whether this Pandit was merely an ordinary Pandit or one who had attained right discrimination (Viveka) and dispassion (Vairâgya). He is not a true Pandit who does not possess right discrimination. If there has been a commission (Âdesha) from the Supreme, then there is no harm in teach-
The Divinely- ing others. Such a Divinely-commis-
commissioned sioned teacher is invincible. No one
teacher. can defeat him. If one single ray from the Goddess of Wisdom falls upon a man,

it brings to him such power that before him the greatest Pandits become like worms of the earth. When a lamp is lighted, swarms of moths rush of themselves towards it without waiting to be called. So he who has received a Divine commission, for him there is no need to seek followers or to make known the time of his lectures. His own power of attraction is so great that people of their own accord crowd around him. Then kings and nobles flock to him saying: "We have brought mangoes, sweets, money, jewels and shawls; of these what will you accept?" To such people I say: "Take them away, I do not want any of them."

Does a magnet ever say to the iron, "Come to me?" No; drawn by the magnet, it goes of itself. Such a man may not be a Pandit, still do not think for a moment that he lacks in knowledge. Is true wisdom acquired by reading books? There is no end to the wisdom of one who has received a Divine commission. That wisdom comes from God and therefore it is endless. In our country in measuring grain, one man weighs and the other pushes small heaps of grain on to him. In like manner when the Divinely-commissioned teacher gives instruction, my Mother, standing behind, pushes toward him the heaps of Divine wisdom and the supply is never exhausted. When the gracious look of the Divine Mother falls upon one, can there be any lack of wisdom? Therefore I ask whether you have received any commission (Âdesha) from the Lord?

Hâzrâ (to the Pandit): Oh! I dare say he must have received something of that kind. Is it not so?

Sasadhar's host: He has not obtained Âdesha, but he is lecturing only from a sense of duty.

Bhagavân: If a man has received no Divine commission, what good will his lectures do? In the course of his lecture a Brâhmo said: "Brethren, I used to drink, I used to do this and that." Hearing this the people began to talk: "What does this fellow say? He used to drink!" Thus this statement produced just the opposite effect in the minds of the audience. Unless the speaker be a good spiritual man, his lectures do not help mankind in any way. A subjudge once said to me: "Sir, you begin to preach, then I will also be ready." I answered: "My friend, listen. There was a large pond in a certain village. Some people used to throw dirt around the water's edge and otherwise defile the pond. Good

Value of lectures without Divine commission.

GOSPEL OF RAMAKRISHNA

men of the village spoke to the offenders and entreated them, but could not produce the slightest impression upon their minds. The offenders continued to violate the sanitary laws. Every morning abuses were showered upon their heads, but all in vain. At last when the municipal authorities put up a notice forbidding everyone to commit such acts and sent a peon with their badge to punish the offenders, from that moment nobody dared throw dirt near the pond."

Badge of authority. Therefore I say a badge of authority is necessary; otherwise no one will listen to your words. A true speaker is one who is authorized by the Supreme and who holds the badge of Divine commission. Every man and woman must obey and bow down to him.

A true teacher of mankind must possess great spiritual power (Sakti). In Calcutta there are many veteran wrestlers. One must try one's strength on such men and not on novices in wrestling. Chaitanya Deva was an Avatâra. Tell me how much of that which he did is now preserved? What good will be done by the lectures of one who does not hold the badge of Divine authority? Therefore I say: "You must first be absorbed in the Holy feet of the Almighty."

GOSPEL OF RAMAKRISHNA

iii

There are infinite ways which lead to the sea of immortality. The main thing is to fall into that sea; it matters not how one gets there. Suppose there is a reservoir of nectar, a single drop of which falling into the mouth will make one immortal. You may drink of it either by jumping into the reservoir or by slowly walking down along its slope. The result will be the same even if you are pushed or thrown into it by another. Taste a little of that nectar and become immortal.

Innumerable are the paths. Jnâna, Karma, Bhakti are all paths which lead to the same **Different** goal. If you have intense longing **paths to God.** you will surely reach God. Yoga (communion with God) is of four kinds: Jnâna Yoga, Karma Yoga, Râja Yoga, and Bhakti Yoga.

Jnâna Yoga is communion with God by means of right discrimination and knowledge in its **Jnâna Yoga.** highest sense. The object of a Jnâni is to know and realize the Absolute. He discriminates between the Absolute Reality and the unreal phenomena by saying: "Not this," "Not this," until he comes to a point where all discrimination between the Real and the unreal ceases and the Absolute Brahman is realized in Samâdhi.

Karma Yoga is communion with God by means of work. It is what you are teaching.

Karma Yoga. The performance of duties by householders not for the sake of obtaining their results but for glorifying the Supreme is that which is meant by this method of Yoga. Again, worship, repetition of the Name of the Lord, and other devotional exercises are also included in it, if they are done without attachment to their fruits and for the glorification of God. The end of Karma Yoga is the same as the realization of the Impersonal Absolute or the Personal God or both.

Râja Yoga leads to this communion through concentration and meditation. It has eight

Râja Yoga. steps. The first is Yama, which consists in non-injuring, truthfulness, non-covetousness, chastity, and the non-receiving of gifts. The second is Niyama, which includes austerities, forbearance, contentment, faith in the Supreme Being, charity, study, and self-surrender to the Supreme Will. The practice of various physical postures is comprised in Âsana, the third; while Prânâyâma or breathing exercises constitute the fourth step. The fifth is Pratyâhâra and consists in making the mind introspective and one-pointed. Concentration or Dhâranâ is the next; Dhyâna or meditation is the seventh, and Samâdhi or the state of superconsciousness the eighth.

Bhakti Yoga. Bhakti Yoga is communion by means of love, devotion, and self-surrender (Bhakti). It is especially adapted to this age.

The path of absolute knowledge is exceedingly difficult. The term of human life at the present day is short and entirely dependent on material food. Moreover, it is almost impossible to get rid of the idea that the soul is one with the body. Now a Jnâni or philosopher may declare: "I am not this body, gross or subtle; I am one with Brahman, the Absolute. I am not subject to the necessities and conditions of the body,— hunger, thirst, birth, death, disease, grief, pleasure, pain." Such assertions, however, will not make him free from these bodily conditions so long as he is on the plane of relativity. He may be compared to a person who is suffering from the intense pain of a wound but who is trying to deny it by mere words of mouth.

When the Kundalini is awakened, true

Bhakti, Divine Love and ecstasy are attained. Through Karma Yoga one can easily attain to various psychic powers. But when Karma Yoga leads to Bhakti Yoga, Divine realization comes. Then all duties, rituals, ceremonials, drop off like the petals of a flower when the fruit has grown. When a child is born, the young mother does not discharge any other duties, but fondles the child the whole day. As she is free from all household duties, so a Bhakta becomes free from the bondage of work after realizing God. The true Bhakta says: "O Mother, Karma with attachment I fear, for it proceeds from selfish motives, and as a man soweth so shall he reap. I see again that work without attachment is exceedingly difficult. If I work through attachment I shall forget Thee; therefore I do not desire such Karma. Grant that my work may become less and less so long as I do not attain to Thee. Till then may I have strength to do unattached the little work that is left for me, and may I be blessed with unselfish love and devotion to Thee! Mother, so long as I do not realize Thee may my mind be not attached to new works and new desires! But when Thou wilt command me to work I shall do it not for myself but only for Thee."

A devotee: Revered Sir, what is Hatha Yoga?

Râmakrishna: <u>Hatha Yoga deals entirely with the physical body. It describes the methods by which the internal organs can be purified and perfect health can be acquired</u>.

Hatha Yoga.

It teaches how to conquer the various powers of Prâna and the muscles, organs and nerves of the body. <u>But in Hatha Yoga the mind must always be concentrated on the physical body</u>. A Hatha Yogi possesses many powers, such as the power of levitation; but all these powers are only the manifestations of physical Prâna. There was a juggler who in the midst of his tricks suddenly turned his tongue upward and drew it back into the post-nasal canal, stopping respiration. Instantly all the activities of his body were suspended. People thought that he was dead, so they buried him. For several years he remained buried in that state. In some way the grave was opened and he regained consciousness. Immediately he began to repeat the same conjuring words with which he had been casting the spell before he lost consciousness. So the practice of Hatha Yoga will bring one control over the body, but it will carry one only so far. Râja Yoga, on the contrary, deals with

GOSPEL OF RAMAKRISHNA

the mind and leads to spiritual results through discrimination, concentration and meditation.

Perfect concentration of the mind is necessary in the path of Râja Yoga. Mind is like the flame of a lamp. When the wind of desire blows, it is restless; when there is no wind, it is steady. The latter is the state of mind in Yoga. Ordinarily the mind is scattered, one portion here, another portion there. It is necessary to collect the scattered mind and direct it towards one point. If you want a whole piece of cloth, you will have to pay the full price for it. Yoga is not possible if there be the least obstacle in the way. If there be a small break in the telegraphic wire, the message will not reach its destination. A Yogi controls his mind, the mind does not control him. When the mind is absolutely concentrated, the breath stops, and the soul enters into Samâdhi.

Concentration.

This state of breathlessness is called Kumbhaka. It can be attained through Bhakti Yoga also. When the emotion (Bhakti) reaches its climax, the breath stops and the mind becomes fixed. If a man is sweeping and some one comes and tells him: "Mr. So and So is dead; have you heard?"

Kumbhaka.

The sweeper, if the dead man be not his relation, will exclaim unconcernedly: "Is that so? Is he dead? He was a good man. I am sorry"; but he goes on sweeping. If, however, he hears of the death of a dear relative, he is so stunned that the broom drops from his hand and he sinks to the ground crying out, "God help me!" At this time his breath stops, his mind is fixed upon his grief and he cannot think of anything else. Again, have you not seen among women how, when one of them is struck with wonder either by seeing or hearing something unexpectedly, her breath will stop, her mind become fixed and the body remain so motionless that the other women will exclaim: "What is the matter? Have you lost your senses?"

At the time of true meditation the body and senses become absolutely still like a piece of wood. When I first saw Keshab Sen

Meditation.

in the Âdi (original) Brâhmo-Samâj, I saw him sitting in meditation with other members; his mind was entirely withdrawn from the external world and his body was perfectly motionless like a wooden stump; then I said to Mathura Bâbu: "This man has hooked the fish." Meditation is possible even with eyes wide open, even when one is conversing with another. Suppose you have a toothache. You may perform all works, but your mind will remain concentrated on the spot where the pain is. Similarly, if you have true concentration on God, your mind will remain fixed even when your body is moving or your mouth is speaking. I used to close my eyes at the time of meditation. Then I thought: "If God exists after closing the eyes, why should He not exist while the eyes are open?" I opened my eyes and saw the Divine Being everywhere. Man, animals, insects, trees, creepers, moon, sun, water, earth, in and through all these the Infinite Being is manifesting Himself. He who thinks upon God for a long time possesses Divine Substance within him. Through him flow Divine powers. A great singer, or one who is perfect in instrumental music or in any other art or science, also possesses a portion of Divine power. This is the doctrine of the Bhagavad Gîtâ,—"Wherever there are signs of greatness, there is the manifestation of Divine power."

A devotee: Revered Sir, what happens after death?

Râmakrishna: Keshab Sen asked me the same question. So long as a man remains in ignorance, in other words, so long as he has not realized God, he will be subject to rebirth; but after Divine realization one does not come back to this earth, nor is he born in any other world. Potters after making earthen pots dry them in the sun. Have you not seen that there are pots which are baked in fire and others that are unbaked? When a pot of unbaked clay is broken, the potter uses the same clay to make a new pot; but if a baked pot is broken, the pieces are of no further use and he throws them away. Similarly, when the ego is not baked in the fire of wisdom, after death it will appear in another form and be born again and again. If a fried grain is planted it will not germinate; in the same manner, he whose inner nature is fried in the fire of wisdom is no longer subject to evolution, but attains to absolute freedom from rebirth.

What happens after death.

In the Purânas the doctrine of dualistic Vedânta prevails, which teaches that the Jiva (the individual soul) is one thing and God is another: "I am distinct and separate from you." This body is like a bowl; mind, intellect and egoism are like water within it, while the Personal God is the sun which is reflected in the water; and this

Dualistic and monistic Vedânta.

GOSPEL OF RAMAKRISHNA

reflection or image of the Divine Being can be perceived by the Jiva in ecstasy. In monistic Vedânta, however, Brahman, the Absolute, is the Reality and all else is unreal like a dream. Egoism is like a stick which lies upon the waters of the infinite ocean of Existence-Intelligence-Bliss Absolute, and makes it appear as divided; but when the stick is removed, the apparent division ceases and the waters of the ocean remain undivided. The knowledge of this indivisible oneness brings the highest state of Samâdhi, where this egoism is entirely obliterated. But the great spiritual teachers like Sankarâchârya * kept a little egoism of knowledge to teach mankind.

---

* Sankarâchârya was the greatest exponent of the Vedânta philosophy in India. He lived about the beginning of the eighth century of the Christian era. His Commentaries on the Upanishads, the Vedânta sutras, and on the Bhagavad Gitâ have shown the profound depth of his philosophical reasoning. He became a *Sannyâsin* when he was eight years old. He wrote his famous Commentaries in Sanskrit at the age of twelve and finished his literary work when he was sixteen years old. Then for sixteen years he preached monistic Vedânta, and established monastic orders and monasteries in the four corners of India. He finished his glorious and eventful career when he reached the age of thirty-two. He

GOSPEL OF RAMAKRISHNA

A true Jnâni, or knower of the Absolute, may be recognized by certain signs. A real Jnâni does harm to no one. His nature becomes like that of an innocent child. As a burnt rope retains its shape and appears from a distance like a real rope, but in truth a breath can blow it away, so the egoism of a Jnâni is merely apparent. A child has no attachment for anything. It may build a toy house; if anyone touches it, it cries; but the next moment it will itself break it to pieces. <u>So a true Jnâni lives in the world, but unattached</u>. He may possess things of great value, but he has no attachment for them. In monistic Vedânta the waking state is no more real than the dream state. A woodcutter was dreaming a happy dream, but being suddenly awakened by some one, he exclaimed with annoyance: "Why did you awaken me? I was a king and the father of seven children. My children were all receiving education in the various sciences. I was seated on the throne and ruling over my country. Why did you destroy so happy and

The signs of a true Jnâni.

Parable of a wood-cutter and his dream.

---

is regarded in India as the Incarnation of Shiva and the embodiment of Divine Wisdom.

delightful a state?" The man replied: "Oh! It was only a dream. What does it matter?" The wood-cutter said: "Get away, you fool! You do not understand that my being a king was as real as my wood-cutting. If it be true that I am a wood-cutter, then it is equally true that I was a king."

Jnâna is to know the Âtman through the path of discrimination: "Not this, not this." When this discrimination leads to Samâdhi, then the Âtman can be apprehended. But Vijnâna is complete knowledge or realization. Some have heard of milk, some have seen it, but others have tasted it. So with God. Those who have heard of Him are still in ignorance; those who have seen Him are Jnânis; but those who have tasted or realized Him are Vijnânis. After seeing God, when one makes acquaintance with Him and realizes Him as the nearest and dearest of all, that is Vijnâna. At first it is necessary to discriminate "Not this, not this," that is, God is not the elements of nature, He is not the senses or sense-powers, He is not this mind, not this intellect, not this egoism; He is beyond all the categories of nature. To go to the roof, one must climb step by step, leaving one step after another. The staircase

Jnâna and Vijnâna.

is not the same as the roof. After coming out on the roof, however, one can easily see that both roof and staircase are of the same material. The same Infinite Brahman appears as the Personal God, Jiva, and the twenty-four categories of nature. You may ask why this earth is so hard and solid, if it has come out of Brahman? His omnipotence can make everything possible.

iv

Râmakrishna (to old Gopâl, Swâmi Advaitânanda): What! Do you still wish to visit holy places?

Gopâl: Yes, Bhagavan, I would like to travel a little more.

Râm Bâbu (to Gopâl): The Bhagavân says, after travelling to many places one should settle down in one spot. This he explains by the parable of the bird on a ship's mast. A bird was sitting on the mast of a vessel as it sailed out to sea. After a long time the bird realized that there were no trees around or land in sight. He flew towards the north to find land, but being disappointed, he returned to the mast, rested a while and flew towards the south. Still finding no shore, he came back again, tired and exhausted. In the

Parable of the bird on the mast.

same manner he went in all directions, but finding nothing but water and water everywhere, he at last rested on the mast and became content.

Râmakrishna: <u>So long as God seems to be outside, in different places, so long there is ignorance. But when God is realized within, that is true knowledge.</u> A man woke up at midnight and desired to smoke. He wanted a light, so he went to a neighbor's house and knocked at the door. Someone opened the door and asked him what he wanted. The man said: "I wish to smoke. Can you give me a light?" The neighbor replied: "What is the matter with you? You have taken so much trouble and awakened us at this hour, when in your hand you have a lighted lantern." What a man wants is already with him; but he still wanders here and there in search of it.

<small>Parable of a man seeking a light.</small>

Râm Bâbu: Bhagavan, now I have understood why a Guru asks his disciple to visit holy places,—to give him experience and to increase his faith in his teachings.

Pandit: Revered Sir, how far did your Holiness go on pilgrimages?

Râmakrishna (smiling): Well, I went to

GOSPEL OF RAMAKRISHNA

Pilgrimages. some places. Hâzrâ went farther and higher up, to Hrishikesha * in the Himâlayas. I did not go so far or so high up. The vulture and the kite soar very high, but their eyes are all the while directed to the charnel-pits below. Do you know what the charnel-pits are? Lust and gold. If in going on a pilgrimage a man does not acquire Bhakti, then his pilgrimage is fruitless; for Bhakti is the end of all; it is the one thing needful.

Do you know what the vulture and the kite are? They are those who talk on lofty subjects and say: "We have performed most of the works enjoined in the Holy Scriptures," but whose minds are immersed in worldliness and strongly attached to wealth, name, fame, and sense-pleasures.

Pandit: Yes, Revered Sir, that is true. Going on a pilgrimage is like casting aside the precious stone worn on the breast of Vishnu and wandering about in search of other jewels.

Râmakrishna: Again, you should know that although you may give thousands of instructions, still they will not produce results until

---

* Hrishikesha is a sacred place of pilgrimage on the banks of the holy river Ganges at the foot of the Himâlayas.

GOSPEL OF RAMAKRISHNA

the time is ripe. A child before going to sleep says to its mother: "Mamma dear, awaken me when I shall feel hungry." The mother replies: "Do not worry about that, my child; thy hunger will awaken thee." In the same manner one yearns after God when the proper time comes for it.

Physicians can be divided into three classes. First, those who, when called in, look at the patient, feel his pulse, prescribe the necessary medicines and then ask the patient to take them. If the patient declines to do so, they do not care. This is the lowest class. Similarly there are spiritual teachers who do not care to know whether their instructions have been practised or whether they have produced good results in their disciples. There are other physicians who not only ask the patient to take the prescribed drug but who reason with him if he refuses to take it. These belong to the medium class. Similarly those spiritual teachers who not only instruct their pupils but reason with them and gently persuade them to follow their teachings, are better than those of the first class. But the best physicians, who belong to the highest class, use force on the patient if he does not listen to their gentle persuasions.

Three classes of religious teachers.

They may go so far as to make him swallow the medicine by force if necessary. Similarly the best spiritual masters use force on their disciples to bring them into the path of the Lord. These teachers belong to the highest class.

Pandit: Revered Sir, if there are such spiritual teachers, like the physicians of the highest class, then why dost Thou say that the spiritual awakening cannot come before the time is ripe?

Bhagavân: Yes, it is true; but suppose the medicine does not get into the stomach? What will the physician do then? Even the best of them are quite helpless. To give proper instruction one must first choose fit vessels.

Fit vessels.

You do not examine the capabilities of your pupils. But I ask those who come to me: "Whom have you to care for you?" Suppose a young man has no father or that his father has left him with debts; how is it possible for him to give his heart and soul to God? Do you hear, my child?

Pandit: Yes, Bhagavan, I am all attention.

The conversation then passed to another subject,—the Grace of God. The Bhagavân said:

Grace of God.

Once a number of Shikh soldiers came to the Temple. I met them before the Temple of the Divine Mother. One of them said: "God is all-merciful." I asked: "Indeed, is it so? How did you come to know it?" "Why, Sir, is not the Lord feeding and taking care of us?" I said: "Is that so extraordinary? God is the Father of us all. If the father does not look after his own children, who will? Shall outsiders from another neighborhood come and take care of them?"

Narendra: Then we should not call Him merciful?

Bhagavân: Am I forbidding you to call Him all-merciful? What I mean is that the Lord is our nearest and dearest and not like a stranger.

Pandit: Priceless are these words!

The Bhagavân here asked for a fresh glass of water. He would not take the one already offered and it was therefore carried away. It appeared that he looked upon it as unfit to be offered to the God in Him, being made impure by the "feverish" touch of some wicked men.

Pandit (to Hâzrâ): You who live with the Bhagavân day and night must enjoy the highest bliss.

Bhagavân (smiling): This day I have had the rare pleasure of looking at the moon of the second lunar day. Do you know why I say the moon of the second lunar day? Sitâ * said to Râvana: "Thou art the full moon, and my Râma Chandra is the moon of the second lunar day." Râvana was highly pleased, for he did not understand the meaning. Sitâ meant to say that the fortune of Râvana had reached its climax like the full moon and that now it must be on the wane; but the fortune of Râma Chandra is like the moon of the second lunar day, which will increase day by day.

Here the Bhagavân rising to take leave, the Pandit and his friends bowed down before Him with great reverence and devotion. He then departed, followed by His disciples.

---

* Sitâ, the faithful and devoted wife of Lord Râma Chandra, who is regarded as an Incarnation of God. She was stolen by Râvana, King of Ceylon, who brought her to his capital, Lankâ. Hence the war described in the epic Râmâyana, which ended with the destruction of Râvana and many of his people.

CHAPTER X

GATHERING OF DISCIPLES AT THE TEMPLE

Srî Râmakrishna was seated on His seat as usual with His face to the north. The western and northern doors of the apartment in which He latterly passed His days looked out on the sacred waters of the Ganges. Balarâm, Râkhâl, and other devotees and visitors were seated on a mat spread out on the floor of the room. They were singing hymns to the accompaniment of musical intruments. One of the songs had particular reference to the six Lotuses marking the different stages of the Yogi's progress toward union with the Universal Spirit. At the close of this song the Bhagavân said:

The six Lotuses mentioned in the Science of Yoga correspond to the seven mental planes mentioned in the Vedânta. When the mind is

GOSPEL OF RAMAKRISHNA

immersed in worldliness, it makes its abode in the **Seven mental planes.** lowest lotus at the end of the spine. Sexual desires rise when the mind is in the second lotus, the sexual organ. When it is in the third, the navel, the man is taken up with things of the world—eating, drinking, begetting children. In the fourth mental plane the heart of the man is blessed with the Vision of Divine Glory and he cries out: "What is all this! What is all this!" In the fifth plane the mind rests in the throat. The devotee talks only on subjects related to God and grows impatient if any other subject comes up in the course of conversation. In the sixth plane the mind is localized between the eyebrows. The devotee comes face to face with God; only a thin glass-like partition, so to speak, keeps him separate from the Divine Person. To him God is like a light within a lantern, or like a photograph behind a glass frame. He tries to touch the Vision, but he cannot. His perception falls short of complete realization, for there is the element of self-consciousness, the sense of "I," kept to a certain extent. In the last or seventh plane it is perfect Samâdhi. Then all sense-consciousness ceases and absolute God-consciousness takes its place. In this state the life of the saint lingers for twenty-one days, after which he passes away. During these days he ceases to take any food. Milk, if poured into his mouth, runs out and never gets into the stomach.

The Bhagavân continued: Some sages, who have reached the seventh or highest plane and have thus attained to God-consciousness, are pleased to come down from that spiritual height for the good of mankind. They keep the ego of Vidyâ, or, in other words, the Higher Self. But this ego is a mere appearance. It is like a line drawn across a sheet of water. Hanumân was blessed with the vision of God both with form and without form; but he retained the ego of a servant of God. Such was also the case with the wise men Nârada,* Sanaka,† Sananda, and Sanat Kumâra of ancient times.

Sages who have reached the seventh plane.

Here the question was asked whether Nârada and others were Bhaktas only and not Jnânis. The Bhagavân replied: Nârada and others had attained the highest knowledge (Brahma-Jnâna), but still they went on like the murmur-

---

* Nârada, see note page 168.

† Sanaka, Sananda, and Sanat Kumâra were the three Rishis or Seers of Truth in ancient India.

ing waters of the rivulet, talking and singing. This shows that they too kept this ego of knowledge. They were Jnânis (knowers), but they talked and sang the praises of the Personal God for the good of others. A steamboat not only reaches its destination itself but also carries numbers of people on board to the same place. Preceptors such as Nârada are like steamboats.

The Avatâras or Incarnations of God are born with Divine powers and Divine qualities.

Avatâras. They can go anywhere and can stay in any state of existence from the highest to the lowest. They can stand on the top of the house and come down by the stairs to the ground floor and can go back to the roof again. They possess the power both to come down and to return. In a seven-story palace a stranger can go only to the outer quarters, but the king's own child, the prince of the house, is free to go to every corner.

As in fireworks there is a kind of flower-pot which sends off one kind of flower for a while, then another kind and still another,

Avatâras and ordinary Jivas. possessing, as it were, an innumerable variety of flowers, so are the Avatâras. Then there is another kind of flower-pot which when lighted burns a little and then goes off all at once. Similarly ordinary Jivas, after long practice and devotional exercises, go up at once in Samâdhi and do not return. There is another class who may be called eternally free. From their birth they seek after God and do not care for anything of the world. We are told of a fabled species of birds called "Homa," which live so high up in the heavens, and so dearly love those regions, that they never condescend to come down to the earth. Even their eggs, which when laid in the sky begin to fall to the earth by the force of gravity, are said to be hatched during their downward course, and the fledglings, finding that they are falling down, at once change their course and begin to fly upward towards their home, drawn thither by instinct. Men such as Sukadeva, Nârada, Jesus, Sankarâchârya and others are like those birds, who even in their boyhood give up all attachment to the things of this world and betake themselves to the highest regions of true Knowledge and Divine Light. Those who come with the Avatâras are either souls who are eternally free or who are born for the last time.

The holy men (Paramahamsas) may be divided into two classes. First, those who declare the Supreme Being to be the Formless One. Trailanga Swâmi of Benares belonged to this class. Generally speaking, holy men of this class are comparatively selfish, because they care only for the liberation of their own souls. Those of the second class say that God is with form as well as formless, and that He manifests Himself to His devotees as a Being with form. Have you ever seen a canal running over into the water of the river with which it is connected? The canal has sometimes no trace left, being entirely one with the river-water. But very often there may be noticed a slight movement in the water which proves its separateness from the river. Pretty much the same is the case with the Paramahamsa belonging to the second class. His soul becomes one with the Universal Spirit. Still the ego of knowledge (Vidyâ) or a slight trace of individuality is kept to mark his separate existence from the Deity.

Two classes of Paramahamsas.

Ego of knowledge.

Again, such a holy man may be compared to a jar or pitcher of water. A pitcher filled with water to the brim gives sound, only when a portion of the water is poured out into another vessel. Similarly the Paramahamsa keeps silent except when his water of wisdom is poured out into the soul of the disciple. Thus he retains the ego of knowledge for the purpose of teaching others.

Again, suppose a person digs a well. He is thirsty and drinks of the water of that well. Yet when his thirst is quenched it is not unusual for such a person to keep the digging implements,—the hack, the shovel, the spade,—for the sake of others who may want them for the same purpose. In the same way a Paramahamsa of the second class, who may have drunk of the waters of Everlasting Life and have thus quenched his spiritual thirst, is often anxious to do good to mankind. With this in view he retains the ego of Knowledge, the ego of Love, and the ego of the Preceptor.

Some persons eat mangoes and then remove all traces of eating by wiping the mouth with a **Helping others.** napkin. They care only for their own pleasure. But there are others who let people know that they have eaten mangoes and are willing to share their pleasure with them. Similarly there are Jnânis who enjoy Divine Communion, and do not think of speaking about it to others; but it was different with the Gopis of Vrindâvan. They not only enjoyed communion with Krishna, the God Incarnate, but were willing to share their happiness with others.

Communion with God may be compared to the process of involution. When one com-
Divine communion. munes with the Supreme Being one's personality becomes absolutely united with the Divine Personality. This is the state of Samâdhi. Then, again, when one returns to the human plane and comes back to the starting-point one sees that the world and the ego or self are evolved from the same Supreme Being; and that God, man and nature are interrelated, so that if you hold on to one of them you realize the others.

Call with Bhakti (love) upon His Hallowed Name and the mountain of your sins shall disappear as a mountain of cotton-wool
Fire of Bhakti destroys sins. will vanish in an instant if it catches one spark of fire. Worship through fear of hell-fire is intended for beginners.

Then turning to some of the company present who were singing, the Bhagavân said: "Will you sing songs which describe the enjoyment that is realized by the human soul after God-vision? Râkhâl (Swami Brahmânanda, one of

GOSPEL OF RAMAKRISHNA

His young disciples), do you remember the song sung the other day at Nobin Neogi's house, 'Be intoxicated with the joy of the Lord'?"

One of the company then said: Revered Sir, may we be favored with a song from Thee?

Bhagavân: What shall I sing? I sing pretty much like yourselves. Very well; when the time comes, I will sing. So saying, He remained silent for a while.

The first song that He then sang was about Sri Chaitanya Deva and Srî Krishna, that is, from the point of view of the Vaishnavas (dualistic Bhaktas). The last was regarding the Divine Mother.

Song

The Devotee and Her Ecstatic Love

1. The waves of the Divine Love come dashing against my body. The swell of the Sea of Love causes the fall of the unrighteous; nay, it drowns the whole universe.

2. I think of diving deep near the bottom of the Sea, but the alligator of ecstasy has swallowed me up. Who is there to feel for me and, holding me by the hand, drag me out of the water?

Song

The Mother of the Universe, and the Machine of the Human Body

1. What a fine machine of the human body hath the Divine Mother made!
   How wonderful are the sports She is playing through the machine only six feet long!

2. Dwelling within the machine, She holds in Her hand the string that sets it in motion; but the machine thinks: "I move by my own will," not knowing Who causes it to move.

3. The "machine" that has realized Her will not have to be born again. She Herself is tied in some machines by the string of Bhakti (love).

ii

At the end of the song the Bhagavân was in Samâdhi. His eyes were fixed and half-closed. His pulse and the heart-beat were suspended. Sense-consciousness had left Him, giving place to pure God-consciousness. Returning a little to the semiconscious state He talked to the Holy Mother, saying: Do not trouble, O Mother!

Come down to this plane. Be still, O Mother! What Thou wishest, O Mother, for everybody shall come to pass! What shall I say to these people?

Nothing can be achieved in the path of spirituality without discrimination (between the **Discrimination and renunciation.** Real and the unreal) and renunciation (non-attachment to riches, honor, sensual pleasures). Renunciation is of many kinds. One kind springs from the acute pain due to worldly misery. But the better kind of renunciation arises from the realization that all worldly blessings are unreal even when they are within reach. Thus, having all, the man renounces everything for the sake of God.

Everything rests upon time. For all religious *Patience* awakening we must wait. But in the meanwhile the precepts of a Guru, the **Time necessary for religious awakening.** spiritual teacher, should be carefully followed, for the impression of these precepts in the mind of a worldly man may be of great help in time of need. Another reason is that constant hearing of those precepts may gradually remove the evil effects of worldly attachment. As the effects of drunkenness can be removed by making the drunkard

GOSPEL OF RAMAKRISHNA

drink rice-water, so the intoxication of the worldly-minded people can be cured by the constant hearing of the precepts of a holy Guru. The number of those who attain Divine Wisdom is very limited. So the Gîtâ says: "Among thousands a few only strive for the realization of God, and among thousands of such seekers after Truth a few succeed in reaching the goal." The more a person is attached to the

Worldly attachment and realization.

world, the less is he likely to attain Divine Wisdom. The less his attachment is, the more is the probability of his getting it. Thus, wisdom may be said to vary directly as non-attachment to the world, its pleasures, its riches, and inversely as attachment to the world.

There are different stages of spirituality. First, there is the state of being struck speech-

Stages of spirituality.

less at the thought or realization of the Absolute Brahman,—Existence, Knowledge and Bliss. This is the utmost point as regards love of God that can be reached by ordinary mortals. Second, there is the state of ecstatic love. This is attainable only by a few. They are human beings with extraordinary, original powers and entrusted with a Divine commission. Being heirs of Divine powers and

GOSPEL OF RAMAKRISHNA

glories, they form a class of their own. To this class belong the Incarnations of God like Christ, Krishna, Buddha, and Chaitanya and their devotees of the highest order.

The two characteristics of ecstatic love are, first, the forgetfulness of the external world, and second, the forgetfulness of one's own body which is so dear to one.

Ecstatic love.

The first is like the unripe mango, the second is like the ripe mango. Ecstatic love of God is like a string in the hands of the Bhakta which binds God. The devotee holds the Lord under his control, so to speak. The Lord must come to him whenever he calls out to Him. In Persian books it is written that within the flesh are the bones, within the bones is the marrow, within the marrow, the last and innermost of all, is this ecstatic love. Srî Krishna is called "*Tribhanga,*" that is, the usual posture of His body is bent in three different angles. Now a soft substance alone can take such an angular shape, so this form of Srî Krishna implies that His whole being must have been made very tender by this ecstatic love.

Chaitanya Deva was the incarnation of Divine Love or Bhakti. He came to teach mankind true Bhakti. He used to have three states of

GOSPEL OF RAMAKRISHNA

consciousness in ecstasy. First, consciousness of the gross and subtle body. At this time he would repeat the Name of the Lord and sing His praises in Sankirtan. Second, consciousness of the causal body alone. In this state he would become intoxicated with ecstatic joy, and retaining partial consciousness of the external, he would dance in company with other Bhaktas. Third, consciousness of the Absolute. In this state he would enter into the highest realm of Samâdhi, and rising above all sense-consciousness, his body would remain apparently lifeless. These states correspond to the five sheaths of the soul in Vedânta. According to Vedânta the gross body includes the material form which is the outermost sheath and the sheath of Prâna or the sense-organs and sense-powers. The subtle body includes two sheaths, mental and intellectual. The causal body is the sheath of joyfulness. Beyond these five is the true Self, the Absolute. When the mind reaches this state, the highest Samâdhi or God-consciousness is the result.

Three states of consciousness in ecstasy.

How to pray is the next question. Let us not pray for things of this world, but pray like Nârada. Nârada said to Râma Chandra: "O

Râma, grant that I may be favored with Bhakti, love, devotion and self-surrender to the Lotus of Thy feet." "Be it so," said Râma. "But wilt thou not ask for anything else?" Nârada replied: "Lord, may it please Thee to grant that I may not be attracted by Thy Mâyâ, which fascinates the creatures of this world." Râma Chandra said once more: "Be it so, Nârada; but wilt thou not ask for something else?" Nârada replied: "No, Lord, that is all I pray for."

How to pray.

Jnâna (knowledge) varies in degree and kind. There is first the knowledge belonging to men of the world—ordinary mortals. This knowledge is not sufficiently powerful. It may be compared to the light of a lamp which illumines only the inside of a room. The knowledge of a Bhakta (devotee) is a stronger light and may be compared to the light of the moon which causes to be visible things outside the room as well as those inside of it. But the Jnâna of an Incarnation of God is still more powerful and it thus may be likened to a yet stronger light,—the resplendent glory of the sun. Such light is the illuminator of the moon as well as of the whole world. Nothing is problematic to the Divine Incarnation (Avatâra). He

Degrees of knowledge.

solves the most difficult problems of life and soul as the simplest things in the world. His exposition of the most intricate questions in which humanity is interested is such as a child can follow. He is the sun of Divine Knowledge whose light dispels the accumulated ignorance of ages.

So long as the man is immersed in worldliness he cannot attain to Knowledge Divine and cannot see God. Does muddy water ever reflect the sun or any surrounding object? Spiritual knowledge is occasionally visible in worldly people, but very seldom. It does not last long. It is like the light of a lamp. No, no, it is like a ray of the sun—as if a ray were coming through a very small hole in the wall. Worldly people repeat the Holy Name of the Lord, but there is no longing in the heart. They have no persistence. Whether they attain or not, they do not care. They are bound by Karma and must reap the results of their works. Is there no remedy for this state, no hope for the worldly man? Yes, there is. Drop a purifying agent, say a piece of alum, into muddy water; the water is purified and the impurities settle down at the bottom of the vessel. Discrimination of

GOSPEL OF RAMAKRISHNA

the Real from the unreal phenomenal universe and non-attachment to the world are the two purifying agents. Thus it is that the worldly man ceases to be worldly and becomes pure.

Worldly people have the knowledge of diversity, which is the same as ignorance. But true knowledge makes one realize the unity of existence. "This is gold, that is brass" is ignorance, while "all is gold" is true knowledge. All differentiation ceases, when true knowledge comes.

Sankara * was a great Jnâni. He had true Self-knowledge; he realized one Brahman every-
Sankara and where and in all beings. He recog-
the Pariah. nized no distinction in caste or creed.
At one time, however, he had the consciousness of difference; he would differentiate a pariah from a high-caste Brâhmin or a sage. He would not touch a pariah after bathing in the sacred river Ganges. One day a pariah was carrying animal flesh along the river bank as Sankara was coming from his bath and the pariah ran against him. Sankara exclaimed: "Sirrah, how darest thou touch me?" The pariah replied: "Neither hast thou touched me

---

* Sankara, same as Sankarâchârya. See note p. 279.

GOSPEL OF RAMAKRISHNA

nor have I touched thee. The Âtman is pure. it is neither body nor the elements of the body. It is far above the twenty-four categories of the universe. Thou art the real Âtman: so am I. How can I touch thee?" Sankara bowed down before the pariah and lo! the pariah transfigured himself into Shiva, the Lord of wisdom. At that moment Sankara's spiritual eyes were open and he realized the absolute oneness of the Âtman. "I am pure and spotless Âtman, eternally free": this is the nature of true Self-knowledge.

<u>Spiritual practices (Sâdhana) are absolutely necessary for Self-knowledge; but if there be</u> **Spiritual practices.** <u>perfect faith, then a little practice will be enough</u>. One must have faith in the words of the Guru or spiritual master. Vyâsa * was about to cross the river Jamunâ. At this moment the Gopis (shepherdesses) arrived. They also wished to go across, but there was no ferry-boat. They asked Vyâsa, "Lord, what shall we do?" Vyâsa replied: "Do not worry, I will get you across the river; but I am **Vyâsa and the Gopis.** very hungry. Can you give me something to eat?" The Gopis had with them a quantity of milk, cream and fresh butter

---

* Vyâsa, see note p. 108.

He consumed them all. The Gopis then asked: "What about crossing the river?" Vyâsa stood near the edge of the water and prayed: "O Jamuna! as I have not eaten anything to-day, by that virtue I ask Thee to divide the waters, so that we can walk across Thy bed and reach the other side." No sooner did he utter these words than the waters parted and the dry bed was laid bare. The Gopis were amazed. They thought: "How could he say, 'as I have not eaten anything to-day,' when just now he has eaten so much?" They did not see that this was a proof of firm faith; that Vyâsa had the faith that he did not eat anything, but that the Lord who dwelt within him was the real Eater.

Stages of spiritual practice. The first stage of spiritual practice is association with spiritual people, the company of holy men. The second stage is faith in things relating to the Spirit. The third stage is single-minded devotion to one's Ideal. The Ideal may be one's Guru, the spiritual teacher, the Impersonal Brahman, the Personal God or any of His manifestations. The fourth stage is the state of being struck speechless at the thought of God. The fifth stage, when the feeling of devotion to God reaches the

GOSPEL OF RAMAKRISHNA

highest point; it is called Mahâbhâva. The devotee sometimes laughs, sometimes weeps like a madman. He loses all control over his body. This state is not attained by ordinary human beings who are not capable of conquering the flesh. It is reached by Incarnations of God who appear in this world for the salvation of mankind. The sixth stage, Prema or ecstatic love, goes hand in hand with Mahâbhâva. It is the most intense love of God and is strictly the highest state of spirituality. The two marks of this stage are the forgetfulness of this world and the forgetfulness of self, which includes one's own body.

After delivering this sermon, the Bhagavân said to His audience that He would be glad to answer any question. But none was asked, so the Bhagavân continued:

Knowledge (Jnâna) cannot be communicated all at once. Its attainment must be gradual. **Attainment of knowledge gradual.** Suppose a fever is of a severe type. The doctor would not give quinine under such circumstances. He knows that such a remedy would do no good. The fever must first leave the patient, which requires time, and then the quinine will take effect. Sometimes the fever will go off without the help of quinine or any other medicine. Precisely the same is the case with the man who seeks for knowledge. To him religious precepts often prove useless so long as he is immersed in worldliness. Allow him a certain time for enjoyment of the things of the world, then his attachment to the world will gradually wear off This is exactly the moment for the success of any religious instructions that may be given to him. Till then all such instructions will be entirely thrown away like pearls before swine. Many come to me and I have observed how some of them are anxious to listen to my words. But others of the company appear to be restless and impatient in my presence. They say to their friends in whispers: "Let us go, let us go. Well, if you wish to stay, we will go to the boat and wait for you there." Spiritual awakening is very much a question of time. The teacher is a mere help.

The meeting then broke up.

ii

Srî Râmakrishna (to a disciple): <u>The fact is, all this desire for knowledge or for freedom depends upon one's Karma in one's previous incarnations</u>.

Karma (past actions).

Disciple: Yes, Bhagavan, it is so difficult to understand one's self. We see the self only as it appears to us. Behind it there may be a hundred previous incarnations. We walk upon the floor of a house but we never stop to see how it is made and what various things are beneath it.

The Bhagavân smiled at the disciple and left His seat. He went out into the veranda next to the western door of His room and for a time looked on the sun which was sinking rapidly towards the horizon. Then He gazed down upon the holy waters of the sacred stream before Him. A disciple was walking alone in front of the Temple on the embankment of the Ganges. He was watching Balarâm and others getting into a boat to return to Calcutta. It being midsummer, the sacred waters of the river were broken into waves. The day was drawing to its close, it was past five, the sky was cloudy and the clouds presented a most wonderful sight, especially towards the north. In the foreground were the Panchavati, backed by a line of tall willow trees, with the silver stream flowing past on their right. In the background were the beautiful dark blue clouds and the dark stream beneath.

The disciple was looking on this charming scene. Suddenly his attention was arrested by the Bhagavân coming from the south in the direction of the Panchavati and the willow trees. As Srî Râmakrishna, smiling like a child of five, came up, the beautiful picture seemed to be more than complete. There was the universe on the one hand, and on the other the One Soul who reflected the universe and saw it in its real nature. Yes, the disciple felt that in that Presence he was as near the solution of the problem of life as he could be. It was this Presence that made everything—the images of gods and goddesses, men, women and children, trees, flowers, leaves, every inch of ground in that Temple instinct with spirituality and full of the Joy of the Lord. Yes, he felt truly that it was the God-Man before him that had thrown an irresistible charm over everything in that wonderful place—over every object, divine or human, animate or inanimate, seen by the outer or by the inner eye, from the dust under His Hallowed Feet to those sacred images worshipped in the Temple or perceived by looking within that other temple, the body of man, that veritable "revelation in the flesh." He felt like one spell-bound in that Presence!

GOSPEL OF RAMAKRISHNA

iii

It was evening. After the usual prayers and other religious exercises enjoined on the pious Hindu were over, there was yet another meeting between the Master and the same disciple. The disciple then asked, referring to the apparently contradictory systems of religious faith among the Hindus: Bhagavan, is this a contradiction: some among the Hindus hold that Srî Krishna is identical with Kâli, the Divine Mother, while others hold that Srî Krishna is the Âtman, the Absolute, and that Râdha is Chitsakti, the self-conscious Power that rules the universe, the Creator, Preserver and Destroyer, the Personal God?

Bhagavân: The former view is that of the Devi Purân. Be it so, but there need be no contradiction. *God is Infinite. Infinite are the Forms in which He manifests Himself. Infinite also are the ways leading to Him.*

Disciple: Oh, I see! The end in view is to get on the roof of the house. The means may be various, as Thou hast often said,—a single rope, a bamboo, a wooden ladder, or a staircase?

Bhagavân: Quite so. That you can under-

GOSPEL OF RAMAKRISHNA

stand this so quickly is due to the Grace of God.
Grace of God. Without His Grace doubt is never cleared up. Our attitude towards God should be like that of Hanumân who said to Râma Chandra: "Lord, I care not for a special time or place for meditation. What alone I am concerned with is to meditate upon Thee."

Suppose you go into a garden to eat mangoes. Is it necessary for you first to count the number **Love of God** of trees in the garden, which may be **the one thing** many thousands, then the number **needful.** of branches, which may be hundreds of thousands? Certainly not; you should at once, on the contrary, proceed to eat. In the same way, it is useless to enter into all sorts of discussions and controversies regarding God, which would only cause a waste of time and energy. One's present and most important duty is to love God, to cultivate Bhakti or devotion.

Disciple:. Bhagavan, I greatly desire that my work in the world should become a little less than now. The pressure of work stands in the way of one's giving one's whole mind to God, does it not?

Bhagavân: Oh yes, no doubt that is so; but

GOSPEL OF RAMAKRISHNA

a wise man may work *unattached* and then work will not do any harm to him.

Disciple: But that depends upon the possession of an extraordinary power of will derived from the realization of God. First realization of God, then work without attachment. Is it not so, Bhagavan?

Srî Râmakrishna: I must say you are right. But the probability is, you must have desired **Power of desire.** these things in your previous incarnations. This reminds me of the story narrated in one of the Sacred Books. It is said that Srî Krishna had made his abode in the heart of Râdhâ: so long there was no *Lîlâ* (the life of sport that he lived in Vrindâvan) But he felt the desire to take the form of a human being; the consequence of this desire was that he came to Vrindâvan. Such is the power of desire. Your duty now is to pray without ceasing for love of God, so that the bondage of work shall gradually fall off.

Disciple: Is it, Bhagavan, the duty of the householder to save against a rainy day?

Bhagavân: Try to follow the precept of **Cast all care on God.** *Jadrichchâlâbha*, that is, availing oneself of things that come naturally in one's way without one's having to put forth any efforts for the attainment of those things. Do not take so much thought for things of that kind, such as saving against a rainy day. Cast your cares on God. What do you think takes place at the time of my Samâdhi?

Disciple: Thy spirit is then in the sixth plane mentioned in the Vedânta. Then Thou comest down to the fifth plane when Thou beginnest to talk.

Bhagavân: I am only a humble instrument in His hands. He is doing all these things. I do not know anything.

Disciple: Because of this wonderful self-abnegation all people are drawn to Thee. Thou didst say that Mâyâ is attachment to one's own relatives and friends, but Dayâ is love extending to all mankind—even to all God's creatures. I do not understand the difference. Is not Dayâ a feeling which makes a man cling to the world?

Bhagavân: Dayâ is not a bad feeling. On the contrary it is elevating and leads one Godward. Do you believe in God with form or without form?

Disciple: I go so far as the attributes. God has attributes. So far I see clearly enough. But is it not a fact that it is impossible to think of the "Formless" without the help of a form? In any case, we have to go through forms and symbols.

Bhagavân (smiling): You see that I lay stress upon the worship of God with form as eminently favorable for the cultivation of devotion.

Disciple: Is Pandit Sasadhar* making any progress in this direction,—in the culture of Bhakti or devotion?

Bhagavân: Yes; but his tendency is in the direction of the path of knowledge. These men belong to a class of their own. They do not see that this way is exceedingly difficult. **Renunciation.** It is sufficient if one can give up the world in the mind. Outward renunciation is not absolutely necessary.

Disciple: What Thou sayest is, as it seems to me, intended for the weak. For men of the highest class is meant renunciation in the strict sense of the word. They must give up the world not only in their mind but also outwardly.

---

* See page 262.

GOSPEL OF RAMAKRISHNA

Bhagavân: You have heard all about renunciation as I have taught it.

Disciple: Yes, Bhagavan, I understand by renunciation not only the absence of attachment to things of this world. It is non-attachment to things of this world *plus* something. That something is the love of God.

Bhagavân: You are right. I am glad that you see this. God-vision cannot be made clear to others. The state of things that comes about may, however, be described to a certain extent. You have no doubt been to the theatre to witness a dramatic performance. Before the performance commences, you must have noticed that the people are very busy talking to one another on a variety of subjects,—politics, household affairs, official business. But no sooner does the drop-curtain go up and mountains, cottages, rivers, men are presented to view than all noise ceases, all conversation ends and each individual spectator is all attention to the novel scene that is being enacted before him. Pretty much the same is the state of him who is blessed with God-vision.

<small>State of God-vision.</small>

Disciple: Ecstatic love of God, as Thou hast said this day, is the string with which to bind the God of love. With such love one may be sure of seeing God. But the question is whether such love is within the reach of the man of the world (Grihastha).

The Bhagavân remained silent.

CHAPTER XI

SRÎ RÂMAKRISHNA AT THE SINTI * BRÂHMO-SAMÂJ

i

BHAGAVÂN SRÎ RÂMAKRISHNA had been asked to attend the anniversary meeting of the Brâhmo-Samâj, which that year was held in the beautiful garden-house of a gentleman named Veni Bâbu.† The morning service was over when the Bhagavân arrived in a carriage with certain of His disciples and took His place on a raised seat set apart for Him on the veranda overlooking a large quadrangle. Crowds of devotees, followers and members of the Brâhmo-Samâj gathered round Him in a circle. The prayers, music and other exercises of a devo-

---

* Sinti, a village about four miles north of Calcutta.

† Veni Bâbu was a follower of the Brâhmo-Samâj. He regarded Râmakrishna as the most Divine man of the age.

tional nature then continued. On hearing the music, Srî Râmakrishna went into Samâdhi and remained motionless for some time. Then regaining His sense-consciousness, He opened His mouth and in rapt tones began to speak thus:

The realization of God is not the same as psychic power. There are many Yoga powers, **Psychic powers.** but do you remember what Krishna said to Arjuna about them? When you see one who exercises any of these powers, you may know that such a one has not realized God, because the exercise of these powers requires egotism (Ahamkâra), which is an obstacle in the path of supreme realization.

There is, indeed, great danger in possessing psychic powers. Totâpuri thus taught me **Danger of psychic powers.** this truth: A Siddha (a man who had absolute control over psychic phenomena) was sitting on the seashore. Suddenly there arose a violent storm, which caused him great distress. Desiring to stop it, he exclaimed: "Let this storm cease!" His command was instantly fulfilled. A vessel was passing at a distance with all sails set. As the wind suddenly died away, the vessel capsized and all on board were drowned. The Siddha was the cause of the disaster and there-

GOSPEL OF RAMAKRISHNA

fore he had to take the sin of killing so many innocent people. As the result of this terrible sin, he lost his power and after death he had to suffer in purgatory.

There was another Siddha, who was very proud of his psychic powers. He was a good man and an ascetic. One day the Lord came to him in the form of a saint and said: "Revered sir, I have heard that thou possessest wonderful powers." The good man received him kindly and gave him a seat. At this moment an elephant passed by. The saint asked him: "Sir, if thou desirest, canst thou kill this elephant?" The Siddha replied: "Yes, it is possible"; and taking a handful of dust, he repeated some *mantram* over it and threw it on the elephant. Immediately the animal roared, fell on the ground in agony and died. Seeing this, the saint exclaimed: "What wonderful power thou possessest! Thou hast killed such a huge creature in a moment!" The saint then entreated him, saying: "Thou must also possess the power to bring him back to life." The Siddha replied: "Yes, that is also possible." Again he took a handful of dust, chanted a *mantram*, threw it on the elephant, and lo! the elephant revived and

The Siddha and the elephant.

GOSPEL OF RAMAKRISHNA

came back to life. The saint was amazed at the sight and again exclaimed: "How wonderful indeed are thy powers! But let me ask thee one question. Thou hast killed the elephant and brought him back to life; what hast thou gained? Hast thou realized God?" Thus saying, the saint disappeared.

Most subtle is the path of spirituality. <u>God cannot be realized so long as there is the least desire for powers in the heart.</u> You cannot thread a needle so long as there are fibres at the point of the thread. Krishna said to Arjuna: "Brother, if thou wishest to realize Me (God), thou must not desire any psychic powers. The possession of psychic power brings pride and egotism, then one easily forgets God. So long as there is egotism, Divine realization does not come."

Desire for powers prevents realization.

There are four different stages in the path of realization. First, that of a beginner, a *Pravartaka*, or one who has just begun to worship God. Those who belong to this class begin to wear the sign of their creed, such as the rosary or the mark on the forehead, and they are very particular about the external forms of their sect. The second stage is that

Four stages of realization.

322

of the neophyte or *Sâdhaka*. Those of this class are farther advanced. They do not parade their beliefs and do not attach so much importance to external signs. Their worship is internal. They repeat the Lord's Name silently, pray without ostentation and feel some longing for God. The third stage is that of *Siddha*. What is a Siddha? One who is firmly convinced in his heart and soul that God exists, that He does everything, that He is the Omnipotent Being, and who has obtained a first glimpse of Him. The fourth stage is that of the *Siddha of Siddhas*. One who has reached this stage has not only seen God but has made acquaintance with Him and has established a definite relation with Him,—either that of a son to his father or that of a mother to her child, or that of friend to friend or of brother to brother, or the relation of husband and wife.

To believe that fire is in the wood is faith. This is one thing, but it is another thing to **Faith and** bring that fire out of the wood, to **realization.** cook something with it, to eat this and to attain peace and happiness afterwards. So to believe that God is in the world and to catch a distant glimpse of Him is one thing; but to come into direct communion with Him, to enjoy His company and taste Divine Bliss is another. No one can set a limit to the various aspects of God which a Bhakta can realize. They rise ever higher and higher.

A devotee: Bhagavan, why can some attain to realization more quickly than others?

Râmakrishna: It depends upon the Samskâras or impressions of previous lives. Nothing happens suddenly or by accident. A certain man drank an ounce of wine in the morning and began to act like a drunkard. People, seeing him, wondered why he should be drunk after taking one small glass of wine. Hearing them, however, another man replied: "Because he has been drinking all night." There have been many instances of sudden conversion. People living in the midst of wealth and luxury have suddenly renounced the world. Such sudden changes are the results of spiritual impressions acquired in the previous life. In the final incarnation of a Jiva, Sattwa qualities prevail: his heart and soul long for realization, the mind becomes unattached to worldly pleasures and constantly remains fixed upon the Supreme Being.

Sudden conversion.

These people here believe in and worship God without form; that is right. (Addressing the

GOSPEL OF RAMAKRISHNA

Brâhmo devotees) Be firm only in devotion to
Firmness of faith necessary for realization. one aspect, either in God with form or in God without form. Firmness in faith is the first thing necessary for realization. Nothing can be achieved without firmness. If you have firm faith in God with form you will attain to Him; similarly if you firmly believe in an impersonal and formless Deity, you will reach Him. Candy will taste sweet whether you bite it straight or crooked. But you will have to be firm and you will have to call upon Him with extreme longing. When a worldly man speaks of God, do you know what it seems like to me? It is just like children quarrelling in their play and taking the name of God in vain; or like a fop walking in the garden, stick in hand, who picks a flower and idly exclaims: "What a beautiful flower God has made!" And even this mindfulness of God exists only for a moment, like drops of water on a red-hot iron. Firmness in devotion to one aspect is absolutely necessary. Dive deep. Without diving into the ocean no one can get the treasure. If you float on the surface, you cannot reach it. Learn to love God. Be absorbed in His love. I have heard your prayers and devotional exercises; but why do

you speak so much of the phenomena which God has made? "O Lord, Thou hast made the sky, the mighty ocean, the moon, the sun, the stars and planets. O Lord, Thou hast made all these, and so on." Why do you dwell upon these things? Seeing the beautiful garden of a rich man, everyone will exclaim: "What a beautiful tree! What a handsome flower! What a large pond and what fine fish in it! What an artistic building! With what rich paintings is the drawing-room decorated!" At the sight of all this everyone is struck with wonder, but how many seek to know the master of the garden? A few only. Those who seek God with intense longing see Him, make acquaintance with Him, speak with Him, just in the same manner as I am speaking to you. I am telling you the truth when I say that God can be seen. Who will listen to me and who will believe me?

Can God be found in the Scriptures? After reading the Scriptures, the highest knowledge one can get is about the existence of a God; but God does not appear to him who does not dive below the surface. Until then doubts are not removed and Divine knowledge does not come. You may read

God and the Scriptures.

GOSPEL OF RAMAKRISHNA

thousands of volumes, you may repeat verses and hymns by hundreds, but if you cannot dive into the ocean of Divinity with extreme longing of the soul, you cannot reach God. A scholar may delude the people by his knowledge of the Scriptures and by his book-learning, but through these he will not attain to God. Scriptures, books, sciences, what good will they do?

Grace of God. Nothing can be acquired without the Grace of the Lord. Yearn after His Grace, devote your energy to obtaining it and by His Grace you will see Him and He will be glad to speak to you.

Sub-Judge: Revered Sir, is He more gracious to some than to others? In that case He would be partial and unjust.

Srî Râmakrishna: How is that? Is a horse the same thing as an earthen pot? Vidyâsâgara **Difference in** asked me the same question. He **powers.** said to me: "Has God given greater powers to some than to others?" I replied: "God pervades all living creatures equally. He dwells in me in the same way that He dwells in the smallest ant, but there is a difference in powers. If all human beings were equal in powers, then why have we come to see you, after hearing of you? Is it because you have two horns on your head? No, it is because you are kind, charitable, learned and have many other qualities greater than in others. It is for this reason that your fame is so great. Do you not know men who alone can defeat a hundred men, and again a man who will run away from a single person?" If there be no difference in powers, why should people respect Keshab Chunder Sen so much? It is said in the Gîtâ, he whom many people respect and honor either for his knowledge or for his musical gifts or for his oratorical powers or for any other reason, in him, be assured, there is a special manifestation of Divine power.

A Brâhmo devotee (to Sub-Judge): Why do you not accept what he says?

Srî Râmakrishna (to the Brâhmo devotee): What kind of man are you? Do you not know that it is hypocrisy to accept an opinion outwardly without believing in it?

Sub-Judge: Revered Sir, shall we have to renounce the world?

Srî Râmakrishna: No. Why should you renounce? **Worship God in solitude.** You can attain to God while living in the world; but at first for a few days you will have to live in solitude and worship Him alone. It is necessary to have a quiet place near your house where you can occasionally be alone for hours at a time and yet go home for your meals. Keshab Sen, Mozoomdâr, and others have told me that they are like Râjâ Janaka, who lived in the world and yet attained to the highest realization. I replied: "It is not an easy thing to be like Râjâ Janaka. Râjâ Janaka was at first a great ascetic and practised extreme asceticism for many years. You could be like him if you practised a little. A man who writes English very fluently has not acquired that facility all at once; he has had to practise for a long time." I also said to Keshab Sen: "Without going into solitude, how can one cure so acute a disease as worldliness? It is like the worst form of typhoid fever. If you keep bottles of chutney and jars of water where a patient is suffering from this fever, he will surely be tempted to eat the one and drink the other and then it will be impossible for the best physicians to cure him. Objects of lust are like the bottles of chutney, and desire to enjoy is like the thirst after water. Worldly thirst has no end. And so long as the object of thirst is kept within reach of the patient, how can he be cured? Therefore I say, withdraw from the place where those objects are and remain in solitude for a time. Then when the disease is cured, you may live in the world without being tempted by it. It is then that you will live like Râjâ Janaka." But in the first stage you must be very watchful. In solitude steadily practise devotional exercises. When a fig-tree is young, it must be protected by a hedge, otherwise it may be eaten up by sheep and cattle; but when the trunk has grown thick, the hedge is no longer necessary. You may tie an elephant to it without hurting it. If after practising in solitude you have acquired true Bhakti (devotion to God) and have gained spiritual strength, then you can go home and live in the world; nothing can corrupt you.

Sub-Judge (with great delight): Revered Sir, these are most beautiful teachings. We need to practise in solitude, but we always forget it and think that we have at once become Râjâ Janaka. It has given me great peace and joy to hear that it is not absolutely necessary to leave the world and that God can be realized even at home.

Srî Râmakrishna: Renunciation, why should you practise it? When you have to fight, it is better to do so from within the fort. You will

GOSPEL OF RAMAKRISHNA

have to fight against the senses, against hunger, thirst and other desires. This fight is easier from within the fort of the world. In this age our life depends upon material food; if you cannot get anything to eat for a day, your mind will be turned away from God. A man once said to his wife: "I am going to leave the world." The wife was very practical and replied: "Why wilt thou wander from house to house for food? When thou art in need of food, is it not better to go to one house than to ten or more?" Why should you renounce? It is so much more convenient to live at home. You do not have to worry about food; then you have your wife with you. Whenever your body needs anything, you will have it right at hand; when you are ill, you will have many to nurse you. Janaka, Vyâsa, Vasishta and others first attained God-consciousness and then lived in the world. They had two swords in their hands,—the one of wisdom and the other of work.

Renunciation and worldly men.

Sub-Judge: Revered Sir, how can we know that true wisdom?

Srî Râmakrishna: When true wisdom comes, God does not appear to be very far. He is no longer there, but here in the heart. He is no longer that but this. He dwells within all. Whoever seeks Him finds Him.

Sub-Judge: I am a sinner; how can I say that God dwells in me?

Srî Râmakrishna: <u>You always talk of sin and sinners; this is the Christian doctrine. Have faith in the Holy Name of the Lord. By the power of faith all sins will be washed away.</u>

Sub-Judge: Revered Sir, how can I have such a faith?

Râmakrishna: <u>First be devoted to God.</u> You have in one of your songs: "O Lord, canst Thou be known without devotion, simply by good works and sacrifice?" That which brings true devotion and unselfish love for God you must pray for with earnest longing in silence. Shed tears of repentance until you have acquired these.

A Brâhmo devotee: Revered Sir, when will they get time? They have to work in their offices.

Râmakrishna (to Sub-Judge): Well, resign yourself to the will of the Lord and draw up a **Resign all** power of attorney in His favor. If **to God.** anyone depends entirely upon some good man, does he do any evil to him? Internally lay upon Him your whole burden and sit calmly, without anxiety. Whatever He has given you to do, do that. A kitten has no self-reliance. It mews and mews and stays where the mother cat places it. She may put it on a soft bed or on the hard floor of the kitchen; the kitten is always content and depends entirely on the will of the mother.

Sub-Judge: We are householders with certain duties; how long shall we have to perform these?

Householder's duties.

Râmakrishna: Of course you have your duties. You will have to bring up your children, sustain your wife, save enough to maintain your family after your death. If you did not do this you would be heartless and cruel. Even great sages like Sukadeva practised loving-kindness. He is not a man who has neither heart nor kindness.

Sub-Judge: How long shall we maintain our children?

Râmakrishna: Until they have passed the age of minority. When the young bird is able to take care of itself, it pecks at the parent bird, if she tries to come near it.

Sub-Judge: What is the duty towards the wife?

Râmakrishna: As long as you live you should

give her spiritual advice and sustain and care for her. If she is faithful, save enough to make her comfortable after your death. But when God-consciousness comes, no worldly duties can bind you. Then if you do not think of the morrow, God will think for you. If you attain to God-consciousness. He will provide for the support of your family. When a Zemindar dies leaving a son under age, a guardian manages the estate for the child. These are legal affairs; you understand them all.

God provides for those who have realized Him.

Sub-Judge: Yes, Revered Sir.

Bijoy: Oh, how great, how wonderful are these words! He who thinks of the Lord with unwavering mind and a heart overflowing with devotion and love for God, is undoubtedly taken care of by the Lord. The Lord carries everything for him like the guardian of the Zemindar's son. Oh, when shall I reach such a state! How blessed are those who have attained it!

A Brâhmo devotee: Revered Sir, can true wisdom be acquired in the world? Can God be realized in the world?

Râmakrishna: You are on the fence; you wish to enjoy both God and the world. Of course God can be realized by one who lives in the world.

Brâhmo devotee: What is the sign of one **Signs of true wisdom.** who has attained true wisdom living in the world?

Râmakrishna: When the repetition of the Name of the Lord will bring tears to the eyes, send a thrill through the whole body and make the hair stand on end. The spiritual eye must be opened. It is open when the mind is purified. Then the presence of Divinity will be realized everywhere and every woman will appear as Divine Mother. Everything is in the mind. The impure mind brings attachment to the world, and the purified mind brings the realization of God. The impure mind of a man becomes attached to a woman. Woman naturally loves man and man naturally loves woman, and from this spring attachment and worldliness.

Every woman represents Divine Motherhood. The same Divine Mother appears in all women **Divine Mother** under various forms. It is said in **in all women.** the Scriptures that Nârada in prayer thus addressed Râma: "O Râma, Thou art Purusha, Thou appearest in the form of all men, and Sitâ, Thy Prakriti, appears in the form of all women. Thou art man and Sitâ is woman.

GOSPEL OF RAMAKRISHNA

Wherever there is masculine form, it is Thy manifestation; and wherever there is feminine form, it is the manifestation of Sitâ, the Divine Mother."

So long as there is attachment to worldliness, and thirst for objects of lust, so long there is **Attachment to the body.** attachment to the body. As attachment to the world grows less, the mind goes towards the Âtman or the true Self and the attachment to the physical body becomes less. When the attachment to the world has entirely vanished, Self-knowledge comes and the Âtman is separated from the physical body. When an ordinary cocoanut is cut into halves, it is very difficult to separate the kernel from the shell; but when it is dried, the kernel becomes separate from the shell by itself. You can feel it by shaking it. A man who has realized God becomes like the dry cocoanut, his soul becomes separate from his body and all attachment to the body leaves him. He is not affected by the pleasure and pain of the body; he does not seek the comforts of the body; he moves from place to place like an emancipated soul. "A true devotee of my Divine Mother attains absolute freedom in this life and is eternally blissful." When you notice that

GOSPEL OF RAMAKRISHNA

tears flow and the thrill comes at the repetition of the Name of the Lord, then you may know that attachment to sense-objects has become less and the devotee is on the path of realization. For instance, if the match is dry it will ignite the moment it is struck; but if it be wet, you can strike it fifty times and yet you cannot get a light. Similarly when the mind is soaked in the water of lust and thirst for worldly objects, Divine enlightenment does not come in it, however hard you may try; it is merely a waste of time and labor. But when that water dries up, spiritual illumination comes instantly.

Brâhmo devotee: By what method can that water be dried up?

Râmakrishna: Pray to the Divine Mother with an earnest and sincere heart; when you see Her, the water of worldly attachment will dry up. Attachment to lust and wealth will drop away from you. If you can feel Her as your own mother, it will come to you at that very moment. She is not like a godmother, but she is your own Mother. Go to Her and importunately ask for what you want. An importunate child hangs on its mother's gown and begs a penny to buy a paper kite. The mother

The Divine Mother will cure worldly attachment.

GOSPEL OF RAMAKRISHNA

may be engaged in talking to other girls and at first she may not wish to give it, saying: "No, your father has forbidden it. I'll speak to him when he comes home. You will spoil everything if you get a paper kite." But when the child begins to cry and will not give in, then the mother says to her companions: "Just wait a minute, let me quiet the child"; she then gets the key to her drawer, opens the money-box, and gives him what he is crying for. Similarly you cry to your Mother and pray to Her, She will surely come to you. (Turning to Sub-Judge) **Pride and egotism.** What is the cause of pride and egotism? Do they arise from knowledge or ignorance? Egotism is the quality of Tamas arising from ignorance. It is a barrier which prevents the soul from seeing God. When it dies, all troubles cease. Of what avail is it to be egotistic? This body with all its comforts and luxuries will not last long. A drunkard, after seeing an image at the Durgâ festival beautifully decorated with jewels and costly ornaments, exclaimed: "Mother, you may decorate yourself with all these valuable things, but after three days they will take you out and throw you in the Ganges." So I say to you all, whether you be a judge or any great personage,

GOSPEL OF RAMAKRISHNA

it is only for a few days. Therefore you must not be proud or egotistic about anything.

People's characters can be divided into three classes,—Tamas, Rajas and Sattwa. Those **Three classes of characters.** who belong to the first class are egotistic; they sleep too much, eat too much, and passion and anger prevail in them Those who belong to the second class are too much attached to work. They love nice, well-fitting clothes and are very neat; they care for a luxurious, richly furnished house; when they sit and worship God, they love to wear costly garments; when they give anything to charity they parade it. Those who belong to the third class are very quiet, peaceful, unostentatious; they are not particular about their dress, they lead a simple life and earn a modest living, because their needs are small; they do not flatter for selfish ends; their dwelling is modest; they do not worry about their children's dress; they are not anxious for fame, nor do they care for the admiration or adulation of others; they worship God, give charity and meditate silently and in secret. This Sattwa quality is the last step of the ladder which leads to the roof of Divinity. A person reaching this state does not have to wait long for God-consciousness.

(To Sub-Judge) You said a little while ago that all men were equal, but now you see how characters vary.

ii

Music for a time interrupted the teaching and Bhagavân Srî Râmakrishna, on hearing it, again went into Samâdhi. The Brâhmo devotees sang the Sankirtan, and when they had finished, all those present resumed their seats, Bijoy taking his place just before Srî Râmakrishna. It was the hour for another Brâhmo service at which Bijoy, who was the leader of the Brâhmo-Samâj, was to read from the Vedas and give an address. Before going to the platform, he asked Srî Râmakrishna's permission, saying: "Bhagavan, grant me Thy blessing, then I shall begin the service."

Râmakrishna: When egotism is gone, everything is accomplished. "I am lecturing and **Egotism and** you are listening;" this sense of ego-**knowledge.** tism you must not have. Egotism proceeds from ignorance and not from knowledge. He who is free from egotism attains knowledge. The rain-water gathers in a low place, it runs off from a high place; similarly the water of wisdom gathers in the humble heart. It is very difficult to be a spiritual leader (Âchârya). One easily loses a great deal by it. When many people show honor and respect, ordinary preachers become egotistic and are easily spoiled. They cannot go further. They merely gain a little fame. Perhaps people will say: "Oh! Bijoy Bâbu is a good speaker or he is very wise," that is all. Never think, "I am speaking." I tell my Divine Mother: "O Mother, I am merely an instrument in Thy hands. Thou dost everything. As Thou guidest me and makest me speak, so shall I speak."

Bijoy (very humbly): Please give me Thy permission. Without Thy permission I cannot begin the service.

Râmakrishna (smiling): Who am I to permit you? Ask the permission of the Lord. When genuine humility comes, there is no fear.

Bijoy repeated his request and Srî Râmakrishna then said: "You can go and begin according to your custom, but keep your mind on God."

Bijoy began the service with a prayer to the Divine Mother. After the service was over, he came down from the platform and again sat near Srî Râmakrishna. The Bhagavân said to him: You prayed to Divine Mother; that was very good. They say that the mother's attraction towards her child is greater than the father's. You can urge your mother more strongly than you can your father. You have a stronger claim on anything that belongs to your mother than on anything of the father.

Bijoy· If Brahman the Absolute be the Divine Mother, then is She with form or without form?

Absolute Brahman and Divine Mother.

Râmakrishna: <u>The Absolute Brahman and the Mother of the universe are one and the same.</u> <u>Where there is no activity of any kind, that is the state of Absolute Brahman, but where there is evolution and destruction, there is the manifestation of the Divine Mother</u>. When the water of the ocean is calm, without a wave or ripple, that is like the state of the Absolute. When the water is in motion and with waves, it is the state of the Creative Energy or Divine Mother. Divine Mother is both with form and without form. You have faith in formless Divinity, therefore you can think of my Mother as formless. When your faith is firm, the Divine Mother will show you how She is. Then you will know that it is not that She is mere

Absolute existence; She will come to you and speak to you. Have faith and you will get everything. If you have faith in the formless Divinity, you must make that faith as firm as a rock. But do not be dogmatic; you must never dogmatize about God. You must not say that He is like this and not like anything else. You may say: "I believe in a formless Divinity, but what else He is, is known to Him. I do not know, I cannot understand." The small intellect of man cannot grasp the whole nature of God. A vessel which can hold a pound only, how can it contain four pounds? If God reveals Himself to one by His Grace and makes one understand His nature, then one realizes Him and not until then. The Absolute and the Divine Mother are one.

Bijoy: How can we attain to the vision of the Divine Mother and the realization of the Absolute?

Râmakrishna With earnest longing and sincerity pray and cry. When the heart will be purified, then you will see the vision as in pure water you can see the reflection of the sun. Upon the mirror of the ego of the devotee is to be seen the reflection of the Absolute Mother of the

Vision of the Divine Mother and the Absolute.

GOSPEL OF RAMAKRISHNA

universe with form. But the mirror should be thoroughly polished; if there be a speck of dirt the reflection will not be perfect. When the sun is to be seen on the water of the ego and when there is no other means of getting a view of the real Sun, so long the reflected image of the sun should be considered as absolutely real. As long as the ego is real, so long the reflected image of the sun is real, not partially but absolutely. That reflected image of the sun is the Divine Mother. If you wish to reach the Absolute Brahman, which is impersonal and without attributes, then start from that reflected image and march towards the real Sun. The Personal God or Brahman with attributes is the one who listens to prayers. Pray to Him and He will grant the highest wisdom, because the same Personal God has the Impersonal aspect also, which is the Absolute Brahman. Divine Energy, which is the Mother of the universe, is another aspect of the same Brahman. All these merge into absolute oneness. The Mother can give Brahma-Jnâna, the knowledge of the Absolute, as also true devotion and absolute love. God is the internal ruler of all. Forsaking egotism, resign your will to His will; you will get everything you desire. When you **mix**

GOSPEL OF RAMAKRISHNA

with other people, you should love them all,
Become one become absolutely one with them.
with all. <u>Do not hate anyone. Do not
recognize caste or creed</u>. Do not say that this
man believes in a Personal God, that man believes in an Impersonal God; this man worships
God with form, that man worships God without
form; this man is a Hindu, that one is a Christian or a Mohammedan. Saying this, do not
condemn one another. <u>These distinctions exist because God has made different people</u> ✗
<u>understand Him in different ways. The difference lies in the nature of the individuals.</u>
Knowing this you will mix with all as closely
as possible and love them as dearly as you can.
Then when you go home, you will enjoy blissful happiness in your soul. Light the candle of
wisdom in the secret chamber of your heart.
By that light see the face of my Absolute
Mother, and by that light you will also see the
true nature of your real Self. When cowherds
All sects of drive the cattle to a pasture from
one family. different quarters, the cows form
themselves into one herd as if of the same
family; but when they return at night, they
separate, each going to its own home. So the
Bhaktas of different sects and creeds, when they

345

meet, are like members of one family, but when they are by themselves, they show their peculiar beliefs and different creeds.

It was late in the evening, and Râmakrishna, entering the carriage accompanied by a few devotees, returned to Dakshineswara.

CHAPTER XII

AT THE HOUSE OF BALARÂM,* A DISCIPLE

i

SRÎ RÂMAKRISHNA arrived from Dakshineswara at the house of His disciple Balarâm about ten in the morning and had His breakfast there. It was this house which the Bhagavân chose to make His chief "vineyard" on that day. Here He had bound devotee after devotee by the tie of Divine Love. It was here that He had so often sung the Name of the Lord and danced at the head of His disciples. It seemed as if another Gourânga † had set up in the house of His disciple Srivâsh a fair for the "buying and selling of Divine Love."

How great was the Master's love for His disciples! There in the Temple of Kâli alone by

---

* See note p. 140.   † See note p. 7.

GOSPEL OF RAMAKRISHNA

Himself He often cried like a child, He so longed to see them. Sleepless at night He would say to the Divine Mother: "O Mother! Deign to draw them into the fold! They are so devoted to Thee! Oh, how I long to see them! Mother, bring them to me or take me to them." Was this the secret of His coming to Balarâm's house so frequently? He declared, indeed, to everyone: "Balarâm is a true Bhakta, he daily worships the Lord of the universe. His offerings are therefore always acceptable." But whenever He came to His house, He would say: "Go and invite my Narendra and other disciples. Offering food to them is the same as offering it to God Himself. These, indeed, are not ordinary men. They are parts of Divinity manifest in the flesh." And many a time had the devotees met there "at the Durbar of God's love."

Mahendra,* who taught in a neighboring school, had heard that Srî Râmakrishna was visiting at Balarâm's house, so having a little leisure he came about noon to see Him. The mid-day dinner was over and the Bhagavân was in the drawing-room resting. His young dis-

---

* See note page 33.

ciples were seated round Him. From time to time He was taking out spices from a small pouch. Mahendra, entering, bowed down and saluted His feet.

Srî Râmakrishna (affectionately): Mahendra! You here! Is there no school to-day?

Mahendra: I have come directly from school. I had just now nothing of importance to attend to there.

A devotee: No, Revered Sir, he is playing the truant.

Mahendra (to himself): Ah me! It is as if some Invisible Force had drawn me to this place.

The Bhagavân then grew more serious and bade them take their seats. He said: For some time past I have not been able to touch any metal. Can you tell me why it is? Once when I put my hand on a metal cup, it was hurt as if stung by a horned fish and the pain lasted for a long while. I had to use a metal pitcher and I thought that I should be able to carry it by covering it with a towel; but no sooner did I touch it than I had excruciating pain in my hand. Then I prayed to my Divine Mother: "O Mother! I shall never touch metal again. Do Thou forgive me this time."

GOSPEL OF RAMAKRISHNA

ii

In the afternoon Srî Râmakrishna was still seated in Balarâm's drawing-room. On His face was a sweet smile, the reflection of which was caught by the faces of the disciples. Girish Ghosh,* Suresh Mittra,† Balarâm, Latoo,‡ Chunilall § and many other disciples were present.

Râmakrishna (to Girish): You would better argue the point with Narendra (Vivekânanda) and see what he has to say.

Girish: Narendra says: "God is Infinite.

---

* Girish Chunder Ghosh, the greatest Hindu poet, dramatist and actor of modern India. He is the founder and manager of many theatres in Calcutta. He is regarded as the Garrick of India. He translated Shakespeare's Macbeth into Bengali and played the part of the hero with wonderful ability and originality. He is a genius and the most devoted householder disciple of Râmakrishna.

† See note p. 177.

‡ Latoo, the devoted servant of Râmakrishna. Although he is illiterate he has reached the height of spiritual ecstasy through his whole-hearted service and devotion for his Divine Master. He is now one of the Sannyâsin disciples of Râmakrishna.

§ Bâbu Chunilall Bose is a gentle householder disciple of Râmakrishna.

We cannot even say that all that we hear or see—be it an object or a person—is a part of God. Infinity is one; how can it have parts? It cannot be divided."

Râmakrishna: God may be Infinite or even greater than Infinite; but by His omnipotent will He can manifest His essence through human form and incarnate Himself among us. Indeed He does incarnate Himself as a human being. How He incarnates we cannot explain by words. One must feel it and realize it. By analogy we can get only a faint idea of it. For instance, if you have touched the horn, leg or udder of a cow, have you not touched the whole cow? But for us human beings the milk is the most important thing and that you can get only from the udder, not from any other part of the body. The Incarnation of God is like the udder, through which flows the milk of Divine Love. In order to give mankind His essence of Divine Love and Bhakti the Lord incarnates from time to time in a human form.

[margin: Divine Incarnation.]

Girish: Narendra says: "Is it possible to fully comprehend God? He is Infinite."

Râmakrishna: That is true. Who can fully comprehend God or even any of His attributes, great or small? Why is it necessary for us to know all His attributes? It is enough if we can see Him and realize Him. Moreover, he who has seen His Divine Incarnation has seen God. Suppose a man goes to the banks of the holy river Ganges and touches the water. He will say: "I have seen and touched the holy river." It will not be necessary for him to touch the whole river from its source to its mouth. If I touch your feet, then I have touched you. If you go to the ocean and touch the water, you have touched the whole ocean. As fire is all-pervading but is more manifest in burning wood, so God, although He is all-pervading, is more manifest in His Incarnation.

Girish (smiling): I, for my part, am searching after fire. I am eagerly looking for the place where I shall find it.

Râmakrishna (smiling): The element fire is more manifest in the wood. If you seek the

Seek God in Man. Divine element, you must seek it in man, for Divinity is more manifest in a human being than elsewhere. Again, if you see a man who is overflowing with Divine Love, who is mad after God, who is intoxicated by the wine of Divine Love, in that man you must know, I assure you, that the Lord has manifested Himself. It is true that God dwells everywhere, but His Divine power (Sakti) is more manifest in some places than in others. In the Avatâra (God-Incarnate) the manifestation of Sakti is very great. Sometimes the manifestation of this Divine power is complete and perfect. In fact Avatâra means the incarnation of Sakti, the Divine Power.

Girish: Narendra says: "He is beyond the reach of mind, words and senses."

Râmakrishna: No, He is beyond the reach of impure mind only, but not of the purified mind (Manas). He cannot be apprehended by ordinary intellect, but purified intellect (Buddhi) can comprehend Him. Mind and intellect become purified when they are absolutely free from attachment to lust and wealth (Kâmini and Kânchan). Then purified mind and purified intellect become one. Indeed God can be realized by the purified mind. Is it not true that the sages and saints have realized Him? They realized the Supreme Spirit in the Self by their true Self.

Girish (smiling): Narendra has been defeated by me in the discussion!

Râmakrishna: Oh no! On the contrary he says: "Girish has such firm faith in the Avatâra in a human form that I feel that I should say nothing against it."

The Bhagavân then expressed a desire to listen to the chanting of hymns. Balarâm's drawing-room was filled with visitors. Everyone watched the Bhagavân, eager to hear what fell from His lips and to mark what He would do next. Târâpada was invited to sing, and sang a song describing the sports of the Shepherd of men, Srî Krishna.

Suresh Mittra, another disciple, was seated at some distance from the Bhagavân. Srî Râmakrishna smiled on him affectionately and pointing to Girish, said to him: Do you talk of the wild life that you did live at one time? Here is one very much more than your match.

Suresh (laughing): That is indeed true, Revered Sir. He is my Dâdâ (respected elder brother) in this regard.

Girish (to the Bhagavân): I never paid attention to my studies in my boyhood. How is it, Revered Sir, that people insist on calling me learned?

Râmakrishna: Do you know what I think about learning and the reading of the Scriptures? Books and Sacred Scriptures all point the way to God. Once you know the way, what is the use of books? Now the time comes for devotional practices in solitude. A person had received a letter in which he was asked to send certain articles to his kinsmen. He was about to order the purchase of those things, when, looking for the letter, he found it was missing. He searched for a long time. His people also joined him in his search. At last the letter was found and his joy knew no bounds. With great eagerness he took it up and went through its contents. But after knowing what things were wanted, he threw the letter aside and set forth to collect the desired articles. How long does one care for such a letter? So long as one does not know its contents. The next step is to put forth one's effort to procure the things. Similarly the Sacred Books only tell us the means for the realization of God. Having once known them, you should struggle hard to acquire them and reach the goal. What is the use of mere book-learning? A pandit may know many sacred texts and sciences, but if his mind is attached to the world, if he enjoys the pleasures of the senses, he has not realized the spirit of the Scriptures; he has studied them in vain.

Râmakrishna then said to Girish: Narendra

GOSPEL OF RAMAKRISHNA

is a young man of very high order. He is interested in everything,—singing, playing on musical instruments, on the one hand, and in the study of the various branches of knowledge on the other. He possesses the virtues of self-mastery, right discrimination, dispassion and many other qualities. (Aside to a disciple) Just look at Girish's devotion to the Lord and his faith in Him.

Nârân,* to the Bhagavân: Revered Sir, shall we not have the pleasure of hearing Thee sing?

Upon this the Bhagavân chanted the Name of the Divine Mother of the universe.

Song

THE BELOVED MOTHER OF THE UNIVERSE

1. O my soul, do thou clasp to thy heart my beloved Mother,
    Let thee and me alone have the pleasure of looking on Her;
    Let Her be seen by none else, by none else!

2. Desires—Oh, get out of their way, my soul; let us enjoy Her presence alone.
    Only let us have the tongue for our sole companion to cry out to Her, saying, "Mother, Mother!"

---

* Nârân was a young householder disciple of Râmakrishna.

3. There are evil desires, there are those which point to us the path leading to worldliness; Oh! Do not let them come near us!
Let the eye of wisdom that leads Godward keep watch, and guard us from evil.

The Bhagavân then sang another song in which He placed Himself in the position of the weary and heavy-laden men of the world, bending under the weight of their trials and sufferings:

Song

THE MOTHER AND HER WEARY CHILDREN

1. O Mother! Thou art made of Bliss Everlasting, why then is it denied unto me?

2. My soul, O Good Mother, knows not anything but the Lotus of Thy Hallowed Feet.
Why then does the Ruler of Death, the King of Justice, find fault with me? Tell me what answer to make to that dreaded King.

3. It was my heart's wish, O Mother, to repeat Thy Sacred Name and cross the ocean of death. Not even in my dream had I the least idea that I should be drowned by Thee in the shoreless ocean.

4. Day and night, O Mother, Thou Consort of Eternity, have I been repeating Thy Sacred Name, which brings salvation unto Thy weary children. But alas! my endless troubles will never leave me. I only regret that if I am not saved, no one else will ever repeat Thy Name.

The Bhagavân next sang about the joy of the Divine Mother:

Song

The Great Mystery

With Shiva the Mother plays always, absorbed in blissful joy.
Deep drunk She is, but falls not.

She dances on the breast of Her consort,
The world quakes under the weight of Her feet.
Both have reached the climax of madness;
Both are fearless and free.

The disciples listened to the songs in deep silence. What struck them was the change that had come over the Bhagavân. He was beside Himself with the joy of the Lord—intoxicated with that unbounded Bliss.

Twilight had fallen. The disciples would not

leave their seats. With heads upraised and eager ears they listened to the sweet Name of the Lord chanted by the Bhagavân, sweeter as repeated by Him than by any whom they had ever heard before. Yes, they had never heard another child calling out so sweetly to its mother, saying, "Mother, Mother!" It seemed as if drops of nectar fell from the lips of the Bhagavân. The infinite sky, the heaven-kissing mountain, the deep blue ocean, the boundless expanse, the deep dense wilderness—what was the use now of going to them in quest of the Divine Father and Mother of the universe? What was the use of fixing one's attention on the "cow's horn" or her feet or any other part of her body? The Master had spoken to-day of the udder of the cow from which to draw the milk of Divine Love. Was it indeed given to those present to behold the vision of God-Incarnate in that very room? What else could have brought into the hearts of the disciples—of those that were weary and heavy-laden—the perfect peace and the joy that are of the Lord? What else could have made this vale of tears overflow with joy? Was it possible that the Man before them was God-Incarnate? Whether He was or not their minds and hearts and souls were His own to deal with just as He pleased! He was already to them the Polestar of this enigmatical life. It was for them now to watch how in His great Soul the Supreme Being, the Cause of causes, was reflected. Thus did some of the disciples think within themselves. They felt that they were truly blessed as they heard the Bhagavân chant the Name of the Divine Mother and of Hari, the Lord God who taketh away all trouble, all sin and iniquity.

The chanting of the Names being over, the Bhagavân prayed to the Mother. It seemed as if the God of Love had taken a human form in order to teach man how to pray. He said:

Mother, I throw myself upon Thy mercy. May the Lotus of Thy Feet ever keep me from whatever leadeth Thy children away from Thee! I seek not, good Mother, the pleasures of the senses; I seek not fame. Nor do I long for those Siddhis (Yoga powers) which enable one to perform miracles. What I pray for, O Good Mother, is pure love for Thee, love untainted by desires, love without alloy, love which seeketh not the things of this world, love for Thee that welleth up unbidden from the depths of the immortal soul. Grant like-

Prayer to the Divine Mother.

GOSPEL OF RAMAKRISHNA

wise, O Mother, that Thy child, bewitched by the fascinations of Thy enchanting powers (Mâyâ) may not forget Thee; yes, forget Thee, entangled in the charming net of Samsâra that Thou hast woven. O, grant that he may never be charmed into loving these! O Good Mother, seest Thou not that Thy child hath none else in the world but Thee? I know not how to chant Thy Name out of deep devotion. Devoid am I of knowledge that leadeth to Thee—devoid of genuine love (Bhakti) for Thee! O, vouchsafe unto me that love out of Thine Infinite Mercy!

This evening prayer—was it called for in the case of this God-Man, for Him who chanted the Name of the Lord day and night, for Him out of whose hallowed mouth there flowed a never-ceasing stream of prayers unto the Most High? Was it then that the Master observed these forms in order to teach mankind how to live and pray?

iii

Girish had invited Srî Râmakrishna to his house. He must come that very night. The Bhagavân said to him: Do you not think it will be too late?

Girish: No, Revered Sir; Thou shalt come away as early as Thou pleasest.

361

It was about nine in the evening. Balarâm had made his offerings ready for Srî Râmakrishna's supper. The gracious Bhagavân would not wound his feelings. He said to Balarâm: "Send over to Girish's house the food that you have prepared for me." Saying this, He set out, followed by His disciples. Going downstairs from the first floor, He became like another being; He looked as if He was lost in the thought of God—as if He had drunk deep! It seemed as if sense-consciousness was beginning to leave Him. A disciple went forward to hold Him by the hand, lest He should miss His footing. The Bhagavân said to him with great tenderness: "If you hold me by the hand, people will say, 'He is a drunkard.' Let me walk alone without any help." He crossed the next turning just a little way from Girish's house. What made Him walk so fast? The disciples were left behind. No one knew what Divine idea had found its way into His heart. What made Him walk like a madman? Was it because He was thinking of that Being who in the Vedânta is said to be beyond the reach of word and thought?

Here was Narendra coming! Many a day had the Bhagavân cried, calling "Narendra,

Narendra," like one gone mad. But now Narendra was there before Him and yet He exchanged no word with him. Was this what people called Bhâva (ecstasy), a state into which Chaitanya is said to have been constantly thrown? Who was there to penetrate the mystery of this Divine ecstasy?

Ramakrishna's ecstasy.

Srî Râmakrishna had come to the end of the lane leading to Girish's house. The disciples were all following. He now spoke to Narendra, saying: "Is it well with you, my child? I had not the power then to talk to you." Every word that fell from His lips was marked by tenderness. He had not as yet come to the door of the house, but all at once He stopped short. He looked at Narendra and said: "This is one of the two,—the human soul, and the other is the cosmos." Was He indeed looking at the soul and the world? If so, in what light? He was gazing on Indescribable Brahman! One or two words had dropped from His hallowed lips, like some solemn texts from inspired Scriptures. Or was it that He had gone to the edge of the Infinite Ocean and stood there speechless, looking on the Boundless Expanse, and had heard one or two echoes re-

iv

verberating from the never-ceasing voice that comes up from the Eternal Deep?

Girish stood at the door of his house. He had come to receive the Bhagavân. Srî Râmakrishna came up with His disciples. At the blessed sight Girish fell at His feet prostrate. The sight was indeed a blessed one and the disciples looked on with awe and admiration. Girish received on his head the dust of His hallowed feet and rose at the Master's bidding. He led the way to the drawing-room, where the Bhagavân and His disciples took their seats. They longed to drink the nectar of His words which brought everlasting life.

He was about to take His seat when He found a newspaper lying by His side. As newspapers had to do with worldly-minded men, with worldly matters, with gossip and scandal, they were unholy objects in His eyes. He made a sign and the paper was put away. Thereupon He took His seat. Nityagopâl * bowed down and saluted His feet.

---

* Nityagopâl was a devoted Bhakta who reached a very high state of spiritual ecstasy (Bhâva). He was a young man who lived like a Sannyâsin, although he did not join

GOSPEL OF RAMAKRISHNA

Bhagavân (to Nitya): Well! and why did you not go there?

Nitya: Revered Sir, I was unable to go to Dakshineswara. I was out of sorts. There were pains all over my body.

Bhagavân: Are you keeping well now?

Nitya: Not very well, I am sorry to say.

Bhagavân: You would better remain one or two notes below the highest in the scale.

Nitya: Company does not suit me. They say all manner of things of me. That puts me into a fright. At times I am quite free from fear and I feel the spirit within me.

Bhagavân: That is only natural. Who is your constant companion?

Nitya: Târak. At times he does not suit the state of my mind.

Bhagavân: Nangtâ * (Totâ Puri) used to say

---

the order. Occasionally he used to come to Srî Râmakrishna to pay his respects and regarded Him as the Incarnation of Krishna.

* Nangtâ was the name by which Srî Râmakrishna called his spiritual teacher in the Advaita Vedânta. The word literally means, "One who does not cover his body with any clothes." Totâ Puri was his real name. He was a Sannyâsin monk of Sankara's school and was a great Vedânta scholar. He reached the highest state of *Nirvikalpa Samâdhi*

GOSPEL OF RAMAKRISHNA

that they had at their Math a Siddha who had acquired some miraculous powers. He used to go about with his eyes fixed on the sky, not caring for his companion Ganesh Gorgy, yet when he left him, he became disconsolate.

By this time a change had come over the Bhagavân. He remained speechless for a while. Returning to consciousness, he said: "You have come, have you? Well, I am here too." Who was there to fathom the mystery of these divine words!

---

after practising for forty years. He used to travel from place to place in India, never spending more than three days in one spot. When he came to Dakshineswara he lived under the trees at the Panchavati and wore no clothes. After seeing Râmakrishna he desired to instruct Him in Advaita Vedânta. Râmakrishna like a child replied: "I shall ask my Divine Mother, and if She gives me Her permission I shall learn of you." The sage Totâ Puri was pleased with His answer. He then stayed with Râmakrishna for eleven months, which was quite unusual for him to do. He gave Him instructions on the oneness of the Jiva with Brahman, and within three days Râmakrishna realized that supreme oneness by reaching the *Nirvikalpa Samâdhi*. Seeing this state Totâ Puri declared in utter amazement: "How wonderful is the Divine mystery! Thou hast acquired in three days what I accomplished after forty years of hard struggle." Since then he regarded Râmakrishna as his Spiritual Brother.

V

Among the disciples who sat at the feet of Râmakrishna, Narendra did not believe in the Incarnation of God, while Girish had a burning faith that God incarnated Himself from age to age in this world of ours. The Bhagavân wished them to discuss the matter before Him.

Srî Râmakrishna (to Girish): I should like to hear you both talk over the matter in English.

The discussion was commenced. It was, however, carried on not in English but in Bengali, with here and there an English word.

Narendra: God is Infinite; it is beyond our power to conceive Him by means of our poor intellect. God is in every human being, but He is not manifest in one particular individual.

God manifest.

The Bhagavân (affectionately): I quite concur. He is in every object, in every human being; only there is a difference in the manifestation of Divine Energy in those objects. The Divine Energy manifest in some objects leads one away from God and is then called Avidyâ (ignorance). When it leads Godward it is called Vidyâ. Again, the manifested energy is greater in some vessels and less in others. Thus it is that all men are not equal.

A disciple: What is the use of all this idle talk?

Bhagavân: There is a great deal of use in it.

Girish (to Narendra): How do you know that God does not take a human body, does not incarnate Himself?

Narendra: Oh! God is surely beyond the reach of words and the finite mind!

Râmakrishna: Quite so; beyond the finite impure mind. But He can be realized by the purified intellect (Buddhi). Purified intellect and purified soul are one. The holy sages (Rishis) realized the pure universal Spirit by their purified intellect and purified soul.

God realized by purified soul.

Girish (to Narendra): If God does not incarnate Himself in a human form, who will explain these difficult problems? He assumes human form to teach mankind Divine Wisdom and Divine Love. Who else has the power to teach in the same manner?

Narendra. Why, He will certainly teach me within the heart.

Bhagavân (affectionately): That is indeed so. He will teach as internal Ruler of the heart (Antaryâmin).

The discussion grew warm. It turned on matters too high for ordinary comprehension: Was Infinity indivisible? What did Hamilton say as to the limit of human knowledge; and Herbert Spencer, Tyndall and Huxley?

Râmakrishna: I for my part do not like these things. God is beyond the power of reasoning; He is something more. <u>I see that whatever is, is God. What then is the necessity of reasoning about Him?</u> I do actually see that whatever is, is God. It is He who has become all these things. This is a stage at which the mind and the intellect (Buddhi) are lost in the Absolute and Indivisible Being. At the sight of Narendra my mind becomes merged in the Indivisible Absolute. What, pray, do you say to this?

Girish (smiling): Surely, Revered Sir, we do not pretend that we understand everything except this.

Râmakrishna: Thereupon at the end of Samâdhi I must come down two notes at least below the highest note in the scale before I can utter a word. Vedânta has been explained by

Sankara.* Another point of view is that of Râmânuja,† who has put forward the doctrine of qualified non-dualism.

Narendra (to the Bhagavân): Sir, may I ask what is meant by Visishtâdvaitavâda (qualified non-dualism)?

Râmakrishna: There is a doctrine called Visishtâdvaitavâda, the view of Râmânuja;
<small>Qualified non-dualism.</small> that is, the Absolute (Brahman) must not be considered apart from the world and the soul. The three form one: three in one and one in three. Let us take a Bel-fruit. Let the shell, the seeds and the kernel be kept separate. Now suppose some one wished to know the weight of the fruit. Surely

---

* Sankara, see note p. 279.

† Râmânuja was the founder of the Visishtâdvaita, or Qualified Non-dualistic School of Vedânta. He was born about 1017 A.D. at Sri Parambattur, a town near Madras in Southern India. He is regarded by His followers as the incarnation of Sesha or Ananta. He wrote Sanskrit Commentaries on the Upanishads, Vedânta Sutras and the Bhagavat Gitâ, and preached His doctrines all over India. He is said to have lived for one hundred and twenty years and died in 1137 A.D. His doctrines were distinct from the Absolute Monistic philosophy of Sankarâchârya. He has now millions of followers among all classes of Hindus in India.

it would not do to weigh the kernel alone. The shell, the seeds and the kernel are all weighed with a view to knowing the real weight of the fruit. No doubt we reason at the outset that the all-important thing is the kernel—not either the shell or the seeds. In the next place, we go on reasoning that the shell and the seeds belong to the same substance to which the kernel belongs. At the first stage of the reasoning we say, "Not this, not this." Thus the Absolute (Brahman) is not the individual soul. Again, it is not the phenomenal world. The Absolute (Brahman) is the only Reality, all else is unreal. At the next stage we go a little farther. We see that the kernel belongs to the same substance as that to which the shell and the seeds belong; hence the Substance from which we derive our negative conception of the Absolute Brahman is the identical Substance from which we derive our negative conceptions of the finite soul and the phenomenal world. Our relative phenomena (Lilâ) must be traced to that eternal Being which is also called the Absolute Hence, says Râmânuja, the Absolute (Brahman) is qualified by the finite soul and the phenomenal world. This is the doctrine of the qualified non-dualistic Vedânta.

I see that Being as a Reality before my very eyes! Why should I reason? I do actually see that the Absolute has become all things about us. It appears as the individual soul and the phenomenal world. One must have an awakening of the spirit within to see the Reality. How long must one reason and discriminate, saying, "Not this, not this"? So long as one has not realized the Absolute Reality. It is not in mere words such as "I see that God has become everything"; mere saying is not enough. By the Lord's Grace the spirit must be quickened. Spiritual awakening is followed by Samâdhi. In this state one forgets that one has a body; one loses all attachment to things of this world; one likes no other words than those relating to God; one is sorely troubled if called upon to listen to worldly matters. The spirit within being awakened, the next step is the realization of the Universal Spirit. It is the spirit that can realize the Spirit.

Spiritual awakening necessary to see the Reality.

After the discussion was over the Bhagavân said. I have observed that discrimination brings only intellectual apprehension of the Absolute, which is far from true realization. The latter can be acquired by meditation in solitude

(Dhyâna); but it is very different from realization through His Grace. If He, out of His Grace, makes us realize what is God-Incarnate and how He manifests through a human form, then it is no longer necessary to reason or explain. Do you know how it is? As in a dark room someone rubs a match on the side of the box and all at once a light is struck. So, if the Lord is gracious enough to strike the light for us, the darkness of ignorance will be dispelled and all doubts will cease forever. Can He be realized by such discussions?

Intellectual apprehension and realization.

The Bhagavân then invited Narendra to be seated by His side. He made many loving inquiries about him and caressed him.

Narendra: Why, Revered Sir, I have meditated in solitude on the Divine Mother for three and four days together, but nothing has come of it.

Bhagavân: All in time; do not be impatient. Mother is no other than Brahman the Absolute. Divine Mother is the primeval energy, when that is without activity I call it Brahman. But when it creates, preserves and destroys the phenomenal world I call it Sakti (energy), or

Divine Mother. That which you call Brahman is the same as my Divine Mother. (To Girish) It is getting late.

Girish: I am afraid I shall have to leave Thee, Revered Sir, and go to my work, unfortunate that I am!

Bhagavân: No, you must serve both parties. Janaka served God unattached to the world and thus looked to the interests of both this world and the next; he drank the cup of milk but did not forget the soul.

Girish: I am thinking, Revered Sir, of giving up my profession.

Bhagavân: No, no; you need not do any such thing. It is all right as it is. You are doing good to many.

Narendra (softly): Just a moment ago he was addressing Him as Lord, God-Incarnate, yet he still has such strong attachment to his professional work.

The Bhagavân had Narendra seated by his side. He fixed His eyes on him. He moved down to sit closer to him. Narendra did not believe that God incarnated Himself, but what did that signify? His love for him was still as great as ever. Touching his person the Bhagavân said to him: Are your feelings wounded?

Never mind; we, too, are of the same mind with you and feel for you.

Bhagavân continued: So long as one reasons and argues about God, one has not realized Him. **Disputations prevent realization of God.** You both were engaged in discussion. I did not like it. How long does the noise continue at a feast to which many are bidden? So long as the guests have not begun to eat. As soon as the viands are served and they begin to partake of them, three-fourths of the noise is gone. Then the more the sweetmeats are passed around, the more the noise subsides. The nearer you come to God, the less you are disposed to argue. When you come up to Him, when you behold Him as the Reality, then all noise, all disputations are at an end. Then is the time for the enjoyment which comes in *Samâdhi*.

Saying this, the Bhagavân gently moved His hand over Narendra's sweet face and caressed him, repeating, "Hari Om, Hari Om, Hari Om."

Then what a miracle passed before the eyes of the disciples! Looking at the Bhagavân, they saw His sense-consciousness beginning to leave Him. Looking again, they saw that it had left Him altogether. In this half-conscious state the hand of the Incarnation of Divine

GOSPEL OF RAMAKRISHNA

Love continued to rest on Narendra's body. Was He breathing into him the inspiration, the power that comes from above? Then yet other changes came over the Bhagavân. He said to Narendra, with folded hands: A song do sing, then I shall get well; how else shall I be able to stand on my feet. "My Nitai! Oh! He is deep drunk, intoxicated with the wine of Divine Love, the love for Gourânga (God-Incarnate)."

A short while and He was speechless again, speechless like a figure cut in marble. Drunk with the joy of the Lord, the Bhagavân went on, saying: "Take care of Râdhâ, lest thou fall into the Jamuna. O thou, mad with ecstatic love for Him who incarnated Himself at Brindâvan, the Lord Sri Krishna!" Once more He was in deep *Samâhdi!* Coming back into sense-consciousness he repeated portions of a well-known song: "O my friend, how far is that blessed woodland, the land where is to be seen my own Beloved One? Look! Here comes the fragrance from the blessed person of my Beloved! I am unable to take a step forward, O my friend!"

Now the Bhagavân had lost all consciousness of the world. He was not mindful of anything or any person in this state. Narendra was seated before Him, but apparently He did not see him. He had lost all sense of time and place. The mind, the heart and the soul had all become absorbed in God. Suddenly He stood up, saying: "Deep drunk with the wine of Divine Love, with love for Gour (God-Incarnate)." A few moments after He took His seat and said: "Yonder is a light coming this way, but I cannot even now say from which way the light comes." It was then that Narendra began to sing:

God-Vision

1. O Lord! Thou hast blessed me with Thy vision and Thou hast driven all my troubles away.
    A charm Thou hast thrown over my soul.

2. Beholding Thee as the Reality, the seven worlds have forgotten their grief!
    Not to speak of my poor self, so worthy of Thy pity and Thy loving-kindness!

Listening to the song the Bhagavân had once more lost all consciousness of the outer world. His eyes were closed. His body and limbs moved not. He was in deep *Samâdhi*. When the *Samâdhi* was over he asked: "Who will take me home to the temple?" A child looking for a companion! Left alone, he saw nothing but darkness about. It was getting late and it was the night of the tenth day of the dark fortnight. Sri Râmakrishna wished to go back to the Temple at Dakshineswara. He seated Himself in the carriage which was to take Him there. The disciples stood on either side of the carriage to see Him off. Even now was He deep drunk with the joy of the Lord! The carriage rolled away. The disciples looked after it for a few moments, then dispersed each to his own home.

CHAPTER XIII

A DAY AT SHÂMPUKUR

Srī Rāmakrishna was living at Shâmpukur at the request of His householder disciples, who had hired a house for Him there.

It was about half-past five in the afternoon of a day in October. Vivekânanda, Brahmânanda, Râmakrishnânanda, Saradânanda, Abhedânanda and other disciples were with Srî Râmakrishna The great national festival Durgâpuja had been celebrated only a few days back but it was difficult for the disciples to take part in the festivities with their whole heart. How could they rejoice when their Master was suffering from a serious malady? Their one thought was to serve Him, to nurse Him, to attend to His smallest wants day and night This devoted and unparalleled service of the Master led the way for the younger disciples (Vivekânanda and others) to the great renunciation of the world of which Bhagavân Srî Ramâkrishna was the ideal example. Through their intense love for the Master they left their homes and sacrificed the duties and pleasures of life that they might give their whole soul to His service.

Notwithstanding His illness, hundreds of people came every day to pay reverential homage to Him. They were eager to receive His blessing and to sit in His presence if only for a few minutes; for His presence brought peace and celestial happiness in the hearts and souls of all. Who had ever seen such unbounded compassion? He was anxious for the welfare of all those who came to Him and was ever ready to help them by removing their doubts and opening their spiritual eyes. This was the time when Bhagavân Srî Râmakrishna showed to the world that He was not a man of this earth, but an embodiment of Infinite Love Divine.

His charm and fascination were so great that everyone who came into His presence would lose the consciousness of time and place. Even men like Dr. Sircar,* who was the busiest phy-

---

* Dr. Mehendra lal Sircar was the best Hindu physician

sician in Calcutta and who usually spent a few moments only with each patient, would remain with the Bhagavân hours together and sometimes the whole day. He had just now been paying Srî Râmakrishna a long visit. Rising to go, he said to the Bhagavân, who was conversing with Syâm Bâbu:* "Now that you have Syâm Bâbu to talk to, I will bid you good-bye."

Srî Râmakrishna: Would you not like to hear some songs?

Doctor: I should like it very much; but your feelings will be too much worked upon and you will go off into a state of ecstasy.

The doctor took his seat once more, and Vivekânanda sang to the accompaniment of instruments:

---

in Calcutta at that time. He was a great authority in medical science and his opinion carried weight among the European physicians of highest repute. He was also the founder of the Science Association in Calcutta, where he occasionally delivered scientific lectures on Physics and Chemistry.

* Syâm Bâbu was a rich Hindu of Calcutta and an intimate friend of Dr. Sircar.

GOSPEL OF RAMAKRISHNA

God and His Works

1. Wonderful, infinite, is the universe made by Thee! Behold it is the repository of all beauty.
2. Thousands of stars do shine—a necklace of gold studded with gems. Innumerable are the moons and suns.
3. The earth is adorned with wealth and corn: full indeed is Thy storehouse. O Great Lord! Innumerable are the stars which sing, "Well done, Lord! well done!" They sing without ceasing.

Kali, the Mother of the Universe

1. In the midst of the dense darkness, O Mother, breaketh forth the light of Thy formless beauty.
   For this the Yogi meditateth in the mountain cave.
2. In the lap of darkness infinite and borne on the sea of great Nirvâna,
   The fragrance of peace everlasting floweth without ceasing.
3. O Mother! who art Thou, seated alone within the Temple of *Sâmadhi*, assuming the form of the Great Consort of the Lord of Eter-

nity, and wearing the apparel of darkness?

The lotus of Thy feet keepeth us from fear;
in them doth flash the lightning of Thy love for Thy children;

And loud laughter adorneth Thy spiritual face.

Doctor (to Vivekânanda): It is dangerous for Him—this singing. It will work upon His feelings with serious results.

Srî Râmakrishna (to Vivekânanda): What does the doctor say?

Vivekânanda: Sir, the doctor is afraid lest this singing bring on ecstasy (*Bhâva-Samâdhi*).

Srî Râmakrishna (to the doctor, with folded hands): No, oh no; why should my feelings be worked upon? I am very well.

But as soon as these words were uttered, the Bhagavân, who was already losing sense-consciousness, went into deep *Samâdhi*. His body became motionless. The eyes moved not. He sat speechless like a veritable figure of wood or stone. All sense-consciousness had ceased to be. The mind, the principle of personal identity, the heart, had all stepped out of their wonted course towards that One Object, the Mother of the Universe.

Again did Vivekânanda pour forth with his sweet, charming voice melody after melody. He sang:

THE LORD, MY HUSBAND

1. How glorious is the beauty! How charming is the face! The Lord of my heart hath come to my (humble) abode.
2. Lo! the spring of my love is running over (with joy)!
3. O Lord of my soul! Thou who art pure love, what riches can I offer to Thee? O, accept my heart, my life, my all. Yes, Lord, my all deign to accept!

NOTHING GOOD OR BEAUTIFUL WITHOUT THE LORD

1. What comfort can there be in life, O gracious Lord!
   If the bee of soul doth not always linger on Thy lotus-feet!
2. What use can there be in countless wealth,
   If Thou, the most precious gem, art not kept with care!
3. The tender face of the child I will not look upon,
   If in that face, lovely as the moon, I see not Thy loving face!

GOSPEL OF RAMAKRISHNA

4. How beautiful the moonlight! Yet I see darkness alone, if at moonrise the moon of Thy love doth not also rise in my soul.
5. Even the pure love of the chaste wife will seem impure, if the gold of her love be not set with the gem of Thy love Divine.
6. Lord, like the sting of a poisonous snake is doubt of Thee, the offspring of ignorance.
7. Lord, what more shall I say to Thee!
Thou art the priceless Jewel of my heart, the Abode of joy everlasting!

Vivekânanda sang again:

THE ECSTATIC LOVE OF GOD

When shall Love Divine enter my heart!
Having all desires fulfilled, when shall I chant the Name of the Lord (Hari) while streams of love-tears flow from my eyes!
When shall my heart and soul be pure! O, when shall I go to the Vrindâvan of love! When will the fetters of the world drop off, and the darkness of my eyes be dispelled by the collyrium of wisdom!
When shall the iron of my body be changed into gold by Thy touch Divine!

When shall I see the world pervaded by God alone, and prostrate myself in the path of Love Divine!

When shall my religious works and daily duties be a thing of the past! When shall my sense of caste and family be gone!

O, when shall I rise above fear, anxiety and shame!

When shall I be free from pride and social customs!

With the dust of the feet of true Bhaktas rubbed over my body;

With the script of renunciation placed on my shoulders, when shall I drink in both hands the water from the river of Love Divine!

Srî Râmakrishna had a special liking for this hymn from the Hindustâni of Zaffir, the Sufi poet:

Hymn

Thou art the refuge and joy of my heart.
 All that is Thou art, all in all Thou art;
Only in Thee have I found my Beloved,
 All that is Thou art, all in all Thou art.

Thou art the dwelling of all Thy creatures.
 Where Thou abidest not can there be one heart,

GOSPEL OF RAMAKRISHNA

In each heart surely Thy Presence has entered;
  All that is Thou art, all in all Thou art.

Either in men or angels triumphant, either in
  Hindu or Mussulman Thou art!
Thy holy will has made everything like Thee;
  All that is Thou art, all in all Thou art.

Whether Mohammedan temples or Hindu,
  Perfectly pure has Thy touch made each part.
All heads before Thee have bowed in devotion;
  All that is Thou art, all in all Thou art.

From the high heavens to earth spread before us,
  From the vast earth to the heavens Thou art,
Wherever I look to my sight Thou appearest;
  All that is Thou art, all in all Thou art.

Thinking and pondering I have seen clearly,
  Searching I have found not another as Thou art;
Now in the mind of the poet has come that,
  All that is Thou art, all in all Thou art.

In the midst of the songs Srî Râmakrishna had come to Himself again. The music was hushed. Then followed conversation with the Bhagavân, which was always charming alike to the learned and the illiterate, to the old and the young, to men and women, to the great and the lowly. The whole company sat mute and looked in silence on His Divine face. Was there any trace now of that serious illness from which He was suffering? Joy alone was there, and radiance of celestial glory. Turning to the doctor, Srî Râmakrishna began:

Do give up shyness, doctor. One should not be shy in repeating before others the Name of the Lord, or in dancing with joy while chanting His sweet name. Do not care what people may say. There is a proverb: "Three obstacles lie in the way of perfection,—shyness, contempt and fear." The shy man thinks: "I, who am so important, how can I dance in the name of the Lord? What will other great people say if they hear of it?" They may say: "What a shame! The poor doctor has lost his head! He has danced while chanting the Name of the Lord!" Give up all such foolish ideas.

Three obstacles in the way of perfection.

Doctor: That is not my line at all. I do not care what people say.

Srî Râmakrishna (smiling): On the contrary,

GOSPEL OF RAMAKRISHNA

you do care very much. Go beyond knowledge and ignorance, then you will realize God. Knowledge of diversity is ignorance. The egotism bred of erudition proceeds from ignorance. That knowledge by which we know that God exists everywhere is true knowledge. But to know Him intimately is realization (Vijnâna).

True knowledge and ignorance.

Suppose your foot is pierced with a thorn, you require a second thorn to take it out. When the first thorn is taken out you throw both away. So in order to get rid of the thorn of ignorance you must bring the thorn of knowledge. Then you must throw away both ignorance and knowledge to attain to the complete realization of God, the Absolute, for the Absolute is above and beyond knowledge as well as ignorance. Lakshman once said to his Divine Brother: "O Râma, is it not strange that a God-knowing man like Vashishta Deva should have wept for the loss of his sons and would not be comforted?" Thereupon Râma replied: "He who has knowledge has also some ignorance. He who has knowledge of one object has also the knowledge of many objects. He who has the knowledge of light has also the

Realization.

Knowledge is relative.

knowledge of darkness, but Brahman the Absolute is beyond knowledge and ignorance and above virtue and vice merit and demerit, purity and impurity."

Syâm Bàbu: Sir, may I ask what remains after both thorns are thrown away?

Srî Râmakrishna: What remains is the Absolute, called in the Vedas *Nityasuddha-bodha-rupam* (the unchangeable, the absolutely pure source of all knowledge).

The Absolute Brahman.

But how shall I explain it to you? Suppose some one asks you what is the taste of Ghee (clarified butter) like? Is it possible to define it? The utmost that you can say is that it is precisely like the taste of Ghee. A young girl once asked a friend: "Your husband is come: tell me what sort of joy you feel when you meet him?" Thereupon the married friend replied: "My dear, you will know everything when you have got a husband of your own; how can I explain it to you?"

In the Purânas we are told that the Mother of the Universe incarnated Herself as the daughter of the presiding god of the Himâlayas Just after she was born, the king of the mountains was blessed with a vision of the various manifestations of the Omnipotent Mother.

Then he said: "O Mother! Let me see Brahman about whom there is so much in the Vedas." The child Incarnate thereupon said: "O father if thou wishest to see the Absolute Brahman thou must associate with the holy sages who have renounced everything. What the Absolute Brahman is cannot be expressed in words." The Tantra has well said: "All things with the sole exception of God the Absolute, have become defiled like leavings of food." The idea is that the Sacred Scriptures of the world having been read and recited with the aid of the tongue have got defiled like food thrown out of the mouth. The Absolute Brahman, however, no one has ever been able to describe by word of mouth. Therefore it is said that the Absolute is not defiled by the mouth. Again, who can express in words the blissful joy that one experiences in the company of the Lord and in communion with the Absolute *Sat-Chit-Ânanda*. He alone knows who has been blessed with such realization.

Addressing the doctor, Srî Râmakrishna continued: True knowledge does not come until egotism is entirely gone.

"When shall I be free?" When "I" shall cease to be. The sense of "I" and "mine" is

ignorance. The sense of "Thou" and "Thine"
Egotism and knowledge. is knowledge. A true Bhakta says: "O Lord! Thou art the doer, Thou hast created everything, I am nothing but an instrument in Thy hands. I do only **Prayer of a true Bhakta.** whatever Thou makest me do. All this is Thy wealth, Thy glory. Thine is the Universe, Thine the family, Thine the relatives. Nothing belongs to me, I am Thy servant. Thine is to command and mine is to serve Thee with my whole heart and soul."

Egotism comes to all those who have studied a few books and have acquired a little learning.

Egotism. I had a talk with Tâgore * about the nature of God. He said to me: "I know all about it." I replied: "He who has been to Delhi does not go about telling others 'I have been to Delhi' and so on. He who is a true gentleman does not boast of being a gentleman."

Syâm Bâbu: Sir, Tâgore has great respect for you.

Srî Râmakrishna: My dear sir, shall I tell you of the vanity of the sweeper-woman in the temple at Dakshineswara? She had a few orna-

---

* Devendra Nâth Tâgore. See note p. 211

GOSPEL OF RAMAKRISHNA

ments on her person and she was so vain that whenever she walked along the road, if she found anyone near she would shout: "Get out of my way! Get out of my way!" What shall I say about the vanity of wealthy people of higher castes!

Vanity.

A devotee: If God is the one Actor in the Universe, then whence come good and evil, virtue and vice? Do they exist by His will?

Srî Râmakrishna: In this world of relativity, good and evil, virtue and vice, exist, but they do not touch the Lord. God is unattached to them—like the wind which is unaffected by the good or bad odor which it carries. His creation is of dual nature, consisting of good and evil, real and unreal. As among trees there are some which bear good fruits, others poisonous, so among human beings there are good men and wicked, sinful men. Wicked people have their place in the world. Do you not see that wicked people are necessary to govern the law-breakers and evil-doers of a community?

The Lord untouched by good and evil.

Syâm Bâbu: Sir, we are told on the one hand that man is punished for his sins, and on the other that God is the sole Actor, all creatures

GOSPEL OF RAMAKRISHNA

being humble instruments in His hands. How shall we reconcile these two things?

Srî Râmakrishna: You talk like a gold merchant weighing things with his delicate balance.

Vivekânanda: What the Bhagavân means to say is that you are talking like one who has a calculating intellect.

Calculating intellect.

Srî Râmakrishna: I say, O Podo, eat these mangoes! What is the use of counting how many mango-trees there are in the garden, how many thousands of branches, how many millions of leaves, and so on? You are here to eat the mangoes. Eat them and go away. (To Syâm Bâbu) You have come into this world to realize God by means of religious works. Your first effort should be to acquire love (Bhakti) for the lotus feet of the Almighty. Why do you trouble yourself with other things? What will you gain by discussing philosophy? Do you not see that four ounces of wine are quite enough to intoxicate you? Why do you then inquire how many barrels of wine there are in the wine-shop? Of what use is such vain calculation?

Doctor: God's wine, again, is beyond all measure. The supply can never be exhausted.

Srî Râmakrishna (to Syâm Bâbu): Further-

394

GOSPEL OF RAMAKRISHNA

more, why do you not execute a power of attorney in favor of the Lord? Let all your cares and responsibilities rest on Him. If any one trusts an honest man, will that man do any wrong? God alone knows whether He will punish sinful acts or not.

Lay cares on God.

Doctor: He alone knows what is in His mind. How can man surmise it? He is beyond all human calculation.

Srî Râmakrishna (to Syâm Bâbu): You people of Calcutta always find fault with Divine Justice. You often complain that God is partial because he makes one happy and another unhappy. You foolish people see in God the same nature as your own. Hem used to come to Dakshineswara with his friends. Whenever he saw me he would say: "Sir, there is only one thing worth having in this world and that is honor, is it not so?" Very few understand that the end of human life is to attain God.

Syâm Bâbu: Sir, is it possible for anyone to show the subtle body? Can anyone show that the subtle body goes out of the gross body?

Subtle body.

Srî Râmakrishna: Those who are true Bhaktas will not care to show you all this. They do not care in the least whether fools will respect

395

them or not. They do not seek the favor of rich people.

Syâm Bâbu: Well, Sir, what is the difference between the gross body and the subtle body?

Srî Râmakrishna: This physical body made of gross elements is called the gross body. *Manas* (mind), the *Buddhi* (intellect), *Ahamkâra* (egoism) and *Chitta*, all these are in the subtle body. The inner body which feels the joy of the Lord and Divine ecstasy is called *Kârana Sarîra* (causal body). The Tantras call it *Bhâgavat-Tanu*, or the body derived from the Divine Mother. Beyond these is the Mahâkârana, the first Great Cause. It is the fourth state. It cannot be expressed by words.

What is the use of hearing all this? Practise and you will know. You repeat the words "*Siddhi, Siddhi*" (hemp-leaves). Will that make you drunk? No, you must swallow some. There are threads of various numbers, No. 40, No. 41, and so on; but you do not know one number from another unless you are in the trade. It is by no means hard for those in the trade to know a particular number from that of another number. That being so, I say, practise a little. That done, it will be easy for you to have correct ideas as to

The importance of practice.

the gross body, the subtle body, the Kârana (the causal body made of joy) and the Mahâkârana (the Great Cause or the Unconditioned).

When you pray, ask for Bhakti, devotion to His Lotus Feet. After Ahalyâ* was made free from the curse called down upon her by her husband, Râma Chandra said: "Ask for a boon from me." Ahalyâ replied: "O Râma, if Thou wilt give me a boon, do Thou grant that my mind may ever be on Thy feet beautiful like the lotus. O, I may be born among swine, but that will not matter."

For my part, I pray for love (Bhakti) alone to my Divine Mother. Putting flowers upon **Prayer for Bhakti.** Her Lotus Feet, with folded hands I prayed: "Mother, here is ignorance, here is knowledge. Oh! Take them; I want them not. Grant that I may have pure love alone. Here is cleanliness (of the mind and body), here is uncleanliness; what shall I do with them? Let me have pure love alone.

---

* Ahalyâ, wife of the great logician, the sage Goutama. She was a devoted wife, but the villainy of her seducer, who personated her husband, made her unchaste. Hence the curse, the effect of which was, it is said, that she was turned into stone. The touch of Râma Chandra made her human once more.

Oh! Here is sin, here is merit; I want neither the one nor the other. Let me have pure love alone. Here is good, here is evil. Oh! Take them; I want them not. Let me have pure love alone. Here are good works, here are bad works. Oh! Place me above them; I want them not. Grant that I may have pure love alone."

If you take the fruit of good works, like charity, you must take the fruit of bad works also. **Dual existence** If you take the fruit of merit, you must take the fruit of sin also. Knowledge of the One (Jnâna) implies knowledge of the many (Ajnâna). Taking cleanliness, you cannot get rid of its opposite, uncleanliness. Thus a knowledge of light implies a knowledge of darkness, its opposite. A knowledge of unity implies a knowledge of diversity.

Blessed is the man who loves God! What matters it if he eats the flesh of swine? On the **Animal food and vegetarianism.** other hand, if a man lives upon vegetables but is attached to the world and does not love God, what good shall he gain?

(To Syâm Bâbu) To live the life of a householder is by no means wrong. But take care that you work without attachment, with your mind always pointing to the Feet of the Lord. Suppose a person has a carbuncle on the back. Now this man talks as usual. Perhaps he attends to his daily work. But pain constantly puts him in mind of the carbuncle. In the same way, although you are in the world, you should turn your mind constantly to God. A woman carrying on an intrigue with a lover thinks of this lover all the time that she is attending to her household duties. <u>Live in the world like such a woman, doing your many duties with your soul secretly yearning for the Lord.</u>

Work with the mind fixed on God.

Syâm Bâbu: Sir, what do you think of Theosophy?

Theosophy.

Srî Râmakrishna: <u>The long and the short of the matter is that people who make disciples belong to an inferior order of men.</u> Again, those who seek for powers also belong to an inferior class, such powers, for example, as the power of getting across the Ganges or the power of reporting here what a person is talking about in a far country, and other psychic powers. It is by no means easy for such people to get pure Bhakti (love) for the Lord.

GOSPEL OF RAMAKRISHNA

Syâm Bâbu: But, Sir, the Theosophists seek to put Hinduism once more on a firm basis.

Srî Râmakrishna: That may be. I am not well posted as to their views or doings.

Syâm Bâbu: Questions like the following are dealt with in Theosophy. What region is the soul bound for after death—the lunar sphere or the stellar mansions?

Srî Râmakrishna: I dare say. But let me give you an idea of my way of thinking. Somebody put it to Hanumân, the great lover of God, "What day of the lunar fortnight is it?" Hanumân replied: "My dear sir, excuse me. I know nothing about the days of the week, the day of the lunar fortnight, or the stars telling of the destiny on a particular day. That is not my concern. I meditate on Râma and on Râma alone."

Syâm Bâbu: Sir, the Theosophists believe in Mahâtmâs. May I ask whether you hold that Mâhatmâs are real beings?

Srî Râmakrishna: If you care to take my word for truth, I say "Yes." But will you be good enough to let these matters alone? Come when I am better. Do but put faith in my words and I shall see that you find peace. Do you not observe that I do not take either money

GOSPEL OF RAMAKRISHNA

or clothes or any other thing? In some theatrical representations well-to-do visitors are expected to encourage the actors by gifts of money during the performance. Here people are not called upon to make such gifts. This is why so many come here.

(To the Doctor) What I have to say to you is this—but do not take offence! You have had enough of the things of the world, money, fame, lectures, and so on. Now give your mind a little to God, and come here now and then. It is good to listen to words relating to God. Such words enlighten the soul and turn it to the Lord.

A short while after the Doctor stood up to say good-bye. But just then Girish came in, and the Doctor was so glad to see him that he took his seat again. Girish, stepping forward, saluted the Bhagavân and kissed the dust of His hallowed feet. The Doctor watched all this in silence.

Doctor: So long as I was here, Girish Bâbu was not good enough to come. He must come just as I am about to go.

There was then a talk about the Science Association and the lectures delivered there. Girish took an interest in these lectures.

GOSPEL OF RAMAKRISHNA

Srî Râmakrishna (to the Doctor): Will you take me some day to the Association?

Doctor: My dear Sir, once you are there, you would lose all sense-consciousness at the sight of the glorious and wonderful works of God, of the intelligence shown in these works and the adaptation of the means to the end.

Srî Râmakrishna: Oh indeed!

Doctor (to Girish): Do everything else, but pray do not worship Him as God. By doing so, you are only bringing ruin on such a holy man.

Worship of the spiritual preceptor.

Girish: Sir, there is, I fear, no help for it. He who has enabled me to get across this terrible sea of the world and the no less terrible sea of scepticism—how else shall I serve such a person? There is nothing in Him I cannot worship.

Doctor: I myself hold that all men are equal. As to this holy man, do you think I cannot salute and kiss the dust of His feet? Look here! (The Doctor saluted and kissed the dust of the Bhagavân's feet.)

Girish: Oh, sir, the angels in heaven are saying: "Blessed, blessed be this auspicious moment!"

Doctor: You seem to think that saluting

GOSPEL OF RAMAKRISHNA

or clothes or any other thing? In some theatrical representations well-to-do visitors are expected to encourage the actors by gifts of money during the performance. Here people are not called upon to make such gifts. This is why so many come here.

(To the Doctor) What I have to say to you is this—but do not take offence! You have had enough of the things of the world, money, fame, lectures, and so on. Now give your mind a little to God, and come here now and then. It is good to listen to words relating to God. Such words enlighten the soul and turn it to the Lord.

A short while after the Doctor stood up to say good-bye. But just then Girish came in, and the Doctor was so glad to see him that he took his seat again. Girish, stepping forward, saluted the Bhagavân and kissed the dust of His hallowed feet. The Doctor watched all this in silence.

Doctor: So long as I was here, Girish Bâbu was not good enough to come. He must come just as I am about to go.

There was then a talk about the Science Association and the lectures delivered there. Girish took an interest in these lectures.

GOSPEL OF RAMAKRISHNA

Srî Râmakrishna (to the Doctor): Will you take me some day to the Association?

Doctor: My dear Sir, once you are there, you would lose all sense-consciousness at the sight of the glorious and wonderful works of God, of the intelligence shown in these works and the adaptation of the means to the end.

Srî Râmakrishna: Oh indeed!

Doctor (to Girish): Do everything else, but pray do not worship Him as God. By doing so, you are only bringing ruin on such a holy man.

Worship of the spiritual preceptor.

Girish: Sir, there is, I fear, no help for it. He who has enabled me to get across this terrible sea of the world and the no less terrible sea of scepticism—how else shall I serve such a person? There is nothing in Him I cannot worship.

Doctor: I myself hold that all men are equal. As to this holy man, do you think I cannot salute and kiss the dust of His feet? Look here! (The Doctor saluted and kissed the dust of the Bhagavân's feet.)

Girish: Oh, sir, the angels in heaven are saying: "Blessed, blessed be this auspicious moment!"

Doctor: You seem to think that saluting

result of hard study. Well, did you not at that time express regret that you had sat up reading until very late at night? Does that prove that reading until the late hours of the night is bad? The Bhagavân may be sorry from the point of view of the patient; He is by no means sorry from the point of view of a Teacher from God anxious for the welfare of humanity.

Doctor (somewhat disconcerted): I confess I am beaten. Now give me the dust of your feet. (To Vivekânanda) This matter apart, I must admit the acuteness of Girish's intellectual powers.

Vivekânanda (to the Doctor): You may view the question in another way. You sometimes devote your life to the task of making a scientific discovery, and then you do not look to your body, your health or anything. Now the knowledge of God is the grandest of all sciences; is it not natural that the Bhagavân has risked His health for this end, and, it may be, sacrificed it? We offer to Him worship equal to Divine worship.

The doctor then saluted the Bhagavân and took his leave. At that moment Bijoy entered and prostrated himself at the feet of Srî Râma-

Doctor: You feel that it is not a right thing to do, do you not?

Srî Râmakrishna: What shall I say as regards the state of my mind during *Samâdhi*? After the Samâdhi is over I often go so far as to ask myself: May not this be the cause of the disease that I have got? The thing is, the thought of God makes me mad. All this is the result of Divine madness. There is no help for it.

Doctor (to the disciples): He expresses regret for what he does. He feels that the act is wrong.

Srî Râmakrishna (to Girish): You have great penetration. You explain it all to him, will you not?

Girish (to the Doctor): Sir, you are quite mistaken. He is by no means sorry that His feet touch the persons of the devotees. No, it is not that. His body is pure, sinless; it is purity itself. He is good enough, in His anxiety for their spiritual welfare, to allow His Hallowed Feet to touch the bodies of the devotees. As a result of His taking their sins upon Himself, His own body, He thinks, may be suffering from disease. Think of your own case. You were once taken ill, so you have told us, as the good friends, may beat me some day with shoes and turn me out.

Srî Râmakrishna (to the Doctor): Do not say that, Doctor. These people love you so much! They watch and look for you like ladies come together in the bride-chamber looking for the coming bridegroom.

Girish: Everyone here has the greatest respect for you.

Doctor (sorrowfully): My son—even my wife looks upon me as hard-hearted, and for the simple reason that I am by nature loath to show my feelings.

Girish: In that case, sir, do you not think it would be better to throw open the door of your mind, at least out of pity for your friends? You well see that your friends do not understand you.

Doctor: Shall I say it? Well, my feelings are worked up even more than yours. (To Vivekânanda) I shed tears in solitude.

Doctor (to Srî Râmakrishna): Sir, may I say that it is not good that you allow people to touch your feet with their body while you are in *Samâdhi*?

Srî Râmakrishna: You do not mean that I am conscious of this?

anyone's feet is something like a marvel! You do not see that I can do the same in the case of everybody. (To a gentleman seated near) Now, sir, oblige me by allowing me to salute your feet. (To another) And you, sir. (To a third) And you, sir. (The Doctor saluted the feet of many.)

Vivekânanda (to the Doctor): Sir, we look upon the Bhagavân as a person who is like God. Let me make my idea clear to you. There is a point somewhere between the vegetable creation and the animal creation where it is difficult to say whether a particular thing is a vegetable or an animal. Much in the same way there is a point somewhere between the man-world and the God-world where you cannot say with certainty whether a person is a human being or God.

Doctor: Well, my friend, matters relating to God cannot be explained by analogy.

Vivekânanda: I say, not God, but Godlike man.

Doctor: You should not give vent to feelings of reverence like that. Speaking for myself, no one has been able, I am sorry to say, to judge my inward feelings. My best friends often regard me as stern and cruel. Even you, my

GOSPEL OF RAMAKRISHNA

krishna. He had been making pilgrimages to various holy places, and Mahima said to him: Sir, you have just returned from a pilgrimage; you have seen many things, kindly tell us about them.

Bijoy: What shall I say? I see now that here I find everything. To go on pilgrimages **Pilgrimage** is useless travelling. There are some **useless.** places where you will find one-sixteenth, or at the utmost one-fourth, of what you see here. In the Bhagavân I find everything in full complement. I have not found anyone who possesses anything more than our Bhagavân.

Râmakrishna (to Vivekânanda): Look what a wonderful change has taken place in Bijoy. His character has become entirely different, as if the milk has been boiled and thickened. By seeing the neck and forehead I can recognize the state of *Paramahamsa*.

Mahima (to Bijoy): Sir, you take very little food, do you not?

Bijoy: Yes, I believe I do. (To Râmakrishna) Revered Sir, hearing of Thy illness I have come to see Thee.

Râmakrishna: What?

Bijoy kept silent for a while and then said.

No one can understand Thy perfection unless Thou givest the power.

Râmakrishna: Kedâr said to me that when he went to other places he starved, but that here he always found food in abundance.

Bijoy (clasping his hands before Râmakrishana): Lord, I know Thee now. I understand Thy glory. Thou needest not tell me of it.

Thereupon Râmakrishna went into Samâdhi. When He returned, He said: "If that be so, let it be so."

Bijoy: Yes, Lord, now I know Thee.

Saying this, Bijoy prostrated himself before Râmakrishna and pressed to his breast the Hallowed Feet of the Lord. Bhagavân Srî Râmakrishna, again losing all sense-consciousdess, entered into God-consciousness and remained motionless like a carven image. Seeing this wonderful sight, some of the devotees shed tears of joy and happiness while others kneeled and began to pray to the Bhagavân. Each one fixed his eyes upon Srî Râmakrishna and, according to the innermost feeling of his heart, realized his Ideal in Him. Some saw in Him the Ideal Devotee, while others recognized the Divine Incarnation in a human form. Mahima, with tears of joy in his eyes chanted: "Behold,

behold, the embodiment of Divine Love!" And after a few minutes, as if catching a glimpse of the Absolute Brahman in Râmakrishna, he exclaimed: "Infinite Existence, Intelligence and Love, beyond Unity and Diversity!"

After remaining in this state for a long time, Bhagavân Râmakrishna came down once more on the human plane and said: God incarnates Himself in a human form. It is true that He dwells everywhere, in all living creatures, but the desires of the human soul cannot be fulfilled except by an *Avatâra* or Divine Incarnation. The human being longs to see Him, touch Him, be with Him and enjoy His Divine company. In order to fulfill such desires, the Incarnation of God is necessary.

Avatâra.

When an Avatâra or Divine Incarnation descends, however, the people at large do not know it. It is known only to a few chosen disciples. Can everyone comprehend the indivisible Absolute Brahman, Existence-Intelligence-Bliss Absolute?

When the Supreme Lord incarnated Himself as Râma, only twelve sages knew it. The other saints and sages knew Him as the prince of the Râjâ Dasaratha. But those twelve sages prayed to Him, saying: "O

Râma.

409

Râma, Thou art the indivisible Existence-Intelligence-Bliss Absolute. Thou hast incarnated in this human form. By Thine own power of Mâyâ Thou appearest as a human being, but in reality Thou art the Lord of the universe."

CHAPTER XIV

COSSIPUR GARDEN-HOUSE

i

BHAGAVAN RÂMAKRISHNA resided for a few months in a large and beautiful garden at Cossipur, about two miles north of Calcutta. Here He was constantly surrounded by His most beloved Sannyâsin disciples and by those women disciples who were especially devoted to Him.

The Sannyâsin disciples were twelve in number.* Most of them were young men of noble families and were graduates of the University at Calcutta. They had left their homes and

---

* Narendra (Vivekânanda), Râkhâl (Brahmânanda), Niranjan (Niranjânanda), Sashi (Râmakrishnânanda), Sarat (Sâradânanda), Bâburâm (Premânanda), Kâli (Abhedânanda), Jogin (Yogânanda), Lâtoo (Adbhutânanda), Gopâl (Advaitânanda), Târak (Shivânanda), Subodh (Subodhânanda).

relatives for His sake. Their one aim in life was to serve their Master, the living God on earth and the Incarnation of Divinity in a human form. The love of Srî Râmakrishna captivated their hearts and souls. Indeed these earnest and sincere disciples were the pillars upon which the Divine Manifestation was about to build the structure of His universal mission. The illness which the Bhagavân had assumed upon His physical form was the means by which He gathered His beloved ones around Him and gave them the opportunity to nurse and wait upon their Divine Master. They sacrificed their personal comfort upon the altar of true devotion and served their Lord with whole heart and soul day after day and night after night. Their devotion was unique and unparalleled in the religious history of modern India. It was these young disciples who afterwards became the world-renowned Swâmis of the Order of Srî Râmakrishna. There were also householder disciples, like Suresh, Balarâm, Girish, Ram, Mahendra and others, who used to come frequently to see Râmakrishna and to serve Him by supplying the household with all necessary things.

ii

Râmakrishna occupied the large room on the second floor of the beautiful house situated in the centre of the spacious garden. He was seated on His bed, which was spread on the floor, and was surrounded by His Sannyâsin and householder disciples. Conversation arose concerning Sannyâs (Renunciation) and a householder's life, and Girish asked: Bhagavan, which is right—to renounce the world with a view to avoid worldly cares and suffering or to worship God living with one's family?

Bhagavân referred to the teaching of the Bhagavad Gitâ and said: He who lives with his family but is unattached to the relations and things of the world, who performs his duties without seeking the results of his works, attains to God in the same manner as one who has renounced the world after realizing that earthly relations and objects are transitory and unreal. Those who renounce the world merely to avoid worldly cares and suffering belong to the lowest class of Sannyâsins. He who has attained to God living in the world is like the man who resides in a

To live in the world or to renounce it.

crystal palace and sees everything of the outside as well as of the inside of the palace.

Girish: Bhagavan, why is it that mind after reaching a very high plane comes down to the world?

Bhagavân: It is natural with the mind of one who lives in the world. Sometimes it is on a high plane and sometimes on a low. Sometimes there is a great upheaval of devotional feeling, then again it subsides, because the attraction of lust and wealth is very strong. A devotee who lives in the world may meditate on God and repeat His holy Name, but again his mind is attracted by the power of lust and wealth, just as a fly sometimes lights on the most delicious sweetmeat and sometimes relishes the taste of filth or of a rotten carcass.

Fickleness of the mind.

It is different, however, with those who have renounced the world. They have detached their mind entirely from lust and wealth and have fixed it upon the Supreme. They constantly drink the nectar of Divine Love. The mind of a true Sannyâsin does not care for anything other than the Supreme. He leaves the place where worldly talk prevails. He listens to discourses about

A true Sannyâsin.

GOSPEL OF RAMAKRISHNA

the highest Spiritual Truth alone. A true Sannyâsin does not speak of worldly matters, he utters no word which has not bearing upon the Spiritual Ideal. A bee sits on flowers only to drink honey. He does not care for any other object. Then, referring to Râkhâl (Swami Brahmânanda), who had a wife and a child before he renounced the world, Râmakrishna said: Râkhâl and others like him have now understood which is good and which is evil, which is real and which is unreal. They have realized that earthly relations are transitory and ephemeral. They will never again be attached to the world. They are like eels which live in the mud but remain untouched by it.

Girish: I do not understand all that. Thou hast the power to make everyone unattached to the world and free from bondage. Thou hast the power to make everyone perfect whether a Sannyâsin or a householder. When the Malaya breeze blows it can transform all trees into sandalwood trees.

Bhagavân: But pithless trees like the banana- and the cotton-tree are not transformed into sandalwood. Similarly those who are worthy will become perfect. Worldliness means attachment to

The worthy will become perfect.

lust and wealth. Many worldly people consider wealth as their heart's blood. But if you take too much care of wealth, perhaps one day it will go entirely out of your possession. In our country farmers build earthen embankments round their fields. Those who do not leave open any passage for water and take too much care of their embankments, invariably have theirs washed off first by the tremendous current of the water; but those who keep one side open, find that their fields become enriched with alluvial deposits and more fertile in the end. They make the best use of their riches who spend them in the service of the Lord and of holy sages. They reap good fruits of their wealth who give freely to the poor and needy and for the good of humanity.

The Bhagavân continued: I cannot use any object that is given to me by physicians and medical practitioners who live upon the painful diseases of other people. However, it is different with those physicians who are kindhearted, charitable and unselfish.

iii

To destroy the pride and egotism of His disciples, Srî Râmakrishna told them to wear the

GOSPEL OF RAMAKRISHNA

seamless ochre robe of the Sannyâsin and to take up the begging-bowl. Being Himself a perfect Sannyâsin, He loved to see His disciples following Him in the path of renunciation.

Taught His disciples renunciation.

On different occasions He sent them out, as Buddha and Sankara had done with their disciples, to beg food from door to door. One morning He called certain among His beloved ones,—Narendra, Sarat, Jogen, Niranjan, Kâli,—and asked them whether they could go forth with the Sannyâsin's begging-bowl and beg uncooked food for Him. It was indeed a great blow to the caste pride as well as to the sense of self-respect of these young disciples. Obeying the Master's wish, however, they took the begging-bowl in their hands, walked from door to door in the neighborhood, collected various articles of food, brought them before their Master and offered them at His holy feet. Bhagavân Râmakrishna blessed them and rejoiced at their sincere and earnest devotion. This was the manner in which the Bhagavân initiated His disciples in the life of absolute renunciation.

iv

One evening Srî Râmakrishna was attended by His faithful servants Sashi (Râmakrishnânanda) and Kâli (Abhedânanda), who were waiting upon Him.

Meaning of His illness.

The Bhagavân opened His mouth and inspired them by saying: The illness of my body is caused by the sins of those who come and touch my feet. I purify the sinners by taking their sins upon myself and suffering for them. He who was Râma, who was Krishna, Buddha, Christ and Chaitanya has now become Râmakrishna. Blessed are those who know this truth. My Divine Mother has shown me that the photograph of this body will be kept upon altars and be worshipped in different houses as the pictures of other Avatâras are worshipped. My Divine Mother has also shown me that I shall have to come back again and that my next incarnation will be in the West.

v

Narendra (Vivekânanda) had extreme longing for the realization of Brahman the Absolute. One day Bhagavân Râmakrishna, addressing Narendra in the presence of other disciples, said: I hold the key of the chest which contains the treasure of the highest realization. I shall not unlock that chest until you have finished my work which I wish you to do.

vi

Pandit Sashadhar came one day to pay his respects to Bhagavân Râmakrishna. Seeing His illness, he asked Him: Bhagavan, why dost Thou not concentrate Thy mind upon the diseased part and thus cure Thyself?

Cure of His illness.

The Bhagavân replied: How can I fix my mind, which I have given to God, upon this cage of flesh and blood?

Sashadhar said: Why dost Thou not pray to Thy Divine Mother for cure of Thy illness?

The Bhagavân answered: When I think of My Mother the physical body vanishes and I am entirely out of it, so it is impossible for Me to pray for anything concerning the body.

Hearing this, Sashadhar bowed at His holy feet and asked His blessing.

vii

The news of Srî Râmakrishna's illness spread like wild-fire among all those who had known

Him or heard of His Divine personality. Hundreds of people came every day to see Him and to pay reverent homage to Him. Some came to receive His blessing, some to kiss the dust of His Holy Feet, some to hear a few words uttered by Him, and others to clear the doubts of their minds. Among these were a few more devoted ones, like Hari, Gangâdhar, Sâradâ, Tulsi, who afterwards joined the Order and were known as Turiyânanda, Akhandânanda, Trigunâtita, and Nirmalânanda. Bhagavân Râmakrishna received them all with equal kindness and was ever ready to help them. Although **His love for humanity.** His physical body was weakened and exhausted, still His desire to help mankind was so great that He often exclaimed: "I would give twenty thousand bodies like this if by that I could help one single soul in the path of righteousness and God-consciousness!"

Dr. Sircar and other physicians gave strict orders to the Sannyâsin disciples to allow no one to come near the Bhagavân, as He needed absolute rest and must have no excitement of any kind. The Sannyâsin disciples followed this advice to the letter and would not allow even the householder disciples to come near Him or touch His holy body. But Srî Râma-

GOSPEL OF RAMAKRISHNA

krishna could not bear this bondage. He burst into tears when He heard of this restriction. His heart melted with Divine Love and He declared that His suffering was infinitely less than that of the worldly people who were groaning under the burden of their worldly cares and anxieties and who had no one to lift them above this mundane existence. His love for humanity was so great that, disregarding His bodily welfare, He called everyone near unto Him in the same manner as Jesus the Christ called all those who were heavily laden and who sought for peace and rest.

Many a time the Bhagavân declared before His beloved Sannyâsin children: Divine Mother is working through this form. She has kept it so long because Her work is not yet finished.

When He could scarcely speak or swallow any food, the Bhagavân said: I am now speaking and eating through so many mouths. I am the Soul of all individual souls. I have infinite mouths, infinite heads, infinite hands and feet. My pure form is spiritual. It is absolute Existence, Intelligence and Bliss condensed, as it were. It has neither birth nor death, neither sorrow, disease nor suffering. It is immortal and perfect. I

His oneness with all.

see the indivisible Absolute Brahman (Sat-chit-ânanda) within me as well as all around me. You are all like my own parts. The Infinite Brahman is manifesting Itself through so many human forms. Human bodies are like pillow-cases of different shapes and various colors, but the cotton wool of the internal Spirit is one. When Jiva (ego) enters into that Spirit and becomes one with it, there is neither pain nor suffering. I am the Infinite Spirit covered by a human skin which has a wound somewhere near the throat. Mind affects the body and is in turn affected by the body. When the body is ill, that illness reacts upon the mind. When one is burned by hot water one says: "This water has burned me," but the truth is that heat burns and not the water. All pain is in the body, all disease is in the body, but the Spirit is above pain and beyond the reach of disease.

<u>My illness is to teach mankind how to think of the Spirit and how to live in God-conscious-</u> **Purpose of His illness.** <u>ness even when there is extreme pain in the</u> body; when the body is suffering from the agony of pain and starvation, when there is no remedy within human power, even then the Mother shows that Spirit is the

master of the body. My illness is to set an example of absolute mastery of the Spirit over matter in this age of materialism and scepticism. My Divine Mother has brought this illness upon this body to convince the sceptics of the present age that Âtman is Divine, that God-consciousness is as true and practical to-day as it was in the Vedic period, that when one reaches perfection, freedom from all bondage is attained. My Divine Mother has shown through Her child what is meant by the various kinds of Yoga and how people of this age can attain to it. She has also shown that all Scriptures are true, that all religions are like paths which lead to the same common goal of the one Infinite Divinity. All of my religious practices, Yoga practices, devotional exercises have been for the good of others and not for my own good. My Mother has set through this form a living example in this age.

"Whosoever will practise one-sixteenth part of what I have said and done will surely attain to God-consciousness in this life."

INDEX

MARGINAL HEADINGS

	PAGE
About the Absolute nothing can be told	254
Absolute Brahman and Divine Mother	342
Absolute frankness	217
A child's "I"	57
A devotee is rich in spirit	185
Agnosticism in Europe and America	250
Ajnânam and Jnânam	119
All desires fulfilled	208
All phenomena unreal	113
All religions lead to God	25
All rituals end in Samâdhi	265
All sects of one family	345
Animal food and Vegetarianism	398
A spiritual leader must renounce the world	258
A true devotee always calm	42
A true Sannyâsin	414
Attachment to the body	336
Attachment to work	238
Attainment of God-vision	242
Attainment of knowledge gradual	308
Avadhuta and a bee	67
Avadhuta and a kite	66
Avatâra	292, 409
Avatâras and ordinary Jivas	292
Abesha of Râmakrishna	261

425

INDEX

	PAGE
Badge of authority	269
Become one with all	345
Bhakta's attitude	147
Bhakti and Jnâna	201
Bhakti Yoga	272
Bigotry is not right	27
Bliss comes in meditation	190
Body and Âtman	219
Body result of past actions	186
Book knowledge and realization	82
Book learning	116
Book-learned Pandits like vultures	104
Bound souls	45
Brahman and Sakti are one	132
Brahman impersonal and personal	132
Brahman indescribable	106
Brahman is Silence	109
Brahman untouched by good and evil	105
Calculating intellect	394
Cast all care on God	314
Character and associations	198
Company of the wicked	42
Compassion and attachment	252
Concentration	275
Concentration and meditation	48
Creation of the world	153
Cure of His illness	419
Danger of psychic powers	320
Days of struggle	207
Degrees of knowledge	303
Delusive power of Mâyâ	157, 259

INDEX

	PAGE
Desire for powers prevents realization	322
Devotee's heart the temple of the Lord	145
Devotion to the Supreme	200
Difference between Soul and God	55
Difference in powers	327
Different aspects of Divinity	30
Different aspects of God	148
Different paths to God	270
Difficult to be rid of "I"	56
Discrimination and renunciation	299
Discrimination of an Advaitin	146
Dispassion	49
Disputations prevent realization of God	375
Distaste for worldly conversation	215
Divine commission	169
Divine communion	296
Divine Incarnation	351
Divine intoxication	230
Divine love and ecstasy	74
Divine love and its various aspects	202
Divine Mother in all women	335
Divine Mother omnipresent	154
Divine Mother the material and the instrumental cause	154
Divine Mother's will	156
Divinity everywhere	210
Doing good to the world	137
Dual existence	398
Dualistic and monistic Vedânta	278
Ecstasy	80
Ecstatic love	301
Ego of knowledge	294
Egoism of a saint	110

INDEX

	PAGE
Egotism	392
Egotism and knowledge	340, 392
Egotism rises from ignorance	235
Effect of lectures on worldly men	264
Evening at the Temple	32, 195
Everything depends on God's will	92
Everything the will of God	223
Example of Janaka	161
Faith and realization	323
Fetters of the soul	73
Fickleness of the mind	414
Fire of Bhakti destroys sins	296
Firmness of faith necessary for realization	325
First cleanse the heart	175
First see God, then help the world	170
Fit vessels	286
Food for a Bhakta	231
Four classes of individual souls	44
Four stages of realization	322
God and the Scriptures	326
God dwells in all	37
God, His devotee and His word one	259
God in everything	39
God is formless and with form	62
God is Infinite	312
God is like a magnet	59
God manifest	367
God Personal and Impersonal	28
God provides for those who have realized Him	334
God realized by purified soul	368
God the Absolute and God the Creator one	191

INDEX

	PAGE
God the one Master	167
God, the sea of Immortality	249
God, the Sun of wisdom	60
God-vision and philanthropic works	171
God-vision the end of all performance of duty	172
Good works and compassion for all	103
Grace of God	286, 313, 327
Hatha Yoga	274
He uplifted womanhood	17
Helping others	295
His Divine powers	20
His love for humanity	420
His mission	10, 18
His oneness with all	421
His Renunciation	16
His Samâdhi	15
His spiritual insight	13
Householder's duties	333
How a householder should live in the world	77
How to fix one's mind on God	65
How to love God	72
How to pray	303
How to recognize a saint	78
Human soul the child of God	204
Humility of Râmakrishna	139
Ideal of a wet-nurse	250
Illustration of a bull's-eye lantern	61
Image worship	63
Intellectual apprehension and realization	373
Intense devotion necessary	164
Is work the aim of life?	240

INDEX

	PAGE
Jnâna and Vijnâna	281
Jnâna Yoga	270
Jnâna Yoga and Bhakti Yoga	113
Karma (past actions)	309
Karma Yoga	271
Kâli, why black?	154
Keshab and his disciples	257
Knowledge is relative	389
Kumbhaka	275
Law of Karma	183
Lay cares on God	395
Lectures and sermons of preachers	245
Life of Srî Râmakrishna by European Scholars	2
Longing to hear about the Supreme	216
Love for all	42
Love of God, the one thing needful	313
Lover of God	191
Lust and gold unreal	70
Madness of Divine love	74
Mahendra's visit to the Temple	22
Many names of one God	26
Mâyâ	114
Mâyâ and Dayâ	182
Meaning of His illness	418
Meaning of Keshab's illness	221
Meaning of Om	96
Means of God-vision	71
Meditation	276
Money is power	52

430

INDEX

	PAGE
Need of solitude.	69
Non-attachment.	112
Non-attachment necessary.	85
Non-dualistic Vedântins.	180
One God has many names.	151
Ordinary spiritual teachers are blind.	169
Parable of a Brâhmin Priest and his boy.	125
" " " man seeking a light.	283
" " " salt doll.	109
" " " woodcútter.	243
" " " woodcutter and his dream.	280
" " " the ant and the mount of sugar.	107
" " " bird on the mast.	282
" " " chameleon.	29
" " " deserted temple.	174
" " " disciple and the mad elephant.	38
" " " elephant and the blind men.	28
" " " false Sâdhu.	205
" " " farmer and his only child.	93
" " " farmer and the canal.	49
" " " father and his dying son.	84
" " " four travelers.	255
" " " monk and the Zemindar.	88
" " " pious weaver.	90
" " " rich man and his Sircar.	120
" " " snake and the holy man.	40
" " " three robbers.	253
" " " tiger.	203
" " " Vedic father and his two sons.	106
Path of Bhakti Yoga best for this age.	172
Path of devotion.	240

431

INDEX

	PAGE
Perfect knowledge brings realization of oneness.	220
Pilgrimages.	284
Pilgrimage useless	407
Power of desire	314
Power of repentance	59
Power of the Lord's Holy Name.	23
Power of the mind.	158
Power of true faith and true longing	72
Powhâri Bâbâ of Gazipur	145
Practice of non-attachment	68
Pray that worldly work may grow less	170
Prayer for Bhakti	397
Prayer of a true Bhakta	392
Prayer to the Divine Mother	161, 360
Pride	75
Pride and egotism	338
Psychic powers.	320
Pure Bhakti and pure Jnâna one	194
Pure heart	59
Purpose of His illness	422
Qualified non-dualism.	370
Râja Yoga	271
Râja Yogi	148
Râma	409
Râmakrishna a Real Mahâtman	4
Râmakrishna as the Divine Ideal of all sects	9
Râmakrishna goes on board the steamer.	143
Râmakrishna leaves Vidyâsâgara	141
Râmakrishna's childlike nature	100
Râmakrishna's ecstasy	143, 226, 363
Râmakrishna's influence upon the mind of Scholars.	7

INDEX

	PAGE
Râmakrishna's love of humor	102
Râmakrishna's Samâdhi	131
Realization	389
Realization of God	14
Relation between Brahman and Sakti	150
Relation between God Personal and Impersonal	31
Relation between Guru and disciples	111
Renunciation	316
Renunciation and worldly men	331
Renunciation not necessary for all	158
Resign all to God	332
Resignation	89
Resistance of evil	40
Right discrimination	79
Sages teach for the good of others	111
Sages who have reached the seventh plane	291
Samâdhi of Râmakrishna	189
Sankara and the pariah	305
Sattwa, Rajas, and Tamas	252
Saving power of God's name	160
Saviours	1
Scriptures and realization	355
Sectarianism and Brahma-Jnâna	256
Seek God in man	352
Selfless works purify the heart	136
Self-surrender and prayer	123
Sense of "I"	51, 118
Sense of sin	159
Servant "I" of a Bhakta	56
Seven mental planes	290
Seven stages of spiritual evolution	53
Signs of one who has realized God	237

INDEX

	PAGE
Signs of true wisdom	335
Solitude a remedy for worldliness	163
Solitude necessary	65
Souls eternally free	293
Spiritual awakening necessary to see the Reality	372
Spiritual knowledge and the worldly	304
Spiritual practices	306
Stages of spirituality	300
Stages of spiritual practice	307
State of God-vision	317
Story of a boy and the cow-house	245
Story of a man and his cottage	246
Subtle body	395
Sudden conversion	324
Taught His disciples renunciation	417
The Absolute and the Divine Mother	259
The Absolute and the phenomenal	95
The Absolute Brahman	390
The Divinely-commissioned teacher	266
The Divine Mother will cure worldly attachment	337
The Divine presence in images	183
The ego of a calf	236
The importance of practice	396
The innermost feelings of a true Bhakta	147
The kingdom of God is everywhere	87
The Lord alone is thine own	121
The Lord smiles on two occasions	120
The Lord, the Ocean of Immortality	135
The Lord untouched by good and evil	393
The madness of love for the Lord	227
The mercy of the Lord	60
The Mother of the universe and Her sports	152

INDEX

	PAGE
Râmakrishna's love of humor	102
Râmakrishna's Samâdhi	131
Realization	389
Realization of God	14
Relation between Brahman and Sakti	150
Relation between God Personal and Impersonal	31
Relation between Guru and disciples	111
Renunciation	316
Renunciation and worldly men	331
Renunciation not necessary for all	158
Resign all to God	332
Resignation	89
Resistance of evil	40
Right discrimination	79
Sages teach for the good of others	111
Sages who have reached the seventh plane	291
Samâdhi of Râmakrishna	189
Sankara and the pariah	305
Sattwa, Rajas, and Tamas	252
Saving power of God's name	160
Saviours	1
Scriptures and realization	355
Sectarianism and Brahma-Jnâna	256
Seek God in man	352
Selfless works purify the heart	136
Self-surrender and prayer	123
Sense of "I"	51, 118
Sense of sin	159
Servant "I" of a Bhakta	56
Seven mental planes	290
Seven stages of spiritual evolution	53
Signs of one who has realized God	237

433

INDEX

	PAGE
Signs of true wisdom.	335
Solitude a remedy for worldliness.	163
Solitude necessary	65
Souls eternally free	293
Spiritual awakening necessary to see the Reality	372
Spiritual knowledge and the worldly	304
Spiritual practices	306
Stages of spirituality	300
Stages of spiritual practice	307
State of God-vision	317
Story of a boy and the cow-house.	245
Story of a man and his cottage	246
Subtle body.	395
Sudden conversion.	324
Taught His disciples renunciation	417
The Absolute and the Divine Mother	259
The Absolute and the phenomenal.	95
The Absolute Brahman	390
The Divinely-commissioned teacher.	266
The Divine Mother will cure worldly attachment	337
The Divine presence in images	183
The ego of a calf	236
The importance of practice	396
The innermost feelings of a true Bhakta.	147
The kingdom of God is everywhere	87
The Lord alone is thine own.	121
The Lord smiles on two occasions	120
The Lord, the Ocean of Immortality.	135
The Lord untouched by good and evil.	393
The madness of love for the Lord	227
The mercy of the Lord.	60
The Mother of the universe and Her sports.	152

INDEX

	PAGE
The nature of disciples must be examined	167
The necessity of practice	266
The omnipotence of faith	125
Theosophy	399
The power of the Divine Mother	133, 155
The realm of the Divine Energy	150
The Siddha and the elephant	321
The signs of a true Jnâni	280
The unripe and ripe "I"	256
The world as a dream	149
The world like a dream	93
The worldly "I"	55
The world unreal	76
The worthy will become perfect	415
Thought of freedom brings freedom	181
Three classes of characters	339
Three classes of religious teachers	285
Three Gunas of nature	254
Three obstacles in the way of perfection	388
Three states of consciousness in ecstasy	302
Time necessary for religious awakening	299
To live in the world or to renounce it	413
Trials of a devotee	184
True devotion and love	58
True knowledge and ignorance	389
True meaning of Gitâ	116
Truthfulness	232
Two classes of Paramahamsas	294
Unity and variety	221
Unity in diversity	115
Value of lectures without Divine commission	268

INDEX

	PAGE
Value of solitude	162
Vanity	393
Various aspects of the Brahman	146
Vidyâ and Avidyâ	104
Vijnâni and Bhakta	114
Vishnu as a boar	260
Vision of the Divine Mother and the Absolute	343
Visit to a poor Brâhmin	211
Visit to Devendra Nâth Tâgore	212
Visit to Keshab Sen	219
Visit to Padmalochana	214
Vyâsa and the Gopis	306
What happens after death	278
What is Bhakti?	132
What thou thinkest, thou shalt become	47
When God is attained worldly attachment vanishes	97
Where Râmakrishna lived	21
Who is a true spiritual teacher?	168
Why God cannot be seen	258
Work and grace	83
Work necessary for God-vision	80
Work without devotion	249
Work with the mind fixed on God	399
Worldly attachment and realization	300
Worship God in solitude	328
Worship of the spiritual preceptor	402
Zoological Garden, Visit to	209

Priority of ...

1) Impersonal Divine: 31, 114, 294

2) Jnana yoga: 56, 64, 115, 117-119, 283, 291-2, 316-17
cf. 173